On Jews
and
Judaism
in Crisis

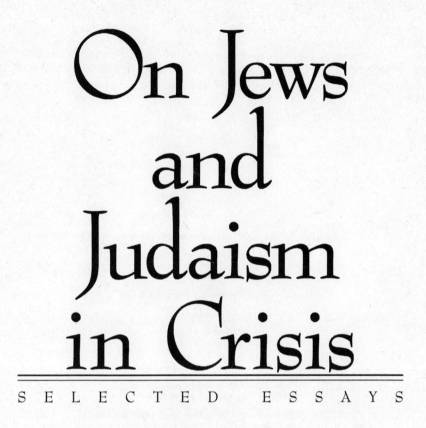

On Jews and Judaism in Crisis

SELECTED ESSAYS

Gershom Scholem

Edited by Werner J. Dannhauser

SCHOCKEN BOOKS · NEW YORK

Ⓢ

Copyright © 1976 by Schocken Books Inc.

All rights reserved under International and Pan-American Copyright Conventions.
Published in the United States by Schocken Books Inc., New York. Distributed by
Pantheon Books, a division of Random House, Inc., New York.

Library of Congress Cataloging in Publication Data

Scholem, Gershom Gerhard 1897–
On Jews and Judaism in crisis.

1. Jews in Germany—History—1800–1933—Addresses, essays,
lectures.   2. Benjamin, Walter, 1892–1940.   3. Germany—History—20th century—
Addresses, essays, lectures.   I. Title.
DS135.G33S297   943'.004'924   75-37010

ACKNOWLEDGMENTS

The author wishes to acknowledge the following:

"With Gershom Scholem" first appeared in *Shdemot* and is reprinted by permission.
"Walter Benjamin" was first published in the *Yearbook of the Leo Baeck Institute*,
Vol. X, London, 1965, and is reprinted by permission of the editor of the *Yearbook of
the Leo Baeck Institute*.
"S. Y. Agnon—The Last Hebrew Classic?" is reprinted from *Commentary* by
permission; Copyright © 1966 (67) by the American Jewish Committee.
"Reflections on Jewish Theology" is reprinted from *The Center Magazine*, a publication of The Center for the Study of Democratic Institutions, Santa Barbara, California, and is reprinted by permission.

Display typography by Stephanie Bart-Horvath

Manufactured in the United States of America

First Schocken Books Edition published in 1976

Contents

Editor's Preface

I

Such is the stature of Gershom Scholem that he scarcely needs an introduction. His incomparable labors in the field of Jewish mysticism (if "field" is taken to mean "field of serious modern study," he must be considered its founder) have not only resulted in the knowledge that mysticism played a much greater role in Jewish tradition than had previously been acknowledged; they have paved the way for the revitalization of a Judaism assaulted on many sides by the credos of modernity.

While the author needs no introduction, a selection of his essays so various as the present one may, nevertheless, benefit from a few prefatory remarks, it being clearly understood that such comments are neither authorized nor authoritative.

II

The earliest of the selections included here appeared in 1916. Thus this volume is testimony to sixty years of the author's continuous and amazing productivity; it is evidence of the great fertility of his mind and thereby additional justification of his stature. While the writings on mysticism can be said to be an indication of the *depth* of Scholem's mind and his capacity to deal profoundly with minute details, this book can be considered an indication of the *breadth* of Scholem's mind at work. He is able to speak with authority about matters literary, cultural, and political; he is at home in the twentieth century as well as the time of Sabbetai Tzvi; one does him less than justice by saying that nothing Jewish is alien to him, though things Jewish do indeed constitute the core of his concerns.

The diversity, then, of the essays herein included sheds additional light on the author's work. Moreover, as if by a way of an "added attraction," they also provide fascinating information about the author's life. Most of his work is austere in its avoidance of reference to himself. Those who know Gershom Scholem know him to be a great conversationalist and an extraordinarily gifted *raconteur*, but he has tended to keep the personal matrix of his writings out of sight. Some of the essays included in this volume are, therefore, a kind of bonus. For example, the interview he granted to a Hebrew periodical provides us with intriguing information about his youth and even affords one a glimpse of his gracious wife; an essay on Agnon in part is a very personal reminiscence about Scholem's life in Germany; the major analysis of Buber's conception of Judaism is also a document of Buber's influence on, and divergence from, Scholem's own work; finally, the two essays on Walter Benjamin are testimony to one of the century's most moving and enduring friendships between men of mind.

III

Custom has it that whenever a collection of an author's essays appears a preface such as this dwells heavily on their "essential unity" or "single theme." Since such statements almost invariably force independent pieces into a mold distorting to them, and since each of the selections was written to stand on its own, the editor has deliberately talked about diversity before mentioning unity. When all is said and done, however, there is little doubt that the essays in this volume possess a certain unity in the sense of having various features in common. Before discussing some of these common features, the editor wishes to maintain that the idea of unity within diversity is certainly not a strange one to Gershom Scholem, whose writings abound with the use of the words *dialectics* and *dialectical.*

To begin with, then, all of the essays in this volume are

written in the twentieth century about the twentieth century. As such, they illuminate some of the many miseries and few splendors of our time as seen not only from the perspective of a Jew, but from a Jewish perspective.

Second, all the essays in this book are either about Jews or about things Jewish, mostly about both at the same time. The connection between this common element and the first is easy enough to establish: no rational person can deny that Jews and Judaism occupy an absolutely crucial place in the history of the twentieth century. Suffice it to mention Hitler and the Holocaust, two phenomena that hang like a dark cloud over much of the material of this volume. In this respect one might consider Scholem's essay "Jews and Germans" to be the most representative piece in the volume.

Third, as follows inevitably from the previous considerations, this is a book about the *crisis* of our time in its various, mostly terrible, manifestations. Some of the pieces deal with the scope and limits of Zionism as a response to that crisis—especially "Jewish Youth Movement" and "Farewell," in which a very young Scholem appears as a Zionist taking Zionism to task for its lack of radicalism,[1] its failure to go to the roots of the problem it seeks to solve, its inability to effect a true conversion in most of its adherents. Other essays are attempts to gain insights into the most unfathomable event of the century, the Holocaust. They assess some of the fictions connected with it, as is evident in Scholem's protest against all prattle about a German-Jewish dialogue; they consider its effects on Israel and on Judaism, as can be seen from "Israel and the Diaspora" and "Reflections on Jewish Theology"; they discuss its impact on eminent men like Buber, Benjamin, and Agnon; they take a position on issues arising in its aftermath, like the author's stand on the Eichmann case and the reactions it produced. In all these instances, Scholem can be seen to examine his own time with an eye unclouded by either sentimentality or cynicism.

1. See Gershom Scholem, *Walter Benjamin—die Geschichte einer Freundschaft* (*Walter Benjamin—the History of a Friendship*) (Frankfurt-am-Main: Suhrkamp Verlag, 1975), pp. 41, 94. This volume, which is as yet available only in German, constitutes an invaluable complement to the two essays on Benjamin included here. Moreover, since it is also to a considerable extent about Jews and Judaism in the crisis of our time, it is to a considerable extent a companion volume to the present one. Its early translation into English would be most desirable.

Fourth, much of the writing in this volume is informed by a polemical and iconoclastic spirit. To put it crudely, Scholem likes to argue; at least he shows no reluctance to use the pen as a weapon in combating what he considers stupidity and wickedness or any unsavory combination of these signs of human frailty.

Finally, almost every selection in this volume (all but the introductory interview and the comments on Eichmann's execution were originally in German) provides irrefutable evidence that the author is a master of German prose. The editor, who is also the translator of most of the essays in the volume, can personally attest to the beauty of Scholem's prose. The prose can, to begin with, be used to show that Scholem is what W. H. Auden said of Henry James: a "master of nuance and scruple." As translator, what the editor has attempted to do here—unsuccessfully—is to recapture the rhythms and richness of sentences that are especially astounding when one considers the fact that their content is of a kind that is usually considered incompatible with graceful writing. Gershom Scholem has shown that the demands of rigorous scholarship and strict reasoning are not necessarily at variance with the demands of literary excellence.

This is not to say that Scholem's style remains static. In sixty years it undergoes noticeable changes (noticeable even in English, it is to be hoped). The two early Zionist essays betray a trace of Buber's influence—readers of the essay on Buber below will gain ample insight into Buber's style. Gradually but surely, thereafter, Scholem develops a voice of his own in a German unmistakably his own. No decline of passion whatsoever is in evidence—consider the statements on the absence of genuine dialogue between Jews and Germans—but the passion is all the more effective because it is disciplined and harnessed to the imperatives of strict argumentation. That the author has a keen interest in beautiful writing is clear from the substance of many remarks he makes; that he writes beautifully himself is evident from the manner in which he phrases his remarks. One might add that Scholem's German probably owes its purity to at least two identifiable factors apart from his genius. First, his style seems to be free of any major Nietzschean influence. Nietzsche's German was indeed remarkable, but its effect on those who came after him tended to be remarkably deleterious. Second, Scholem left

Germany at the beginning of the 1920s and was thus spared any contamination by the corrupted German of much of the twentieth century. No doubt exists, for example, that the Nazis both with and without clear intent left a horrible scar on their mother tongue. One need not dwell on the irony of the fact that today's most classic German may well be written by a Jew living in Israel.

IV

In 1973 the editor suggested to Gershom Scholem that his writings on "Jews and Germans" should be made available to English readers in book form, along with some other selected essays of his. He met with the editor in October 1973, at which time a tentative table of contents for his volume began to emerge.

The author, to be sure, expressed doubts in regard to two of the longest essays included in this book. He feared that the essay on Buber and the essay titled "Walter Benjamin and His Angel" might resist translation. Having read these essays with particular admiration, believing on some quasi-philosophical level that anything in German prose could be translated into English prose, and being brash, the editor thereupon declared that he could and would translate these essays—if Scholem himself offered help. The latter was willing.

The editor arrived in Jerusalem to teach for a semester at the Hebrew University in the fall of 1974; during the next six months, this book took shape. Gershom Scholem was extravagantly generous with his time. He checked over all the essays in this book translated for the first time for this volume, making numerous greatly helpful suggestions and changes.

As far as the two essays on Benjamin and Buber were concerned, he did more than check them over; he became an active collaborator, going over this editor's drafts page by page, and indeed line by line. Editor and author spent a number of afternoons poring over these translations, frequently sitting under Klee's *Angelus Novus*. It is to be hoped that the outcome of these labors not only proved Gershom Scholem right in assessing the difficulty with which these essays would yield their sense in

English, but also proved the editor right in presuming that the essays were possible to translate.

To say they were possible to translate is not to say they were easy to translate. Two examples of problems encountered must suffice; both are connected with the essay titled "Martin Buber's Conception of Judaism."

First of all, the early Buber, whom Scholem quotes extensively, wrote with a distinct and unmistakable style, partaking of bombast and other excess. Scholem's essay takes note of the excesses by quoting examples of them rather frequently. All translators know that a deficiency of style, inextricably tied as it is to the grammar, rhythm, and syntax of the original language, is particularly difficult to capture in another language. The reader himself must judge the success of the outcome.

Certain German words, secondly, tend to defy rendition into English at all, and do defy rendition by one constant equivalent. The word *Gestalt* is a good example. The sensible decision to keep it untranslated in English texts has been adopted in the case of another word abounding in Buber's texts and in Scholem's essay on him: *Erlebnis*. The alternative, to use a footnote each time it occurs, would be far too cumbersome. The problem is that German has two words for the English term *experience*: *Erfahrung* and *Erlebnis*. An *Erfahrung* can be passive; it can frequently be translated as *practical experience*. An *Erlebnis* is active; it can sometimes be rendered as a vital, vivid, or living experience; frequently it almost means *adventure*. A man who has gained rich and maturing experience throughout a lifetime is a man of *Erfahrung*; a man who has fully participated in a major event has had an *Erlebnis*. At Scholem's suggestion, and with the editor's full concurrence, a decision was reached to leave the word in German and to explain its use in the passage the reader has just read.

One must add that Gershom Scholem's labors were not confined to technical matters of translation. A perfectionist, he made use of the occasion to change a term here or there, as well as to make minor additions or deletions where he saw fit. A single example must suffice. The information that Buber gave a lecture in Polish in Jerusalem as late as 1943 is not contained in the original German version, nor is it the product of the editor's fancy; it was added by the author himself. Since Gershom Scholem has reviewed and revised the editor's translations, the present versions are to that extent the most authoritative to be found. That is also to say that the editor is not responsible for substantive deviations from the German, though he is certainly to be blamed for those passages in which justice has not been done to Gershom Scholem's exemplary German.

V

In working on this volume, the editor has incurred a number of debts. The staff of New York's Leo Baeck Institute proved most cooperative during two days of background research. The executive editor of Schocken Books, Seymour Barofsky, patiently put up with inevitable delays and was always helpful.

The editor is most obliged to Fania and Gershom Scholem. Mrs. Scholem was ever a perfect hostess and displayed the magic gift of producing coffee or Scotch at the exact moment they were required. She also managed to protect the editor against her husband's inability always to suffer fools and foolish questions gladly. As for Gershom Scholem himself, he performed more than the tasks mentioned previously. Offering more knowledge and wisdom than the editor, alas, could absorb, he performed the *mitzvah* of turning a bad Jew into a slightly better one.

WERNER J. DANNHAUSER

With Gershom Scholem: An Interview*

The Self-deception of Assimilation

Muki Tsur: Kurt Blumenfeld once defined German Zionism as post-assimilatory Judaism. To what extent does this reflect your own biography?

Gershom Scholem: Blumenfeld's definition holds for most, not all, the German Zionists. Some were beyond the bounds of assimilation. The Jews who came from Eastern Europe were not all assimilationist or on the brink of assimilation. Their children constituted a considerable part of the Zionist camp in Germany. This definition does not hold for Jews who came from Orthodox homes. After all, in Germany there was a considerable minority of pious Jews who had not exactly been ravaged by assimilation-ism, for obvious reasons; although some of the forms of assimila-tionism were to be found in such homes. These elements were an organic part of the soil that produced the Zionist movement, which I joined in 1911.

But the definition "post-assimilatory Jew" applies to me. I am a member of a family that had lived in Germany—in Silesia—for a long time, and came to Berlin at the beginning of the nineteenth century. I myself was a fourth-generation Berliner. The transition in our family from Orthodoxy at the beginning of the nineteenth century to almost total assimilation at the beginning of the twentieth was a matter of three generations—from my grandfather, through my father, to my own generation;

* From *Shdemot: Literary Digest of the Kibbutz Movement*, No. III (Spring, 1975), pp. 5–43. The interview was conducted by *Shdemot*'s managing editor, Muki Tsur, and the former managing editor, Abraham Shapira. Translated from Hebrew by Moshe Kohn.

in the third generation, assimilation was complete—or so it seemed.

The Jewish post-assimilatory renaissance meant a revolt against the life-style of the parents' home or of the circle of families like it. This was a conscious breakaway, a volitional act, a decision—albeit a childish one (I was fourteen at the time) though I didn't consider myself a child. Spiritually, I matured early. My decisions of that period were not clearly formulated, but the fact is that there was a decision to make a post-assimilatory break. At the time, I did not have an abstract-conceptual awareness of assimilationism. My awareness was an emotional one. This I shared with my contemporaries who joined the Zionist youth movements. If I had become a Zionist six or seven years later, I would no doubt have possessed the refined intellectual tools needed to understand what was happening. I went through many stages after that original break before I was able to formulate what was happening.

Muki: What did you break away from?

Scholem: The revolt, or the break—in instances like mine—was against self-deceit. A person living in a liberal-Jewish, German-assimilationist environment had the feeling that those people were devoting their entire lives to self-delusion.

We did not come to Zionism in search of politics. It is important to understand that for my contemporaries in Germany, Zionism was only to a limited degree (it would be wrong to say not at all) a political Zionism. Some of us, to be sure, went on to become real political Zionists, but the Zionist choice was a moral decision, an emotional one, an honesty-seeking response. The honesty did not express itself in the desire for a state, but in a revolt against the lie that Jewish existence was. Jewish reality seemed alive, flourishing, but those who went over to Zionism saw that reality as rotten. Zionism was a revolt against the life-style of the run-of-the-mill bourgeoisie to which my family belonged. This was the milieu in which hundreds of thousands of young Jews grew up in Germany.

Muki: Wasn't there the possibility of going over—out of the same motives—to the Revolution?

Four Brothers, Four Ways

Scholem: Of course that possibility existed. In those years only a minority of the youth joined the Zionist movement, whereas the great majority was assimilationist and chose self-deceit—that is: the total Germanization of the Jews. Another small minority—which included my brother Werner—joined the Revolutionary camp.

We were four brothers. Two of them took after my father. One of them was even more German than my father, a right-wing German nationalist, a *Deutschnationaler.* The other one merely wanted everything to be all right; he had no special ideals. My third brother, who was two years older than me, opted for the Revolution. He was killed in Buchenwald by the Nazis, as a former Communist Party Reichstag [German Parliament] deputy. This brother of mine, who at first had thought that Zionism might be the way, one day wrote a letter to that Zionist youth organization saying that he had found something broader than the narrow little thing called Jewish nationalism; he had found: Humanity. He became a left-wing radical socialist and took part in all the splits of the Social Democratic Party in Germany, finally landing with the Communists in 1921. Six years later they expelled him as a Trotskyist, along with most of the Jews in the Communist movement. (Actually, the overwhelming majority of the leading Trotskyists were Jews—something that people today like to gloss over, the way people always gloss over unpleasant facts.)

That was before World War I. Why was one brother attracted to German Social Democracy and the other to Zionism? I don't know. This is the sort of personal decision that nobody can explain.

My Social Democrat brother was the third son. He was the only one of my brothers with whom I was close. I never had any serious conversations with my oldest brothers. The eldest (he is six years older than I) is living in Australia, and he is still what he was. In 1971 he told me, "What, Hitler is going to tell me what I am?!"

I wasn't drawn to the Revolution. I had stormy debates with

my brother. I told him, "You're deluding yourself the same way
Papa is deluding himself. You are deluding yourself by imagining
that you represent Germany's exploited industrial workers. That's
a lie. You don't represent a thing. You're the son of a middle-class
bourgeois Jew. That makes you furious, so you go wandering off
into other fields; you don't want to be what you are. You say: The
Revolution (that was the general slogan of the time) will solve all
problems, especially the national problems." At that time we did
not yet know—we weren't that wise yet, neither he nor I—that
the Revolution, as the historical reality we became familiar with,
had not solved a thing. (I am now speaking of the Revolution, not
as an abstract concept, but as a concrete idea we had seen in
reality.)

Jews Are Only Good for Going to Synagogue With

Muki: How do you explain your break with your home?

Scholem: Of course, I can't explain why a fifteen-year-old boy
decides as he does. Something impels him, draws him, after a
situation of emptiness; after being surfeited with things that he
felt lacked vitality.

The members of the assimilatory generation angrily rejected
the charges of their children. Papa certainly didn't enjoy hearing
me tell him he was deceiving himself. This resulted in our total
estrangement from each other. When I came home and said, "I
think I want to be a Jew," Papa responded by quoting the maxim
that was so popular among German Jewry: "Jews are only good
for going to synagogue with."

When he started talking to me in that vein, I got angry and
said, "That's all a lie!" This feeling continued to develop in me
during those prewar years and all through the war, during that
critical period for the world as a whole and for the Jews in
particular. In the end, there was nothing we had to say to each
other—nothing that interested me or interested him. I an-
nounced that I was going to study Hebrew: that was how my
decision to rebel expressed itself. I wasn't sure yet whether I
wanted to be an observant Jew. But a Jew I wanted to be.

Muki: Was it a decision to be a Jew or to be a Zionist?

Scholem: For me there was no difference between the two. When I woke up one fine morning . . . how did I wake up? Before I arrived at this Jewish turn, I had been interested in history. One day I happened on Graetz's book, *History of the Jews.* Although he would not admit it, he was a national Jew, on the threshold of Zionism. This becomes clear when you read his book, especially the German version. It is clear that Graetz did not like Gentiles. They sensed this, and it did him considerable harm.

On the other hand, I grew increasingly critical of my milieu. According to the ideology on which we were reared—to the extent that we were reared at all—we were Germans; true—we were told—we are Jews, and we brought the world monotheism, but Christianity is only a watered-down version of Judaism, and there isn't such a fundamental difference between the two.

I noticed that in all my years at home, till my father threw me out on account of my Zionism, I had never seen a German Christian in our home. Ours was an ordinary, middle-class bourgeois home, neither rich nor poor. But no Christian ever set foot in our home, even though Papa had a theory that everything was all right.

As a young man, Papa had been active in a movement that had wide popularity among the petite bourgeoisie: the gymnasts —*Turnerschaft,* in German (a word, incidentally, that was coined 160 years ago). Papa was active there before the rise of organized anti-Semitism. It took several decades for anti-Semitism to become organized. In Germany it began in the 1880s—just at the time Papa had started becoming active. Berlin was a very liberal city at the time, under a liberal government. Anti-Semitism began to make headway in those circles and started raising its head. Most of the organizations that had Jewish members started discreetly making them feel unwelcome. Papa sensed this and stopped being active, but he did not resign. He remained a member of that organization all through the years. Our family was in the printing business; we owned two printshops, Grandpa's and Papa's. In Germany there were employers' associations and joint organizations with the workers, such as group health plans. Papa was also active in those.

As I said: except for a formal fiftieth-birthday visit, for

example, no Christian member of any of the organizations in which Papa was active ever set foot in our home. And I sensed it.

"Do you want to return to the ghetto?" they argued with me. I replied, "You are the ones who are living in the ghetto. Only you won't admit it. Where are the Gentiles? I've never seen a single one of them come to your homes for a social call."

My grandfathers had received an Orthodox upbringing. They had grown up Orthodox, and all of them made the transition to German society without cutting themselves off completely. I was a little boy when they died—four and nine years old—so I had no close ties with them. My parents were already a product of that transition of lower-class Jews of Silesia to the Berlin petite bourgeoisie.

There was not an iota of Jewish observance in our family. Friday night was observed as family night. The uncles—my father, his brothers and their families—would get together the way they used to do at my grandmother's, who had since died. Afterward, they continued to get together, more or less, the way assimilated families do. We didn't observe the Sabbath proper but Sabbath Eve—just as we didn't observe Passover, Shavuot, or Sukkot, but only sat together at an all-family Seder on Passover Eve. Though one of the uncles, who knew how to read Hebrew without knowing what he was reading, would recite the Haggada in some kind of singsong, and everybody sang *"Ehad mi yodea"* and *"Had gadya."* We made something of a mess of it. The melodies were more popular and better remembered than the words. But many families didn't even have these Sabbath Eve get-togethers.

Papa worked on Yom Kippur, and didn't go to synagogue. That was an advanced degree of assimilation, because most of the assimilating Jews went to synagogue on Yom Kippur. There are numerous degrees and shades between observance and estrangement.

I signed up at the Jewish community library in Berlin, and I started reading Judaica. That was a big step for me. Very soon I told myself, "I want to learn Hebrew." In the lessons in Jewish religion conducted in the school I went to, we didn't learn the Hebrew alphabet. Papa and Mama objected to my Hebrew studies. I looked for somebody to teach me. I wanted to learn Hebrew because of my interest in Judaism. It seemed very rational to me. Today I ask myself whether it was really all that rational. What interested me then was to find a way to the Jewish primary sources. I was not content with reading *about* things. This has characterized my whole life.

Muki: Was your decision influenced by anti-Semitism?

Scholem: I can't say that I suffered from anti-Semitism as a boy. I had virtually no encounters with anti-Semitism, and those I did have did not leave a deep mark on me, although at that time—thirty years after its beginning—the anti-Semitic movement in Germany had already gathered real strength.

There's Nothing to Be Learned from the Zionists

Muki: How did you learn Hebrew?

Scholem: I taught myself. I went to my former teacher in Jewish religion (in those classes at school, incidentally, we read selected Biblical passages in German), and I said to him, "Are you prepared to teach me to read and write Hebrew?" Twice a week I and one of my friends would stay after school for an hour, and we learned. We learned quickly. I wanted to learn. It interested me. I did it with a passion. I also taught myself Hebrew grammar.

Muki: But you also rebelled against the Zionists.

Scholem: Correct. I got to know the Zionists in Germany. I went to meetings—especially of Zionist youth groups. I was an active member of one of those groups for several years. This group—to a considerable extent under my influence—developed into the most radical group in German Zionism. Some of its members were later to found Kibbutz Bet Zera in the Jordan Valley.

I wanted to learn. That is how the awakening of my Jewish interest expressed itself. I wanted to know who the Jews were. I didn't know exactly, but neither did the Zionists.

The German Zionists were generally ignoramuses. One of Papa's brothers was a Zionist from the outset. After Grandpa died, he took over the printshop. He was also one of the founders

of Bar-Kochba (today known as Maccabi), the sports organization. Nordau spoke of a Judaism of muscles, of Jewish sports
education.

My uncle printed the World Zionist Organization's newspaper, *Die Welt,* and the organ of the German Zionist Organization,
the *Jüdische Rundschau.* He was a real Zionist, but he didn't
know much about Judaism. I saw immediately that there was
nothing to be learned from him, even though he was somehow a
Zionist, by feeling. He wanted to be a Zionist, but he drew no
conclusions from that. So—although I was twenty-five years
younger than he, I didn't care for his Zionism. In my family
circle, they laughed at my uncle's Zionism—"Zionist" was
something funny to them—but that didn't bother me one bit. It
seemed perfectly all right to me that he said he wanted to be a
Jew, but that wasn't enough for me—I wanted to learn, and those
Zionists had nothing to teach.

So I joined a Zionist youth club.

Muki: Which one?

Scholem: Jung Juda [Young Judea]. They were high-school
juniors and seniors. The Zionist university students busied
themselves with propaganda activity and preparing cadres that
would carry on with Zionist activity on the campus after
matriculating. I started going there with my brother in 1912.
There I met observant Jews for the first time. Although my
maternal grandfather had founded a synagogue in West Berlin,
there was not a single observant Jew in my family circle.

During Passover 1913, one of them told me that Talmud
classes were being started in one of the Berlin Jewish communal
religious schools. I asked, "Do I know enough to participate?" He
said, "Try. We don't know anything either." So I went. A small
group of pious Conservative rabbis had started a class for
sixteen-year-olds, who were no longer required by law to take
religious lessons. They wanted to teach Gemara, Mishnah, things
that weren't taught in the Jewish communal afternoon schools.
The Jewish Community Council was opposed to the project and
refused to pay the teachers' salaries. It is impossible to understand today what the Jewish community councils were like at the
time they were run by the anti-Zionists.

Those teachers were real idealists. They worked without pay.

About ten people from all Berlin attended that class. I was one of them. We learned every Sunday from 7 A.M. to 1 P.M.—Mishnah, Gemara, Torah with Rashi's commentary, Bible. It seems that the year before that, in which I had learned by myself, had sufficed to put me on a par with those who had had seven years of afternoon religious school!

The teachers were Orthodox men, some of them pro-Zionist, some anti-Zionist. One of them had a great educational influence on me. He was a great-grandson of Rabbi Akiva Eiger: a very observant man, a bachelor who had never married because the girl he wanted had married some rich fellow instead of him, the poor rabbi; he was a real idealist. He was not a great scholar, but he was a marvelous teacher, a tremendous pedagogue. He was such a good person, a loner, so full of goodwill. He was happy that we young people—eight out of the ten of us Zionists—came to him. I owe these teachers of mine a great deal. I once wrote about this teacher of mine, Dr. A. J. Bleichrode, of blessed memory.

Mrs. Scholem: Many years later, we were participating in a class in Jerusalem, and one of the people there was asking such questions that if one of us had asked them, Scholem would have made short shrift of us. But he answered this gentleman with extraordinary patience. We had no idea who he was. When the session was over, Scholem said—in the words of Rabbi Akiva to his disciples when they unknowingly tried to keep his wife from approaching him: "Whatever I possess and whatever you possess —we owe to Him." That was Rabbi Bleichrode. He got to sit and study in Jerusalem a few years longer—study under Scholem.

Agudat Yisrael

Scholem: I not only studied under him, I even joined the Agudat Yisrael [today the most extremely Orthodox of the parties represented in Israel's Parliament].

Muki: Agudat Yisrael?

Scholem: Agudat Yisrael was founded in 1911, the year I became a Zionist, as a competitor to Zionism. Organizationally, structurally, and in its slogans, Agudat Yisrael was a total imitation of Zionism, except that it was Orthodox. It was not yet anti-Zionist then the way it became at the end of World War I and in the 1920s. It was very powerful in one activity: studying. What is more, of course—and this must always be said to the credit of the Orthodox—they never took a single penny of tuition fee. I studied for ten years—from 1913 to 1923—in Germany and Switzerland, with rabbis or Orthodox lay scholars, and not one of them ever dreamt of taking as much as a half-pfennig from me. We must give full credit to those circles for their great idealism. Every student who taught spoken Hebrew had somehow to earn money to pay for his studies at Berlin University. So to learn to speak Hebrew you paid money, but if you wanted to learn "Torah"—Bible, commentaries, Talmud, medieval Hebrew literature—it never cost you a penny.

I left Agudat Yisrael because I didn't want to be Orthodox. I hesitated about becoming observant. For some reason it didn't appeal to me. Judaism interested me very much, but not the practice of observances. In that respect, the only thing that attracted me was the synagogue, and I went for some years—at first every Friday evening, and then every Sabbath morning. When I was a high-school student, I often went to a synagogue that had an organ. Afterwards I went to an Orthodox synagogue without an organ. I liked both of them. To this day I don't quite understand what people have against an organ. On the other hand, I enjoyed the style of prayer in the old Orthodox synagogue in Berlin. The Orthodox thought I would be a great *baal teshuva* [penitent] like Ernst Simon—today Hebrew University Emeritus Professor of Education—and they received me nicely. But *kashrut,* for example—kitchen Judaism—held little attraction for me. My first wife was from a very Orthodox family, though she herself was not Orthodox. We married in Eretz Yisrael one month after I arrived here (she had come half a year earlier). We discussed whether to keep a kosher home—that variety of Judaism made no sense to me. My father had said to me, "Why don't you become a rabbi? If you want *Yiddishkeit* so much, then become a rabbi and you'll be able to keep busy with *Yiddishkeit* all your life." I told him, "I don't want to be a rabbi." Papa didn't understand what I wanted: *Yiddishkeit* without anything? I called it Zionism.

I studied Hebrew without a sense that one day I would really know it. I thought it was extremely difficult, that I would never master it. But after four or five years of intensive study I found that it was possible to master Hebrew.

The Zionist Youth Movement

Muki: How did the Zionist youth movement impress you?

Scholem: It's hard for me to say. I had few experiences there. I belonged to Jung Juda as long as it existed. It was a small group—only twenty or thirty people—and eventually developed into a radical circle. It consisted of Jewish students, some of whom belonged to other Zionist organizations that did not attract me because they had taken over strong assimilationist influences. They thought that because of their Jewish pride, and in order to safeguard Jewish honor in the eyes of the Gentiles, we had to organize ourselves the way the Gentiles did and carry the war back to them in their style. That repelled me. I was not a member of any students' association. I was an "asocial" anarchist. Perhaps the real, secret reason was that I didn't like smoking. When they all sat there smoking at the Jung Juda meetings, I would get a headache. I hate smoke-filled rooms. It may be that I didn't go to those students' associations not for any of the profound reasons I mentioned, but for a physiological reason.

There were Zionist youth groups that imitated the rebellious German youth by going on outings and hikes: back to nature. One of the important organizations of this sort was the Blau-Weiss [Blue-White], an organization of young Jewish hikers in ferment. Most of my friends joined, but I didn't. My attitude to them was that of a very critical outsider.

Why? In 1917, when I was 19, I wrote a long and formidable article in their group-leaders' journal, in which I argued that people were deluding themselves if they thought that a person's Jewishness was nurtured by sending him out to look at nature instead of by study. I argued that it was necessary to learn the Jewish primary sources, and that the Jewish youth movements had to change their ways. I thought they were confused. Confusion was my favorite word in my first years of Zionist activity. I waged war against this confusion. It seemed to me that the Zionists were creating assimilation within Zionism, imitating alien frameworks, singing 400-year-old mercenaries' songs. This excited all the others, but not me; it didn't interest me one bit. In the first years they said, "Of course, we agree; that is what we all wish, but we have no time for it." I said, "This comes first. It is forbidden to engage in propaganda so long as the propagandist is not setting an example." The whole discussion centered around this matter of setting an example, on educating, on what one has to do to be worthy of being an educator. To tell you the truth, I wasn't interested in becoming an educator.

Youth Movements: From Romanticism to an Order

Muki: There were two phases to your revolt against the Jewish youth movement. The first was against its romanticism; and the second—later on—was against the way it organized itself as an "order." Do you see any connection between these two phases of the youth movement?

Scholem: There was a dialectical logic to this process. The Blau-Weiss people started as romantics and ended up fascists. As you know, it isn't popular to say that Zionism has fascists, too. But I think it does, even in Israel.

The way from the romanticism of Blau-Weiss to Walter Moses' fascist order was a typically dialectical one, with things developing intensively and vigorously in a very short time. The transition took five years, the way it happened in the opposite direction with Hashomer Hatzair.

The transition in Hashomer Hatzair from romanticism to Marxism took place from 1924 to 1929. By 1930 they were already Marxists. With some, it started in Galicia, when a large part of the Galician Hashomer Hatzair left Zionism; we are not told that very many of the Hashomer Hatzair people in Galicia left Zionism and went over to Communism, but it's a fact. This was an intensive development of things that were in a state of high tension.

Muki: Did you openly express your criticism of the movements' second generation?

Scholem: What I wrote against the romantic aspect was crystalized in several articles that I wrote between 1916 and 1918. They evoked considerable comment. I criticized the counterfeit romanticism, which was German romanticism in Zionist guise rather than relating itself to Eretz Yisrael. Against the second phase I wrote only one thing: the big pronunciamento against Walter Moses' Blau-Weiss.

This is a long text that I wrote in 1922, when the fascistization that caused an immediate crisis was already on the scene and three years before the total decline of the Blau-Weiss. When their first *olim*—some fifty or sixty boys—came to Eretz Yisrael, there was an immediate collision with the Histadrut. That was in 1925. The following year the Blau-Weiss disbanded officially. Walter Moses opened the Dubek cigarette factory in Tel Aviv.

Opposition to the War

Muki: What stand did you take on World War I?

Scholem: During the war years I was close to my brother. The two of us were part of a small minority in Germany that opposed the war, and we certainly were not partners to the general war enthusiasm—my brother for Socialist reasons, and I for Zionist reasons, though our common attitude brought us closer to each other.

At the beginning of the war, I and several of my friends wrote a letter to the German Zionist newspaper protesting against a patriotic article written by a certain Zionist who was then a follower of Martin Buber's and is still living with us in Jerusalem. He concluded his article approximately thus: "And so we went to war not despite our being Jews but because of our being Zionists." This sentence made me furious. I protested against the publication of such a statement. There are people in the Zionist movement—I argued—who think that this is not our war; perhaps we ought to do our duty and enlist—but I doubt even that. Be that as it may, in this war of Germany's, Russia's, or England's, the question with respect to Jewish interests is whether or not they coincide with Germany's. In our letter, we questioned whether they did. We protested against the publication of that pro-German letter simply because censorship made the editors afraid to express any other point of view. We considered the Zionist movement's endorsement of Germany's war against Britain as scandalous. That was at the beginning of 1915.

Muki: Was Buber a German patriot?

Scholem: In a way, yes. This is a very complicated matter, a strange chapter in Buber's life. One of the things that preoccupied me in my Zionist youth was Buber. All through 1914, after I left Agudat Yisrael, I was greatly influenced by Buber. But after a year I left him—not him personally, but his way of looking at things. I read all his writings. He was very popular then among the Zionist youth, because they thought that Buber was Zionism. But I was very disappointed by his stand on the war. The things he was publishing then got me very angry; I was especially angered by the writings of the Buberites. I knew some of them.

My rebellion against Buber's way of looking at things developed because I was convinced that a person who writes as bellicosely as he was writing could not be a true teacher. Buber was a tremendous force in Germany then; he had a profound influence on the youth. But after the war he was also a disappointment—not only to me, but also the romantic youth, who at a certain point were prepared to swallow whatever he felt like feeding them. Buber said very big things, things that looked very extreme, very radical, but it seemed to me that he drew no conclusions from them. When the time came to plan and act, he joined forces with the religious socialists in Germany instead of with the people of Degania. This surprised me, for I thought that after the war Buber would go—as all of us should have gone—but he did not go—as others did not—to Eretz Yisrael.

During the war (1915–16) I brought out an underground newspaper called *Blue-White Spectacles,* whose aim was to see and show things through Zionist spectacles. It contained antiwar poems and articles, etc. It was a Zionist newspaper for activist youth, preaching radical Zionism. I published an antiwar poem of my own. The newspaper was printed by lithograph, in Papa's printshop. I still have the three issues that appeared.

That letter to the editor that I mentioned fell into the wrong hands, and in 1915 I was expelled from school. I was then seventeen. As a result I gained a year, starting university at seventeen.

Muki: You were expelled from school and accepted at the university?

Scholem: In Prussia there was a special law for the benefit of the Junkers. In the landed nobility, the eldest son would be an army officer, the second son studied law and became a senior bureaucrat, and the third son inherited the estate. He did not study and did not have to be smart, but still, for social reasons, they wanted him to be a somebody. So they issued a regulation whereby anybody who had reached age sixteen and completed ten years of school could enroll at a university faculty of letters or agriculture as a regular student for four semesters but could not sit for examinations. This was intended to give the youngest sons some "polish." If this law had been widely publicized, all the gifted young Jews would have gone right to university. This was expressly stated in the university regulations—but who reads regulations? Between 1915 and 1919 I studied mathematics at university. I was good in math, but I realized that that was not my forte. Why did I study math when I already knew that after the war I would leave for Eretz Yisrael? I thought of being a teacher and prepared myself for that. Later, when I knew Hebrew, I bought myself math books that had been published by the Hebrew Gymnasia in Jaffa. I committed them to memory, so that I would be able to be a high-school teacher in Eretz Yisrael.

Cast Out of the House—and Playing a Part

Meanwhile, I underwent all kinds of crises. Early in 1917 my brother was arrested for participating in an antiwar demonstration. And Papa threw me out of the house. He said, "It's all the same—socialism, Zionism—it's all antipatriotic." He sent me a registered letter ordering me to leave his household by March 1, 1917. He made me a one-time gift of 100 marks and said, "Go fend for yourself. I am under no obligation to support you. Do what you wish, or do nothing."

I went to live with Zalman Shazar, who was eight years older than me. He didn't own a thing, and neither did I, but we lived marvelously. We lived in a kosher boardinghouse in which none of the boarders were kosher. The others were all Russian Jews; I was the only *Yekke* [German Jew]. I stayed there till they tried to draft me into the army [that summer]. For two years I had evaded conscription.

Muki: How?

Scholem: When I was called up, I decided I wasn't going to serve. I wanted to learn to shoot—I was no pacifist—but I didn't want to fight for Germany. Three months later I was sent home as an incurable schizophrenic: that is what the official documents said.

Muki: You put on an act?

Scholem: I put on an act without knowing what I was acting. I played myself, only more so. The game I was playing required a tremendous effort of concentration and keeping up the tension, and a tremendous will to succeed. I spent six weeks in a lunatic asylum where I had been sent for observation and checkups. There they ruled me totally insane. Those were the six most intense weeks of my life because I was healthier than the doctors. The problem was to keep them bluffed. My behavior was guided by materialistic calculations: how not to be found out by them when, for example, they would look me in the eyes and say to me, "What are you doing? What kind of act are you putting on here?" I had never read a book on mental ailments, and I was guided solely by intuition. And it worked.

Papa had to take me back because the doctors made him. But I didn't want to go on living in his house, so I went to Jena to study math. At Jena I had to sign my discharge papers, which included a chit saying I was insane, an incurable schizophrenic. (They were not supposed to show this to me!) At that time this was called "adolescent insanity." At Jena I taught Hebrew to a few girls, Zionist students, and I "converted" Toni Halle (who was later the principal of the Tichon Hadash High School in Tel Aviv) to Zionism. One of my pupils was a girl medical student—a Zionist—from Erfurt. One day I asked her, "What is dementia praecox?" She stared at me and said, "Do you have it?" "Yes," I said. "Have you come across it in your studies?" she said. "No," I said, "I just want to know how you eat it." She gave me some books to read and took me to a psychiatric clinic. There I saw a real case of what I had been playacting. Then I saw what a powerful intuition had guided me.

When I was summoned for a reexamination, I got a blanket exemption from military service and then a passport to Switzerland. I spent a year and a half there, with my friend Walter Benjamin.

Into the World of the Kabbalah

Muki: How did you come to study *kabbalah?*

Scholem: Simple, in one respect. In another respect—impossible to explain. In what way simple? I started reading Judaica intensively. I was impressed, and I started getting interested in details. I happened to have an excellent memory—for numbers, dates, all sorts of silly things. I read, and I started getting interested in *kabbalah* already in 1915. I still have the first notes on the subject, and the books I bought that year—Hebrew and German. I still use the copy of the Zohar I bought that year. I didn't understand it. I wanted to know, and I couldn't find a person who could teach Zohar. My rabbi couldn't. My childhood friend, Aaron (Harry) Heller—later one of Israel's leading physicians—and I asked him to teach us *kabbalah.* He suggested that a small group of us read the *musar* [ethics] book *Reshit Hokhmah* together. We learned till he stopped. He said, "Children, I can't explain the quotations from the Zohar. I don't understand them." He was an extremely straightforward man.

I also read Graetz's chapters on the *kabbalah.* I liked Graetz very much as a historian, but I was extremely critical of his attitude to the *kabbalah.* It was clear to me that the kabbalists could not possibly have been the kind of scoundrels, swindlers, or idiots he described.

In the nineteenth century not a single sensible thing was written on *kabbalah.* Certainly not by the Jewish *Maskillim* [modernists of the Enlightenment]. There were just one or two philosophers of the German Idealistic school who had dealt with the subject. There was, for example, a devout Catholic of a special, weird sort of liberal bent, who had written four volumes in German on the *kabbalah.* I felt that he had a closer affinity to the subject than the *Maskillim*. I quickly realized that the subject of *kabbalah* disturbed the Jewish historiography of the nineteenth century—all the schools in Italy, Germany, Galicia, Hungary, and Moravia that had produced the great Judaica scholars of the time.

Then it was still something latent: I read all around the subject, but it hadn't quite gripped me. I started teaching myself to read the Zohar. Strange, but it was impossible to find a teacher. I was able to read the Talmud, I knew Aramaic; it's possible to learn Aramaic—there's nothing superhuman about it. True, I was busy with other things; reading Judaica and Hebrew. But my interest in *kabbalah* gradually intensified. Even though I didn't identify with it, I wanted to know what there is to this *kabbalah*.

When I was in Switzerland in 1919, I made notes on *kabbalah*. Even before I knew anything, I jotted down things on what interested me in *kabbalah* philosophically, on what I thought it should be. And indeed, most of my jottings proved to be wrong, but they influenced my approach. I considered whether it was worthwhile devoting a few years of intensive study to *kabbalah*. In any case, Judaism as a living phenomenon attracted me. I wanted to enter the world of *kabbalah* out of my belief in Zionism as a living thing—as the restoration of a people that had degenerated quite a bit. I was a great admirer of Y. H. Brenner [the Hebrew fiction writer and thinker who was killed in the Arab riots of 1921 at age forty]. I was certainly one of only about ten persons in all Germany to have read Brenner in Hebrew. Brenner's Hebrew was rather difficult: one also had to know Talmud well, for he used Aramaic. Altogether, I don't understand how a young person today can read his novel *Shekhol Vekishalon (Breakdown and Bereavement)* without knowing the Jewish primary sources.

I debated with myself whether it was worthwhile investing a concentrated effort in studying *kabbalah*, studying the Hebrew and Aramaic primary sources, and doing Ph.D. work on it, instead of continuing with mathematics.

I didn't know whether to go to Göttingen, the mathematicians' Mecca, or to Munich, the only place with a large collection of kabbalistic manuscripts (the collection is still there). Finally, I decided to go to Munich and do a Ph.D. in *kabbalah*. I had an excellent topic, a philosophical one.

Muki: What theme did you want to treat?

Scholem: I wanted to write on the linguistic theory of the kabbalists. An excellent idea. When I got down to work, I saw that I didn't understand enough and I stopped writing. I wrote that particular essay a few years ago—exactly fifty years after having given up. At that time I didn't know I would be dealing with *kabbalah* the rest of my life. I had thought of writing of other things. I wanted to write on the Book of Lamentations and the *kinnot* [Tishah Be-av dirges] as a literary genre. I had a metaphysical theory on the essence of the *kinnot*. At that time I wrote a number of things which I have never published: a commentary on the Book of Jonah, another one on Job—or rather, a basis for a commentary on Jonah and Job—metaphysical reflections of mine that were suppressed.

In the months before going to Switzerland, in 1917–18, it became clear to me that I was interested in those kabbalistic matters. I was interested in the question: Does halakhic Judaism have enough potency to survive? Is *halakhah* really possible without a mystical foundation? Does it have enough vitality of its own to survive for two thousand years without degenerating? I appreciated *halakhah* without identifying with its imperatives. This question was tied up with my dreams about the *kabbalah*, through the notion that it might be *kabbalah* that explains the survival of the consolidated force of halakhic Judaism. That was certainly one of my obvious motives.

I didn't know the answers to those questions, but I had all kinds of notions and assumptions.

Gradually I taught myself to read the Zohar—never mind understanding; the important thing was to break through. It took a long time to master the text. I felt a certain sympathy, but I was also repulsed by many features of *kabbalah*. I did not, God forbid, think that that was truth, that was philosophy. But I thought it was worthwhile examining it all also from the philosophical aspect. There were two levels I was interested in for the sake of arriving at an understanding of Judaism:

"historiosophy"—the dialectic manifesting itself in spiritual processes—and the philosophical-metaphysical sphere. I tried to arrive at an understanding of what kept Judaism alive.

I suppose I have some sort of predilection for mysticism. I never sneered at the mystics, and I do not share the views of those who do. They had a certain something that we lack.

Muki: Did those first thoughts ever come back to you—especially with regard to the philosophical aspect?

Scholem: Yes. Very much so. I have referred to it a number of times in my writings—sometimes in hints, sometimes very explicitly. I have written quite a bit on this in my analyses of the thoughts of kabbalists or of kabbalistic systems.

I worked on several presuppositions. In the course of the work, the premises proved wrong or changed. But whenever I approached a subject, I did so with a curiosity that had something uniquely mine in it. Perhaps it was that I wanted to get to know a Judaism of which I was ignorant and there was nobody to explain it.

I was prepared to assume that, philosophically speaking, there are certain things which perhaps the mystics knew and other people don't know. I thought that in a few years I would go on to another field of Jewish thought.

Franz Rosenzweig's Judaism

Muki: What did you think of Franz Rosenzweig's attempt to answer these questions?

Scholem: I was very critical. What impressed me was the force of his thinking. But two aspects of his thinking got me angry. One was the ecclesiastical aspect he gave Judaism in his book; the way he saw Judaism as a kind of pietistic Protestant church. The second was the Jewish-German synthesis he wanted to create. I have never been able to tolerate that. The German-Jew that Rosenzweig set up as an ideal was intolerable to me. Very soon I found myself in a very acute personal crisis in my relations with Rosenzweig.

Muki: Did you know him personally?

Scholem: Of course. When Rosenzweig started getting inter-

ested in Judaism, he heard about me. I was some sort of freak
phenomenon. People told him: There is this young Scholem
fellow who has gone out of his mind, a Jew from a nonobservant
family, who doesn't want to put on *tefillin* [phylacteries] and all
that, but who is sitting and studying Hebrew and busying himself
with Judaism, and wants to know what it's all about, and is a
passionate Zionist.

Rosenzweig had been in an army hospital together with a
man who had been influenced by me when I was battling the
Blau-Weiss. This man had told him about me. He sent me his first
writings: translations of prayers from Hebrew into German. They
are very interesting, and in some respects very strange. As a
translator he was a unique phenomenon. We met several times.

Once we had a terrible scene. I attacked him—and not
gently—for his Jewish-German harmony, which I utterly rejected. He wasn't a Zionist. He was much more fanatical and
radical than me. Very authoritarian: he couldn't tolerate anyone
rebutting opinions that were important to him. He thought he
wouldn't be able to go on living if he should have to choose
between Germanness and Jewishness. He was ten years older
than me and nine years younger than Buber. After that scene
between us in 1922, he became very ill. If I had known he was
sick, I wouldn't have started that discussion about Germanness
and Jewishness. It was an obsession with both of us—for me a
negative one, and for him a positive one. In 1927, when I was in
Frankfurt, Ernst Simon told me that Rosenzweig would be very
glad if I paid him a visit. I went.

Muki: And you talked?

Scholem: He was mute by then. I spoke and he answered in
short sentences—by signals that his wife wrote down.

Muki: Did you have the impression that he was happy about
your visit?

Scholem: Certainly.

Between Conservatism and Change

Muki: Besides the two reservations that you mentioned, was
there anything in Rosenzweig's thought that gripped you?

Scholem: The Star of Redemption is a profound and very important book, despite the difficulty in imagining that we will accept it as the Jewish theological system. I think that Judaism is in for changes of form. Certain historical forms aren't destined to survive forever, and I strongly doubt whether the traditional Jewish forms are going to survive in their present form, although it certainly is desirable that something should—and reasonable to assume that something will—remain. Whether a little or a lot, I don't know. My views, in any case, were and are very far from the church conception of Judaism. If you ask me today whether —in light of all that has happened in the last fifty years—I believe that the Jewish future lies in the traditional Orthodox framework, my answer is no. Rosenzweig's view was a conservative one. He lived in a fixed traditional liturgical year. I think there will be a crisis of birth or a crisis of passage into oblivion; time will tell. But Rosenzweig's direction—of crystalizing tradition in what I call church form—is very far from what is happening in Israel in the area of Jewish renewal.

I don't know what form will crystalize here, whether there will be some synthesis of the conservative forces and the forces of change. The situation may be much more dangerous than we think, but I don't believe a new church will come into being. I see something today that I didn't see fifty years ago: the threat of death, of oblivion, in the processes unfolding here. As for the Diaspora—I don't see productive forces that will manifest anything Jewish that will endure, anything of enduring value.

But whether we will show that potential here—that depends on a whole complex of matters that do not hinge on us alone. When you look at the secularization process, at the barbarization of the so-called new culture, you can perceive grave processes in which it is difficult to discern any seed of future, any fructifying seed. But who knows? Maybe there is no other way of undergoing crises. Degeneration for the purpose of regeneration.

The Way to Israel: Between Romanticism and Realism

Muki: What motivated you to come and settle in Eretz Yisrael?

Scholem: I really thought that a Jew has to go to Eretz Yisrael, even if we were going to be a small sect there. We didn't know there would be millions. Who knew? The problem was a personal, not a national, one. I don't know what my problem would have been if I had come from among the impoverished Jews of Poland. But for a German Jew like me, it was a personal problem: is this the way?

I believed that if there was any prospect of a substantive regeneration of Judaism, of Judaism revealing its latent potential —this could happen only here, through the Jewish person's reencounter with himself, with his people, with his roots.

Muki: In Germany before coming to Eretz Yisrael, did you meet any people who had been here?

Scholem: Quite a few. During World War I there were several dozen Eretz Yisrael Jews—"Palestinians"—in Germany.

Muki: What did they say about the country?

Scholem: They had all come to Germany before the outbreak of the war and had got stuck there. Among them were talkers—speechmakers—at Zionist youth meetings. They spoke about Eretz Yisrael as romantics. If they didn't speak as romantics, they talked foulmouthed talk. That is how I learned to curse in Hebrew—something the primary sources didn't give you. Sometimes they spoke of the difficulties, the unpleasantnesses, but generally speaking, they were patriots. I didn't see any others. Those who had no intention of returning to Eretz Yisrael certainly didn't bother to meet with the Jewish youth. The vast majority of them returned.

There were also some German Zionists who had gone to Eretz Yisrael before the war and returned to Germany.

Muki: For example?

Scholem: The engineer Josef Loewy. He had spent several years in Eretz Yisrael before the war and had received his call-up orders from the German army. Loewy had lived in Haifa and Tel Aviv for several years. He spoke realistically, not romantically, about the country. He was embittered and told awful things about the leaders of the *yishuv* [the Jewish community in Eretz Yisrael]. He had complaints about both the workers and the bourgeoisie. He said that all or most of the bourgeoisie engaged

in forcing up real-estate prices. He said that real-estate speculation was *the* evil that would ruin Eretz Yisrael.

Once Harry Heller and I sat up all night with Josef Loewy.
We told him that we wanted to go to Eretz Yisrael after
completing our studies. He tried to convince us that we had
better realize what we were heading for. There was corruption.
There were people—he mentioned names: I still remember
them—he said, "What are they doing? They're speculators. They
live on speculation—Zionist speculation and real-estate speculation." The lands problem was the most concrete, the main
problem preoccupying the Zionists in those years—to the extent
that they at all related realistically and seriously to Eretz Yisrael
matters. Books appeared in Germany that people of the different
Zionist camps had written on this subject. There were debates
whether the Jewish National Fund ought to be the only
instrument of the Jewish people returning home; whether
real-estate speculation should be banned by Zionist legislation
and discipline.

Those who were against leasing lands and against the ban on
private ownership of land remained silent. They were on the
defensive, for the Zionist mood was against them. They didn't
speak; they just bought land. The role that real-estate speculation
played in the country's development is still a subject of bitter
debate. When I came, there were stormy debates on the matter.
The bourgeoisie favored speculation (naturally, they gave it other
names). As we know, there was a sector of the population that
got rich from it—and called it development. Some say this was
one of our biggest catastrophes. And some said the opposite; that
if not for this, nothing would have developed here, because the
means and capacity of the Jewish National Fund then could not
have achieved what private means did. I guess both sides were
right.

Muki: Between the romantic and the realistic versions, which
attracted you most then? What was your own approach to the
reality in Eretz Yisrael—the romantic or the realistic one?

Scholem: My sympathies lay with the Left, even though I
didn't believe then that the Socialist question was cardinal to the
success or failure of the Jewish national renaissance. Among my
notes I have found many jottings attesting that I came here with

the idea that the situation here was very critical and all the rest of it was of no consequence. That was certainly my stand—neither romantic nor realistic.

I was among the supporters of land nationalization. This is what made me one of the fools who doesn't own any land, because I refused to buy land, even though I could have done that instead of buying books. But for reasons of conscience I didn't do so. Now I'm in the ridiculous position of being perhaps the only old-timer in Eretz Yisrael who doesn't have a piece of land he can call his own.

My inclinations then were toward the *halutzim* [agricultural laboring pioneers], and the innovators, and those striving for regeneration. As far as I can recall, I didn't care for the bourgeois concerns.

What drew me to Hehalutz [the Zionist pioneering youth], despite its being a very weak movement, was its seriousness, sense of responsibility, and will and readiness to cope with something concrete. People came and said, "We shall do." Coping with the concrete removed them from romanticism and gave the whole thing a dimension of depth that the dream did not possess.

Muki: What remained of that experiment?

Scholem: It is impossible to say how many people vanished from the scene and then suddenly turned up in Paris and London, New York, Los Angeles, and Toronto. The centrifugal attraction continued—it was like a migration of dunes—and not much remained of it. But historically speaking, what was done in Eretz Yisrael is the only existential thing created by that generation, and not what was drawn off to the Diaspora.

Secular Messianism

Muki: Do secular movements contain a religious element? In your eulogy for Rosenzweig ["Franz Rosenzweig and His Book *The Star of Redemption*," delivered at the Hebrew University in 1930], you referred to socialism and psychoanalysis.

Scholem: Yes. I said dialectical materialism has occupied the seat of the Quality of Justice, psychoanalysis has occupied the seat of the Quality of Mercy, and God Almighty has been banished from them both. He contracted Himself till nothing of Him remained revealed.

Muki: Can you point to any social movements that you think have assumed a messianist posture? Do you see Communism as a messianic movement?

Scholem: Socialism has messianic pretensions of that sort. According to some of its observers, devotees, and critics, it has in it a great deal of secular messianism. It is a moot question whether that is correct. There is an element of truth to it, but how much is a very big question.

Many young people took Communism as a substitute for messianism. There have been times, places, and circumstances in which many people—not only Jewish youth, to whom this certainly applies—saw a messianic dimension in Communism. The zeal with which they threw themselves into it had some of the enthusiasm of the messianists to it. And this is where the whole thing collapsed. Messianism is really a very big and complex matter, not at all simple.

I've written about this twice in my books. I've defined what I thought was the price the Jewish people has paid for messianism. A very high price. Some people have wrongly taken this to mean that I am an antimessianist. I have a strong inclination toward it. I have not given up on it. But it may be that my writings have spurred people to say that I am a Jew who rejects the messianic idea because the price was too high.

I think that the failure to distinguish between messianism and secular movements is apt to trip up movements of this sort. Such a mix-up becomes a destructive element. The misapplication of messianic phraseology injected a false note into the minds and self-image of the devotees of those secular movements.

Walter Benjamin

Muki: Could you speak of your connection with Walter Benjamin? Did he represent an aspect of the same problem? Was the closeness and the tension between you and Walter Benjamin a kind of reenactment of your relations with your brother and with the secular messianic movement?

Scholem: On a sublimer plane it is possible to answer yes. But only to a degree. Benjamin, at least in his later years, had a strong element of inclination toward secular messianism, whose concepts were taken from the world of Jewish messianism.

At the same time, I don't know to what extent a man like Benjamin was careful not to confuse religious and political concepts. I submit that to a certain extent even he confused the two, for toward the end of his life he did, in fact, too much identify the two spheres with each other. This is evident in some of his last writings. There were times when he knew the distinction very well and was careful about it, and was not prepared to discuss matters of history in terms of redemption.

On the other hand, the debate with a thinker like Benjamin was conducted on an altogether different plane from the one on which I argued with my brother. My brother was much less profound and dialectical than Benjamin. My brother did not at all believe in the possibility of an utter rout. He didn't take it seriously. A man like Benjamin took this possibility seriously. Toward the end of his life he fell into total despair—as is evident in his published last letters.

But this is a very delicate matter. It's hard for me to judge. I wasn't with Benjamin in those years. I was here and he was there. He went, in his way, to historical materialism, and I did not, being certain that it held no promise whatever, and that he gave himself to something that was incapable of producing anything good or useful. I still think so.

Muki: What was his attitude to you and your preoccupation?

Scholem: I don't know, I can't tell you. After 1923 I saw Benjamin only twice. After I came to Eretz Yisrael, Benjamin still sometimes toyed with the idea of coming. There are many documents attesting that. I was not surprised that he didn't come, though I wanted him to. I have no clear idea what he thought of me. As I said, in those years I saw him only twice. Once for several weeks in Paris in 1927, and once for a few days in Paris in 1938. That's all.

If I did speak about myself, then it was about the findings of my researches that I spoke. He was the first person I told—in 1927—that I had discovered a new world in Sabbatianism. I had just returned from Oxford, and I met him in Paris, and I told him. It made a tremendous impression on him. That is what I spoke about—my work. I did not speak much about myself. I reminisce at length about that man of genius in a special book. [*Walter Benjamin—die Geschichte einer Freundschaft* (Frankfurt-am-Main: Suhrkamp, 1975).]

The Relationship to Psychoanalysis

Muki: In your Rosenzweig eulogy in 1930, you spoke of the power of grace embodied in the modern world in psychoanalysis, and of the power of justice embodied in historical materialism. Did you see any connection between psychoanalytical ideas and any psychological ideas in the kabbalistic view of the soul?

Scholem: I've never undergone analysis, so my approach to it isn't a direct one but that of an outsider. As for the abstract aspect of psychoanalysis—the trouble is that I knew Freud's first writings. As a young man, I had read some of them.

Muki: When?

Scholem: Between the ages of twenty and twenty-five. In those years I was not one bit interested in the assumptions of psychoanalysis. As to its therapeutic value, I had no personal experience of it, so I was unable to judge. When I told people that I had not been convinced by the theses in Freud's book on the interpretation of dreams—which I had read carefully—they told me, "Oh, you can't judge that in the abstract; if you haven't undergone analysis you are unable to judge." I reject that contention. It is like the Hasidim arguing that a non-Hasid can't write a history of Hasidim; that a nonbeliever can't judge "from the outside." Whoever says that is, in my opinion, an irresponsible driveler or an apologist.

There are some people—like Theodor W. Adorno and others—who did not undergo analysis and still were drawn to the ideas of psychoanalysis. Walter Benjamin never underwent analysis, but later in life he apparently started being influenced by psychoanalysis. When I was going through the papers he left, I found a number of sociological-philosophical notes. He was interested in social psychology as a means of understanding historical and social processes, and even used concepts drawn from the later Freud—concepts that, to tell the truth, seem to me to be fundamentally metaphysical.

I have read almost nothing of the later Freud. This may be a shortcoming in me, but what I have read is simply awful. *The Future of an Illusion* is an absolutely terrible book. If not for the fact that Freud's name is signed on the book, everybody would reject it as a feeble production, without any solid foundation.

In treating the history and world of the *kabbalah*, using the conceptual terminology of psychoanalysis—either the Freudian or the Jungian version—did not seem fruitful to me. Even though I should have had a strong affinity to Jung's concepts, which were close to religious concepts, I refrained from using them. For twenty-five years I lectured at the Eranos meetings, and in that circle there was a considerable Jungian influence. But in those lectures I deliberately shied away from all psychoanalytical and Jungian psychopathological concepts. I was not convinced that those categories were useful. I particularly avoided using the theory of archetypes, of which I remain highly sceptical.

Psychoanalysts of all schools whom I have met in my travels and in Jerusalem have said, "What you're saying is pure psychoanalysis." For example, the chapter on Abulafia in my book; what I have written about transmigration of the soul. What I was saying seemed to them to corroborate what they were saying. I hope that I gained by not resorting to their lexicons to explain the concepts or symbols of the kabbalists.

Max Brod's friend in Prague, Jiri Langer, a Hasid of the Belzer Rebbe who later converted to Freudianism, wrote a book on analysis and *kabbalah* called *The Erotics of Kabbalah*. He made a mishmash out of the two things in terms of Freudian concepts. The book appeared in Prague when I started my serious research in 1923, and I was deeply disappointed by it. Precisely in those matters where he tried to use Freudian concepts I found no substance. Most of it was utter nonsense, despite the fact that the book wasn't written by a boor but by a learned man who also understood mystical literature.

Avraham Shapira: How do you feel about Erich Neumann?

Scholem: I greatly esteemed Erich Neumann the man, but I often didn't understand what he was saying. He was a man of powerful intellect and deep feeling, but I found no possibility of using the analytic concepts and the categories he constructed on the basis of Jungian thought. I have tried to plumb his *magnum opus, The History of the Development of Human Consciousness,* but I can't say I have understood it.

The psychoanalysts of the different schools have always thought I was saying exactly what they required, and I was delighted that someone was finding my writings useful. But they were written in clear awareness of the principles of historical criticism. I have said that many times. I think that if we understood history better, we would need fewer psychological hypotheses to explain historical phenomena. The use of psychological concepts in history is somewhat of an emergency exit.

Muki: Aren't the two related?

Scholem: There is a reciprocal relationship between them. There are always psychological explanations of events. In my book on Sabbetai Tzvi you'll find quite a bit of that. Of course, the two are not completely separated. But historical analysis and knowledge of processes promise more than very hypothetical psychological premises. I have read many writings of leftists attempting to unite Marxism and psychoanalysis. In those books or essays, which were written by extremely clever people, I have found precious little truth. The attempt to match up psychoanalysis with Marxism is an attempt to express the Quality of Mercy and the Quality of Justice in a psychological world instead of in the theological world of tradition. I am very skeptical about that.

Muki: If you had to write the history of the period from World War I till today, to examine the group that went with you and parted from you, how much of a role would you assign to the psychological factor in the decisions whether to come to Eretz Yisrael and remain here, whether or not to remain a Jew?

Scholem: I don't know. I can't answer that question. The decisions about which I may be able to judge by understanding events or the people I lived with were, in my opinion, moral decisions, not psychological ones. Of course, you might say that a moral decision is psychologically based. I'm not sure of that. I have strong reservations about psychological categories in this respect. At times I can understand them as biographical decisions, but it is very hard to say whether the biographical element is also a psychological element. Take the erotic influence, for example. That is not a psychological influence. Often people arrive at decisions because of a woman's charm—this has always existed and still exists—but I am somewhat doubtful whether psychology exhausts the abundance and the depth that there are in Eros.

It is a moot question whether a person's distaste for a particular society or milieu is a moral or a psychological reaction. The Zionist response of Jewish youth in Germany had a powerful moral element, notwithstanding the possibility of describing it as a psychological reaction. I think there is no moral nuance to the various psychological urges at play in man. Moral considerations are essentially nonpsychological.

Muki: Sometimes the moral calculations are also critical calculations, like the distaste you mentioned. Is this the kind of criticism you have in mind when, in writing of Walter Benjamin, you say that there is purity in destruction? Are you referring to the moral side of criticism? Is the urge to destroy the basis for rejecting an immoral reality?

Reason as a Destructive Instrument

Scholem: Yes. I think that people generally use the instruments of Reason to criticize a tradition or a milieu. This is a very legitimate use, because the instrument of Reason developed in man largely on the critical, destructive side. When Reason is isolated from the other possibilities in the complex of human urges, in the whole human psychological network, it transpires that its task is to criticize. In history it has done so quite successfully. In the area of construction, Reason has had relatively few successes. Other forces have had far more outstanding and decisive successes in construction than Reason. Reason is a dialectical tool that serves both construction and destruction, but has had more notable successes in destruction. The devotees of Reason have tried to build networks of positive thought—but these networks are far less enduring than criticism;

that is, creative destruction. I know that this is a very painful
point, and many admirers of Reason (of whom I am one) do not
like to hear this. But I am inclined to think—in summing up my
researches in history, religious history, philosophy, and ethics—
that Reason is a great instrument of destruction. For construction, something beyond it is required.

Muki: What is that?

Scholem: I don't know. Something that has—something
moral. I don't believe there is an enduring rational morality; I
don't believe it is possible to build a morality that will be an
immanent network for Reason. I confess that in this respect I am
what would be called a reactionary, for I believe that morality as
a constructive force is impossible without religion, without some
Power beyond Pure Reason. Secular morality is a morality built
on Reason alone. I do not believe in this possibility. This is an
utter illusion of philosophers, not to speak of sociologists.

Shapira: Was this the view of Walter Benjamin? We got onto
this subject via Walter Benjamin.

Scholem: I am not Walter Benjamin. I am Gershom Scholem.
The great mission of Reason is to be critical, in both the natural
and the social sciences, history, and psychology. Walter Benjamin
was a very complex person. He had an ingenious intuition; he had
blatantly religious ideas that were camouflaged behind a network
of Marxism till the end of his life. I don't know whether his
religious views were liquidated in a network of social, psychological, and analytic concepts, or whether they simply hid themselves, as though the generation was not worthy of having them
revealed to it. It isn't a simple matter.

The "conversion" of the Hashomer Hatzair people—the
process of their adhesion to the Marxist world—is, in my opinion,
an example of a decision that was moral in essence. I don't say
that the decision was a correct one; on the contrary, it was a
tragic error when those comrades accepted something that was
forbidden for them to accept. They did not see things right, and
they did so for moral rather than political reasons.

Anarchism held many attractions for me, especially its
positive utopianism. But it, too, always filled me with terror. I
knew that it stood no chance of realization, given the data of the
human race, in history. This is a kind of messianic vision to which

the transition is not possible with the forces functioning in history.

To this day I would say that the only social theory that makes sense—religious sense, too—is anarchism, but it is also—practically speaking—the least possible theory. It doesn't stand a chance because it doesn't take the human being into consideration: it is based on an extremely optimistic assessment of the human spirit; it has a messianic dimension, a transhistorical one.

Shapira: In your essay "Redemption through Sin," you seem to regard pseudomessianism as a positive phenomenon, though without identifying with it. And in your book on Sabbetai Tzvi, you write that the Sabbatian messianic type "leads directly to nihilistic conceptions of religious values." Isn't this a contradiction of your view of the positive aspect of destructivism?

Scholem: I don't know if it is or not. I maintain that the spectacle of a pseudo-Messiah cannot be tolerated by Jewish tradition as a positive phenomenon, but I do not say that it is not a possible and legitimate aspect of Jewish tradition. I was able and ready to write what I have written in both essays. In the Sabbetai Tzvi book I also showed how strong was the element of hope for something positive even in the words of the Sabbatians. In the closing chapters of the book I tried to show, through precise examples, the extent to which the Sabbatians saw the positive element in negative things. It is clear that as far as traditional values are concerned, this was negative. But I have never stopped believing that the element of destruction, with all the potential nihilism in it, has always been also the basis of positive Utopian hope. Of course, from the standpoint of the values of official traditional Judaism, this conception is negative.

Zionism: A Calculated Risk

Muki: You have spent your entire life among secularists. What has been your attitude toward secularism?

Scholem: I have always considered the transition through secularism necessary, unavoidable. But I don't think that Zionism's secular vision is the ultimate vision, the last word. Without the secular awakening we should not have got as far as we did. A direct nondialectical return to traditional Judaism is impossible, historically speaking, and even I myself have not accomplished it.

I have always considered secular Zionism a legitimate way but rejected the foolish declaration about the Jews becoming "a nation like all the nations." If this should materialize, it will be the end of the Jewish people. I share the traditional view that even if we wish to be a nation like all the nations, we will not succeed. And if we succeed—that will be the end of us.

I cannot free myself from the dialectical lesson of history, according to which secularism is part of the process of our entry into history; entry into history means assimilating into it. Since I do not believe in "like all the nations," I do not see ultimate secularism as a possibility for us and it will not come to pass. I do not believe that we are going to liquidate ourselves. There is no reason for the Jews to exist like the Serbs. The Serbs have a reason to exist without theology, without an ahistorical dimension. If the Jews try to explain themselves only in a historical dimension, they will of necessity find themselves thinking about self-liquidation and total destruction. If the things Uri Avneri [editor of *Ha-olam Hazeh*], Yonatan Ratosh [poet and "Canaanite" ideologist], and the Matzpen people say materialize, the Jewish people will find itself without any impulse to continue existing.

Muki: Will secularism lead to a religious return?

Scholem: Like all destruction, secularism is both liberation and risk. But Zionism was a calculated risk in that it brought about the destruction of the reality of Exile. The foes of Zionism certainly saw the risk more clearly than we Zionists.

Muki: In opposing "like all the nations," you accept Ahad Ha-am's view?

Scholem: Correct. In this respect I am an Ahad Ha-amist and religious, but more religious than Ahad Ha-am. I don't believe in a world of total secularism in which the religious factor will not manifest itself with redoubled strength.

Muki: In our conversations, you have spoken of various stages of cutting yourself off: from your father's house, from a particular version of Zionism, from Buber, from psychoanalysis and Marxism, from a certain way of life in Eretz Yisrael. Cutting oneself off is an act of saying farewell—farewell as an act of criticism.

Reason as a capacity for criticism exposed you and confronted you with the need to make decisions: your curiosity about your Jewishness, your Zionism—that entire moral dimension about whose sources it is impossible to speak.

Scholem: All those cutoffs you mention are correct, but I have never cut myself off from God. I don't understand atheists; I never did. I think atheism is understandable only if you accept the rule of unbridled passions, a life without values.

I am convinced that there is no morality that has any inner meaning unless it has a religious basis. I don't believe there is such a thing as the absolute autonomy of man, whereby man makes himself and the world creates itself.

Muki: Then you accept Dostoyevsky's view that "if there is no God, everything is allowed"?

Scholem: Yes. I have heard people say that this statement of Dostoyevsky's is vicious and scandalous. I do think that here Dostoyevsky can teach us something, but we don't need him to understand this. Without God there is no such thing as values or morality that carry any real, binding force. Faith in God—even if it doesn't have a positive expression in every generation—will reveal itself as a force, even by means of not manifesting itself. I do not believe in moral relativism. The day may come when it will be forbidden to speak of God. But then the faith in Him will grow. A secular regime opens up more possibilities for the manifestation of those positive forces in man that are linked to something with a spark in it. I believe that God will then manifest Himself all the more strongly, though I'm not sure that that will be a world of the *Shulhan Arukh*—though that is not out of the question.

Muki: Were the major decisions in your life—to be a Jew, to come to Eretz Yisrael, to deal with *kabbalah*—linked to the religious dimension?

Scholem: Yes.

Muki: Did you turn to Jewish history rather than theology because of its dialectical facet?

Scholem: That is an exaggeration. I wasn't, as a young man, as wise as you think. I was much more naïve. I was riding high on a moral-religious awakening. I was far from nihilism. My sympathy for anarchism, too, was a moral one. I believed in anarchism as

Utopia. I wasn't an atheistic anarchist. I thought that the organization of society under absolute liberty is a divine mandate. I was not the only one of that Zionist generation of the Third Aliyah to believe that. In my youthful jottings you will not find a single clue to a dialectical understanding of processes. I came to see the force of dialectics only gradually, in the course of careful study, especially after I came to Eretz Yisrael and saw the contradictions in the constructive processes here: the inner contradictions of the revival of the secular language and the silence overpowering the language. I did not learn dialectics from Hegel or the Marxists, but from my own experiences and from pondering the labyrinths of Zionism as I was trying to implement it.

I was one of those who took the Biblical passage "And you shall be unto Me a kingdom of priests, and a holy nation" [Exodus 19:6] as the definition of Zionism. In 1918 already I mentioned it in one of my articles. If I was capable of putting down a thought like that without a second thought, then clearly I was naïve and not dialectical. The concept of "holy nation" is what interested me. Although I have since learned a great deal, I cannot say that there is nothing to this passage.

Shapira: Muki asked you how the dialectical element in your conception was created or crystalized, and you answered that it wasn't there at the outset but that it did not come through study of historical processes. Isn't this a conclusion that results from the consideration of historical studies?

Scholem: It came to me chiefly through what you have defined as existential experience of life in Eretz Yisrael. I considered myself a person who had come here to do something about implementing Zionism as I innocently understood it. But I saw that it was all really a very complex matter.

Shapira: Is it also possible to say that the dialectical conception of history and of the process of social and individual existence suit your "soul-root"—to use the kabbalistic term?

Scholem: I am not prepared to answer that. You can answer it; maybe one could put it that way. Otherwise I would not have invested forty or fifty years of intensive labor and thought in the way I did more or less. I assume that if I have done what I have done, it may be deduced that it isn't alien to me, to my "soul-root." I wrote in my Hebrew essay, "The Science of Judaism," that the petit bourgeois side of Judaism consisted in its ignoring the paradoxes contained in the living realities of Judaism, of the Jews in the world, of the Jewish reality in history, of the ideas themselves, and in reducing it all to an abstraction. I never did care for traditional national Jewish theology.

An Encounter with Kabbalists in Eretz Yisrael

Muki: When you came to Eretz Yisrael, did you find kabbalists here?

Scholem: Yes. When I arrived I visited the kabbalistic Bet-El Yeshivah, which was still intact in Jerusalem's Old City.

Muki: Did they know that you were dealing with *kabbalah?*

Scholem: One of them knew. I was in personal contact with him: Gershon Vilner.

Muki: Was that a real community?

Scholem: By my time, it no longer was really a community, as it had been some 100–150 years earlier. Bet-El has a history. A number of interesting things have been written about it. They owned no material possessions and didn't need any. Ascetics don't need much to live. What they desired was a share in the World-to-Come—the possession that really matters. Documents have remained, including "contracts" in which they undertake to share with each other their spiritual possessions—the Splendor and the Glory of the World-to-Come, not the dollars. They were banded together in a kind of mystical community in which they lived in absolute and total spiritual partnership. Their leader and great light was Rabbi Shalom Sharabi, a Yemenite, an Oriental mystic, who—in the view of the Sephardic Jews—was the greatest kabbalist after the Ari [Rabbi Yitzhak Luria]. He was known throughout the Orient. When I visited Bet-El it was impossible to determine whether their undertaking was really continuing. It was difficult to get inside their world. Perhaps if I had conducted myself as an Orthodox Jew, I would have learned more about them.

There were several Ashkenazim in Bet-El. Outside this group, I remember at least three Ashkenazim in Jerusalem who were famous kabbalists, but by no means Hasidim. They were mainly from Lithuania—from the Vilna and Bialystok areas.

The most famous was Rabbi Shlomo Eliashov, the outstanding kabbalist of the generation before mine. He died here at age eighty, around the time I arrived. Ashkenazi *kabbalah* was very, very remote from the Sephardi conception. Ashkenazim who joined Bet-El had to change their way completely and switch over into a kind of Oriental gear.

Muki: How did that group impress you?

Scholem: It's difficult to say. Sometimes I would go to their prayer services, which were very impressive. I have a pamphlet from the year 5665 [1904–1905] which contained a detailed report of the exorcizing of a dybbuk by Rabbi Benzion Hazan, a kabbalist from Baghdad, himself a product of Bet-El, one of the heads of the Jewish Quarter when the Old City of Jerusalem surrendered to Jordan's Arab Legion in 1948. It was he who conducted the negotiations with the Legion. He died in the 1950s.

What remained of Bet-El was something like Yoga. I had the feeling that I was dealing with a group of Eretz Yisrael Jewish-style Yoga practitioners.

Muki: Who was that man you met?

Scholem: He was called Gershon Vilner. That wasn't his real name, of course, but Gershon Cohen or something of the sort. But as he was from Vilna, everybody called him Vilner.

Muki: What was his attitude toward you?

Scholem: I can't say, really. When I met him I was twenty-six and he was about seventy. I told him I wanted to learn *kabbalah*. He looked a long time and checked—looked at my forehead lines—and only then spoke to me. He said, "I am prepared to teach you, but only on condition that you do not ask questions." That made a tremendous impression on me (I wrote about it in my Eranos lecture, "*Kabbalah* and Myth," my first lecture there, where I refer to "a friend of —," meaning myself). I told him, "I should like to think about it." Then I said, "I can't." He was a remarkable Jew, a shining personality.

Muki: How long did you study under him?

Scholem: I didn't study. We only held conversations.

Assimilation—Then and Today

Muki: You mentioned Jewish Yoga and Oriental influence. For you or the Jews of your generation, being an assimilationist meant joining European culture. During the year I spent as an emissary in the United States in 1971–72, I met young Jews who were trying to assimilate to a culture that was a mixture of East and West. A bit of Buddhism, a touch of Yoga, some Christianity —a strange concoction. Young Jews who are assimilating not into American culture but into a culture that is rejecting Western culture.

Scholem: But that is out of disappointment with American materialism; that is a reaction to vulgarity. I had a pupil who became a Conservative rabbi. He was here in the late 1940s or early 1950s. He knew his Judaism and had a warm Jewish heart. One day I got a letter from him saying he had seen the light in the teachings of Ramakrishna.

Muki: A large percentage of the followers of Ramakrishna are Jews.

Scholem: Ramakrishna didn't know how to read or write. He died in 1886, aged about fifty, in Bengal. He is considered one of the great figures. Romain Rolland wrote a famous book about him. I have a translation from the Bengali of his conversations—a verbatim record written down by his disciples in the last five years of his life. The publication of the book was subsidized by a German Jew who had made his money from real-estate investments in Switzerland, then moved to California and got very rich, and continued to live by his belief. The book is an authentic document—one of the most interesting religious documents I know.

My student wrote me that he was able to go on conducting himself as a Jew without doing violence to his religious inclinations. He also wrote poems in Hebrew. I don't know where he is now—in California or in the East. (He has since shown up in Jerusalem, where he got married early in 1975.)

One day the whole thing blew up. As I said, my student was a rabbi. I don't know whether he was active as a rabbi, but he was in search of spiritual life. One day his guru told him to stop putting on *tefillin*. And as you know, once you accept a guru, you have to do his bidding, the same as with a Hassidic *rebbe*. My student told his guru, "But you explicitly told me that there is no contradiction between observing Jewish ritual—observing all the Commandments—and the path to the goal." The master replied, "Yes, I said that. But meanwhile you have reached a different plane. What I said was correct when I said it. Now it is no longer correct. Now you have to stop."

It is quite a widespread vogue among young people. It is generally superficial, though in some cases it goes deep. Spiritually, it is hard to tell them anything, for they are looking for something that is out of this world. What we are doing here in Eretz Yisrael doesn't interest them, is remote from them.

The poet Allen Ginsberg once visited me. A likable fellow. Genuine. Strange, mad, but genuine. I took a strong liking to him. My wife and I had a very interesting conversation with him, and in her inimitable way she asked him, "Why don't you come to live here?" (I never ask anyone this question. People know whether and when it is time for them to come: that's basic. If people want to come, then it is possible to talk to them about it. But I don't have it in me to tell anyone that he must come to Eretz Yisrael. But my wife is different.) He looked at us and replied, "Me? Your great ideal is to build a new Bronx here. All my life I've been running away from the Bronx, and here I come to the Jewish State and find that the whole big ideal of the Zionists is to build a giant Bronx here. If I have to go back to the Bronx, I may as well stay in the original one." We said to him, "What if you're mistaken?" But there is something to what he said.

He said: "I'm going to India for ten years"—and three months later he was out of India. In a person of that sort there is a kind of reaction to the real state of neglect of American Jews. But there are people of that sort right here in Israel, too.

The Pendulum Swings between Imitation and Creation

Muki: In our literature we have always spoken of assimilation as a reaction to external pressure of a minority culture confronting a majority culture. Here in Israel the Jews are the majority culture, yet there is assimilation here, too—rejection of Judaism, or indifference to it. Judaism is seen as a function of our minority status—something we don't need here, being the majority. There is no desire to turn Moslem or Christian, but to be a world-standard engineer, computer scientist, cineaste, or poet. Doesn't this rather mess up the whole Zionist theory?

Scholem: This is only a natural conclusion. We are paying the price of our slogans. We wanted to change something in the Jewish people, and this desire has been a primary factor in our success. But we also wanted something else: to preserve continuity along with the change, continuity that doesn't express itself by changing forms. This we did not achieve. This continuity today expresses itself only in dogmatic conservatism, on the one hand, or in indifference to the Jewish cultural heritage, on the other.

Whether there is something in between, whether anything will be created out of this—some new synthesis—is not yet clear. There is no telling yet whether the dream won't just smash itself up on technology.

I have just been reading Shlomo Zemah's book, *Dape Pinkas*. It is a very bitter book, but it contains some thought-provoking things, and it has made an impression on me. He writes that in 1905—eighteen years before I came here—there were in Eretz Yisrael only five families that actually spoke Hebrew in their daily life. All the rest is a lie, a kind of Zionist myth. When I arrived in 1923, the atmosphere had changed. I came into a beginning that had different perspectives—not of degeneration, but of something new. We called it renaissance.

Now things have changed again. There are the beginnings of what you call technological assimilation, universalist assimilation. Look at the style and the content of the writing in our literary supplements. Thirty years ago no one would have printed such stuff. They would have laughed and said, "Go to Paris." I laugh at it, but also cry a little. This is a necessary part of the dialectic we are in now. The problem is that the pendulum has to swing the other way, too. Imitation is cheap. A year in Paris is enough. Firmness like the late Shlomo Grodzensky's° is not to be had at a bargain.

° A literary critic and editor (1904–1972) of the *Yiddisher Kemfer* in New York and of several Israeli publications after his settling in Israel in 1951.—Ed.

It is possible that we are condemning too hastily, because we don't see the seeds beneath the surface. We only see the swing of the pendulum that is turning our life here into a grotesquerie. I think that this passage through secularism to some new florescence is unavoidable. It is in the very soul of what we are doing here. If I had to see assimilation as the end of the process, as the final outcome of the process called "Jewish national renaissance," then I have no other word for it but grotesquerie. But I don't accept this as the last word. Fads have a way of suddenly passing.

In my fifty years of living in Eretz Yisrael, I have identified fully with both the land's secularism and its religiosity. There is nothing Jewish that is alien to me. I accept the secularistic processes, just as I hope for opposite processes.

I don't think we are able to give conceptual form, expression, to the chaos, because we wanted to shape something out of it. We saw secularism as raw material, a state out of which something new and endurable would be created. We didn't know whether we would succeed. The upshot is perhaps not what we had overoptimistically anticipated. But historical processes generally lead to outcomes altogether different from those they seem headed for at the outset.

For example: Christianity as a historical phenomenon bears virtually no resemblance to original Christianity as a religious phenomenon. I suppose that is true of all the historical religions. Very rarely will you find something that is an exact reflection of its roots. The Judaism of today, too, is not the Judaism of Moses. I don't believe that better thinkers than me are able to describe fully what is happening in this generation. What is developing and happening here is not expressible in the form of an endurable method or thought. I think that our lack of vocabulary and paucity of concepts are objective matters, not subjective. This is not because of any weakness on the part of philosophers; it is inherent in what is happening. We are unable to explain to ourselves what sparks functioned and sustained whatever remained alive in all these processes. It is altogether a riddle how Judaism and the Jewish people have held out. A large part of the Jewish people has almost always fallen away. So it is important to find out what has sustained us.

Muki: Zionism is not a messianic movement. What is the

element that Zionism has contributed to these processes? What is the "spark" in Zionism?

Scholem: That is a delicate question: whether Zionism has anything in it that will lead to something new. I believed in that hidden core in Zionism. Whether I was right or not, I don't know.

I was a member of the Brit Shalom [a movement for Jewish-Arab reconciliation started in the 1920s] from its inception till its decline. But that was for "external" purposes. "Domestically," I was something else. The Brit Shalom people were Zionist humanists who thought that the survival of Zionism in Eretz Yisrael was in danger. Perhaps Brit Shalom was wrong; I don't know. I have no desire to judge. There are many facets to the history of Brit Shalom. The Arab question was a controversial one, and our approach to it caused us to be suspected of liquidating Zionism—a charge that I think is unjustified. The debate will not be easily settled. And today people are certainly prepared to judge the whole thing more coolly. But this matter has never been crucial for me. For me it was a symbol of conduct.

I once thought that perhaps there is a hidden facet to the historical process taking place here that may have a religio-metaphysical aspect.

Muki: Yet you have also written that the Zionist movement is not a messianic movement.

Scholem: The central point of my "esoteric" view of Zionism, that found its expression in what I said in public, too, was indeed what you say. Ever since becoming an adult and starting to think systematically about Zionism, I have thought that the crucial thing is that Zionism is a process—a most legitimate process. Zionism is not a messianic movement. And that is its secret. Because as a messianic movement it is doomed in advance to failure.

I never wished to believe and I did not believe that it had to fail. Though neither did I believe that it would necessarily succeed. Maybe it will, and maybe we are commanded to do everything possible to make it so, but there is no guarantee of it. Of one thing I was certain—and I repeated this in all the notes I jotted down for myself up to 1935—and that is that the process unfolding here before our eyes was legitimate, because it was based on an assessment that was outside the messianic plane.

I should like to read you what I wrote in 1929 in *Davar* [the

daily newspaper of the Histadrut—the Eretz Yisrael General
Labor Confederation] when the Brit Shalom was under heavy
attack. I was replying to an article by Yehuda Bourla [the
novelist, who died in 1970]. I wrote:

> He argues that we are turning our backs on the Jewish
> people's political redemption (that was the general argument
> against us). The truth of the matter is that that is a very foggy
> argument, in need of clarification. What sort of political redemp-
> tion is meant? Does Bourla mean the messianic idea in a political
> form, as he hints in his opening words? If that is the case, then I
> submit that that is not a problem of Brit Shalom but of the entire
> Zionist movement. I, a member of Brit Shalom, am opposed, like
> thousands of other Zionists who are not associated with Brit
> Shalom and who are far removed from its views, to mixing up
> religious and political concepts. I categorically deny that Zionism
> is a messianic movement and that it is entitled to use religious
> terminology to advance its political aims.
>
> The redemption of the Jewish people, which as a Zionist I
> desire, is in no way identical with the religious redemption I hope
> for for the future. I am not prepared as a Zionist to satisfy political
> demands or yearnings that exist in a strictly nonpolitical, religious
> sphere, in the sphere of End-of-Days apocalyptics. The Zionist
> ideal is one thing and the messianic ideal is another, and the two
> do not touch except in pompous phraseology of mass rallies, which
> often infuse into our youth a spirit of new Sabbatianism that must
> inevitably fail. The Zionist movement is congenitally alien to the
> Sabbatian movement, and the attempts to infuse Sabbatian spirit
> into it has already caused it a great deal of harm.

This was written in 1929. I certainly am not turning my back
on the Sabbatian movement. Since then, I have devoted forty years
to its study. But I think it would be catastrophic if the Zionists
or the Zionist movement erased or blurred the borders between
the religious-messianic plane and political-historical reality.

I think that the Jewish people's entry into the plane of history
means the acceptance of responsibility for itself, its achievements
and its failures. Action on the political plane of secular history is
something different from action on the spiritual-religious plane. It
would be disastrous to confuse the two.

The mystical side of Zionism concerns something that is

growing without being messianic: it comprises elements that do not cross the border into the eschatological but stay in the realm of the realizable, which are sure to have symbols of its own in history, in the everyday external world, in the world of action, etc., something that can work, such as in the revival of the language as a language that is suited for people to speak, live, and think in it.

Perhaps I was mistaken; I may now be mistaken—but who knows whether there is such a hidden core in Zionism? I don't. When Buber, near the end of his life, wrote extremely bitter things about the State of Israel, in a little book, *Addresses on Judaism*—writing that he saw no religious aspect whatever to the State—he wrote this out of an attitude of negation. I wrote a reply saying it was difficult to understand how a man like Buber knows the borders between the sacred and the profane; saying that I did not know them. His reluctance to look historical reality squarely in the eye had driven him to exaggerate, I said, adding that I was surprised at him, for this went against the inner logic of his own thought, his own system.

I am not sure whether I was being consistent when I argued that. But I haven't changed my mind. The greatness of the Zionist movement has been that it was a movement that accepted historical responsibility, that undertook tasks and accepted responsibility for our actions, without any messianic pretensions.

Muki: On the other hand, if I have understood you correctly, you maintain that the religious, the mystical side of Zionism exists but does not manifest itself on the political plane.

Scholem: It hasn't manifested itself. But one bright day it will do so. Perhaps we will be privileged to see it manifest itself. But meanwhile—well, that is why I have never dealt with this matter.

"I Don't Call Myself a Secular Jew"

Muki: When we were studying *kabbalah* with you at the Hebrew University, the class consisted of both religious people and secularists.

Scholem: I was addressing myself to all of them. I spoke in a manner that no one knew just where I stood.

Muki: But the reactions were different. To put it in extreme terms, the secularists took the philosophical-religious side of the *kabbalah* more seriously than the religious people, who took the *kabbalah* as no more than a chapter in the history of religion that had no significance for their own faith. The secularists sought some living spark in *kabbalah*. Of course, this is a generalization. How do you explain this?

Scholem: I explain it the same way I explain the fact that I devoted fifty years to research in *kabbalah*. I don't consider myself a secularist. My secularism fails right at the core, owing to the fact that I am a religious person, because I am sure of my belief in God. My secularism is not secular. But the fact that I addressed myself to *kabbalah* not merely as a chapter of history but from a dialectical distance—from identification and distance together—certainly stems from the fact that I had the feeling that *kabbalah* had a living center; it expressed itself according to the time, and that in another form it could, perhaps, have said something else in another generation. Something unknown of this sort must have motivated me beyond all the philological games and masquerades at which I excel. I can understand that something of this sort inspired my secularist listeners the way it inspired me.

To the religious traditionalists, the whole thing was quite suspect. To me it isn't suspect at all, because to me the question was whether the *halakhah* as a closed system had the power to sustain itself without a special mystical vitality that prevented it from becoming totally fossilized; and we have already spoken of this.

This question of the *halakhah* has often been in the background of my thoughts on *kabbalah*. I have refrained from writing much on the *halakhah*, actually, because I do not wish to pose as an expert on a matter of which I have only a general understanding but which I have not mastered. Though from a historical standpoint, it is clear to me what *halakhah* is and how one does or does not "swallow" it. Here I can understand the different reactions you're hinting at. I did not feel them so much. Among my best students there were unequivocally religious people. My approach was that of a person trying to think and to formulate concepts that would express symbolic thinking.

Muki: It was precisely because of and by means of the

historical-rational garb in which you presented *kabbalah* that I was able to create a bridge to the *kabbalah*'s nonrational world.

Scholem: The garb in which I presented the matter was historical, not rational. In my university lectures, I dealt with historical analysis.

Muki: We are confused, lost, searching. Strange images that I encountered in the *kabbalah* were not as strange as the history around me, as this twentieth century of ours. Did the *kabbalah* feed your inner world—you have lived through such stormy years in such a strange world?

Scholem: I can't say. Maybe it fed me more than I'm willing to admit. I suppose that I considered *kabbalah* as one of the possibilities for Jewish survival in history, that gave a dimension of depth to those who decided to remain Jews. I saw that there was something to *kabbalah*, but I did not see it as the be-all and end-all. I was not out to be a promoter of *kabbalah* but to state what I understood and did not understand. Historical processes generally lead to quite different results than they seem headed toward at the outset.

I cannot say that if I had to decide today on matters of principle, I would decide according to the instructions of the kabbalists. I would decide as a person trying to decide on the basis of a positive attitude to morality, public morality. We are not, after all, at liberty not to bother ourselves, not to bother our moral, political, and personal thinking power in order to arrive at historic decisions concerning our future in this country. I don't think the Talmud will help us much, even though I am far from denigrating the Talmud; on the contrary, I am a great admirer of the Talmud, and I find it extremely interesting. But I don't think that the Talmud or the *kabbalah* will provide us with the answers to the fateful questions which Zionism has posed and which we have to struggle to find the answers to.

There's Mystery in the World

Muki: I was not referring to the political-messianic dimension but to a different aesthetic aspect—to the linguistic style of our

strange era. The kabbalists were struggling with ineffable things
—the sense of chaos all around—and precisely this speaks to us,
even though it was written in a different conceptual world than
ours.

Scholem: If you ask me, I say that the kabbalists had a
fundamental feeling that there is mystery—a secret—in the
world. The world is also—but not only—what is apparent to us.
The kabbalists were symbolists. What attracts you here to the
kabbalists—in any case, what attracts me—is that a rather small
group of people were able to create symbols that expressed their
personal situation as a world situation. It was clear to them that
what we would call *technology* could not be the last word; that if
technology wishes to survive, it must reveal a symbolic dimension. What makes the *kabbalah* interesting is its power to
transmute things into symbols. And the symbols are not subjective. They are an objective projection of the inner side of a
miserable, grotesque, and weird Jewish externality.

This is what I would affirm in *kabbalah* and reject in
technology. Technology thinks it can banish the symbolic dimension from reality.

Modern man lives in a private world of his own, enclosed
within himself, and modern symbolism is not objective: it is
private; it does not obligate. The symbols of the kabbalists, on the
other hand, did not speak only to the private individual—they
displayed a symbolic dimension to the whole world.

The question is whether in the reality in which today's secular
person lives, this dimension will be revealed again.

I was strongly criticized when I dared to say that Walt
Whitman's writings contain something like this. Walt Whitman
revealed in an utterly naturalistic world what kabbalists and
other mystics revealed in their world.

Today we are living in an altogether different time. Technology is proceeding—leaping—forward with giant strides, but the
problem remains.

If humanity should ever lose the feeling that there is
mystery—a secret—in the world, then it's all over with us. But I
don't believe we'll ever come to that.

Jewish Youth Movement[*]

In recent years and up to this very hour, we have not had among us a Jewish youth movement: no movement which would be felt and sustained by young people as Jews. We have this and that organization, and we often and at length hear talk of them and their programs as the embodiments and standards of the Jewish youth movement; but what one looks for in them in vain is often not only Judaism and youth, but rather, again and again, movement. Without exception these organizations, the great and small ones, lack the characteristics of a movement: wholeness, spirit, and greatness. They may be necessary in many respects and their persistence justifies itself because of this, but in one respect decisive here, they are not necessary: they are not continually reborn out of the flow of movement.

It is true that there was a Jewish youth movement during the first years of the Zionist movement, so long as Herzl's idea had life and form, but the content was bound to dwindle when the spiritual situation changed, and to this day no new and generally recognized idea has been born; thereby, however, the seed was sown among the new generations that has now sprouted all too splendidly: the confusion which, along with its overcoming, must be discussed here. The youth of yesterday and today have been incapable of creating a change in this respect; on the contrary, youth has become ever poorer in strength and substance; all it says, thinks, and does is shadowy; all is merely skeletal, the object of lectures and discussions, program, and guiding principle, but

[*] "Jüdische Jugendbewegung," *Der Jude*, Vol. I, No. 12 (March, 1917), pp. 822–25. Translated by Werner J. Dannhauser.

in truth nothing effective and living. So little was a youth movement present, and so little had it won power over the will of minds, that in the decisive moment our youth succumbed to the war. That has been the final and greatest triumph of confusion and the deepest fall we have experienced. It proves something.

The new youth has been hastened in its coming-to-be (*Werden*) by the war. A new generation faces the task: to become a movement.

One thing has always been present—and this should not be forgotten—and is once more present today: *yearning*. But it cannot be emphasized too strongly: one builds no houses from yearning, a movement cannot base itself on the fact that one speaks again and again of yearning, that the latter is the content, form, and expression of the movement. If life is not generated from it and it does not bear fruit, so that from a truly Jewish yearning a true devotion will come forth, an entry and descent into Judaism, it falls into the hands of eternal death. It may happen that on one great day our yearnings will come together and breed enthusiasm, so that we will depart and imagine a movement among us; but if we have not received the impulse to build it, it will truly have been a cold fire and will perish quickly. This, however, has hitherto not yet been realized: that yearning helped to create content. Those few among us in whom their yearning has in truth awakened life, for whom Judaism became not only a banner but an order to march, have had a path prepared for movement; for movement is within them, and thus it may also arise among them.

It is not as if the demand were that everyone who later enters the movement must already come to it in a state of completion; no, for the movement will secure him substance because he will coalesce with it and identify with it, so that it will most certainly be nonsense to speak of the movement and its bearers as two different things. But today that is not the problem. We are speaking not of those who stand without or of those to come but, rather, of those who stand within; of those and to those who today sit proudly and arrogantly on their "movement" and are of the opinion that one only has to do a little (or much) more work and shaping, confusers and confused ones; and of us, who know that we still have no movement and who ask how shall we create one. Or, if that does not depend on us, how shall we participate in it? For it may be that the final spark that leaps between the moved individuals and gives the movement its divine seal and perfection is not in our hands. But just as the exact sciences distinguish between the *necessary* and *sufficient* conditions of a phenomenon, so here too: the realization of our demand is the necessary presupposition and is within our power, not, however, that which makes it into a sufficient one. But we do not doubt that when we have done what is ours to do, God will do what is His.

Certainly, if God does not build the house, the builders labor in vain; however, if the builders do not labor and do that which is their task and is possible, but stand aside swaggering and are of the opinion that they are done, then surely God will not build.

The demand can essentially be expressed in, and developed from, one word: wholeness. Youth is not whole, it is confused. And first and foremost we demand that the persons who come to us shall indeed have to learn anew, for there is no other way whatever than this one out of the confusion of the present, and whoever wishes to bring that confusion into our circle proves that he has remained outside. If our position is not completely different from that of the confused, then we have no right to proclaim any "decision." The youth today confronting the task of becoming a movement is also faced with the task, as precondition, of becoming different in the final and innermost sense: unconfused.

To track down these things is not impossible today, as Hugo Bergman° seemed to think in the first number of this journal, but rather more possible than ever before. For since some, from circles one often calls radical, by way of a welding together of the most curious things, have from the outside driven the confusion to a dizzying height of paradox with their "consistent" Zionism,

° Samuel Hugo Bergman was born in Prague in 1883 and by 1903 was already publishing articles on Zionism. He emigrated to Palestine in 1920 where he became professor of philosophy and eventually the first rector of the Hebrew University. His scholarly reputation rests primarily on his work in epistemology, but he has also widely written on Jewish themes.—Ed.

the separation is clearly presented and demanded for anyone who cares to see. The infinite paradoxes that have awakened our rage and indignation have taught us to think of *our* way. Our way, that is to say: to move ourselves toward Zion *as* wholeness and *in* wholeness.

Today youth is still most intimately entangled in tactics: the demands that are raised are only piecemeal and timid, and none has the courage and strength of wholeness; the standpoints we assume are attempts to cast furtive glances in all directions, and the courage to occupy the one and only standpoint is stifled by internal and external reasons. By internal ones, for one is comfortable and the ideologies of comfortableness are many. It is uncomfortable to make whole demands on oneself when from the very start one only wants to fulfill half; one does not demand Zion when one means Berlin. By external ones, for it is untactical. The sacrifices we demand are disjointed and superficial, for to demand whole sacrifices fills our youth, which has propaganda at heart, with dread.

Everywhere we have heard the objection: one must not frighten away those who stand on the outside. A diabolical argument! But that is how it is with us: everything turns around those who stand on the outside, for them everything is cut to order, every breath of consideration taken by the "movement" and every labor. That Zionism does not end but rather begins with the Basel program, that is a recognition now and then defended but the consequences of which youth has hitherto not been prepared in fact to draw. The commitment to Hebrew has not been connected, insofar as it has found any echo at all in Germany, with the insight that a youth movement not fundamentally Hebraized is no longer thinkable today; Hebrew is held to be a more or less important avocation. It would be a sad task for a statistician to determine how long one takes among us from the avowal of a youth movement to the actual taking up of Hebrew, even as a sideline. It is certain that among such youth no wholeness of Judaism and no fullness of content can be born if the road on which this result has been reached—tactics and prudence—is not abandoned.

The wholeness of dedication is not present, for the people who are with us are divided. One is not in the movement but in clubs, and the whole of a member is more than he reveals to the "movement" in the club; he does not have Zion as a goal, but rather Zion and something or other, from land reform to the theory of numbers, and this not as something subordinate but as something with equal rights, something extra that is also present. That, however, must not be: one goal must we set above ourselves, to which everything—but absolutely everything, even if it be the theory of numbers itself—is subordinated. The wholeness of which we think must not consist of many constituent parts, but only of one piece. And this means that we must find the courage for restrictions, for one-sidedness. If our youth were not so completely bent on preserving its many-sidedness—it suffices to point to the relevant problem of "German Jewishness" (*Deutschjudentum*)—we would be farther along; if syntheses were not always sought but dogmas erected, if there were not always reconciliation but battle, if in the hour of danger alliances were not always formed with the others—the others in and around us—then a great strength would rise as the tide, and the rising tide might be followed by the breakthrough of the movement. The rippling away of our creeks in all directions will never turn into a roaring waterfall.

If the will to clarity and greatness, to the final consequence, to seeing through the blue-white glasses ("*blau-weisse Brille*") is not found, the confusion will not be overcome. And this long will youth lack the right to a true propaganda: until it itself has become what it propagates. Today we cry much and loudly, on all streets and into all ears, but these are the cries of the confused and divided, cries from the surface, and they drown without support in the whirlpool of our time and are not heard. The youth for which we hope, however, will be able to go forth and cry differently—and we are far from seeing this as at all superfluous —for its cry will come from the depth and be clear. One is not permitted to call if one wants to stand both here and there, in Berlin and in Zion. We, however, will know where we have to stand if our cry is to be heard.

Farewell[*]

*An Open Letter to Dr. Siegfried Bernfeld
and against the Readers of This Journal*[*]

My dear Dr. Bernfeld:

Lying before me are the first two issues of the journal *Jerubbaal*, of which you were good enough to invite me to become a collaborator. According to the picture that the Jewish youth movement presents to everyone who can see—a dismal picture which was brought into sharper relief rather than concealed by the activity that for a time developed around it—according to this picture I could not indulge in any illusions about how a journal would be constituted that speaks from out of this youth, to this youth, and not against it. For indeed that against which passion is summoned up here is not worth the trouble: the one suitable object of combat, however, this writing youth, glorifies its absoluteness to itself in hymns of praise.

The picture that was to be expected has unfurled in the most fearful way and annihilated all hopes. It is no longer harmless stupidity, mindless, narrow-minded pedantry (so amusing to combat) that acknowledges itself and the honesty of which precludes all damage; no, this youth has kept in step with all the other movements of our time: it has ideas. It cannot be refuted, for there is nothing great it does not declaim, no objection or demand to which it cannot reply: but we also say and want that. Why should Zion be missed in it, when it proclaims Zion as the

* "Abschied," *Jerubbaal, Eine Zeitschrift der jüdischen Jugend,* I (1918–19), 125–30. Translated by Werner J. Dannhauser.

standard of its life? This youth is, morally viewed, a globe: one must put oneself in its center in order to recognize its mendacity, for from the outside it is unassailable and every other position within it distorts one's perspective. No cut or thrust against it is of any use any longer except for one thing: to see through it. It cannot be refuted; it can only be overcome. The only way of this overcoming that cannot be perverted is silence. Thus what I can say here is nothing positive, which, rather, can come to view only as the basis of my negation. Labor is oral teaching, and nothing of it can be committed to writing except the method, and it is exclusively the method of my silence that I wish to, and must, express here, not in order to convert—in this surrounding an impossibility for every word that does not possess prophetic purity—but rather to bear witness to a youth that receives, unfolds, and transmits Zion and the Torah silently, a youth that after this one necessary word of separation in *Jerubbaal* will become visible in the one and only manner worthy of it: in silence.

The great demand of Zionism, which is eternally one, to be a holy people, has a presupposition the misunderstanding of which is in a real sense the chimerical basis for that objective mendacity against which witness is to be given here. Community demands solitude: not the possibility of together desiring the same, but only that of common solitude establishes community. Zion, the source of our nationhood, is the common, indeed in an uncanny sense, the identical solitude of all Jews, and the religious assertion of Zionism is nothing other than this: the midst of solitude happens at the same time to be where all gather together, and there can be no other place for such a gathering together. As long as this center is not restored to radiant brightness, the order of our soul, which honesty bids us to acknowledge, must be anarchic. In *galut* there can be no Jewish community valid before God. And if community among human beings is indeed the highest that can be demanded, what would be the sense of Zionism if it could be realized in *galut?* Therefore, if the demand of Zionism is to be met, this cannot happen by way of community. And this is the *petitio principii* that portends the curse of Zionism: the pseudo-Zionist lie of community referring itself to an affirmative will. It is the characteristic content of the youth movement, the inner absurdity of which betrays itself in the absolute shapelessness that is its necessary consequence. This anticipation of community has its origin in the metaphysical horror people have of the strict demands of Zionism, the demands of which are no longer courageously negated in the old manner. One suspects that Zionism, unfolded in its purity, is the most fearful judgment of that disorder to which this youth, which basically does not know solitude at all and if it knows it cannot bear it, has condemned itself.[1]

Something else is connected with this: just as youth cannot be solitary, it cannot be silent. The silence in which word and deed unite is alien to it, for it has never beheld the pure word and the pure deed. Human beings, however, who are unable to observe silence are also in the last analysis unable to speak with each other. They do not understand each other for their language has neither form nor foundation: it is chimerical. Thus arises that fearful perversion that is the sphere of the Jewish youth wishing to be a movement: chatter. In it all things mingle in an indiscriminate manner and are perverted: Zion to the state of the future, Judaism to spirit (or whatever the hundred names for it may be), vision to living experience (*Erlebnis*), and so one could draw up the endless—and yet steadily remaining at the nadir—dictionary of the terminology of chatter.

The most fearful of these perversions announces itself in our days: it is that of labor. The legitimate concept of labor is nameless. Chatter is able to name labor and is preparing to substantiate it. Labor has no ideology, but the pure deed is an idea. The weakness of Zionist labor, about which committees and commissions lament, is based on the substantiation, so extremely illuminating to Zionists, of labor through chatter. For this, after all, is its principle: anything can be exchanged for anything and nothing will be changed. Why, then, should not labor be exchanged for demagogy or any other concept of this sphere? So, too, Hebrew has been robbed of its meaning,[2] for the Hebrew of

1. The documents of this disorder follow each other—at least since the book *Vom Judentum (Of Judaism)*, which has become a veritable triumphal arch of confusion—in unlimited succession and geometric progression of their nullity, and not a word would need to be wasted on them if the devastating effects which, for example, much of the Blau-Weiss literature exercises, did not awaken sorrow and lament.

2. When at the last meeting of the German Zionists a speaker expressed this simple and serious truth, he was treated to a very stormy scene by one of the attending "Hebraists."

the chatterers could never become the revelation of a community that proves its reality by the possibility of being silent in Hebrew.

Youth has no language. That is the reason for its uncertainty and unhappiness. It has no language, which is to say its life is imaginary and its knowledge without substance. Its existence is dissolved past all recognition into a complex flatness. It has lost the criteria of its own reality when it lied to God by chattering and made intoxication the speechless measure of its sham existence. To restore language to youth: that is the task. It demands another way than that of language, which can no longer lead to youth, since in chatter it has perverted the highest principle of language, on which all understanding rests: that of revelation itself. No going along with it can help; only our radical renunciation of the youth movement itself in the name of our task can save us from going under. For we are on a sinking ship, and no jubilation and no satisfaction about the "general direction" can deceive us about the fact that we are not traveling to Zion but are going under in Berlin: "They cry *shalom, shalom,*—but there is no peace."

There is only one place from which Zion can be reached and youth restituted: solitude. And there is only one medium, brought to radiance by labor, that will be the source of renewal: the existence that must be the argument against a youth that has desecrated words. That is the true help: that each averts the intoxication of living experiences (*Erlebnisse*), the pitiful abundance of the chatter and upbringing of others, for which he has no calling, and in seclusion seeks to bring order into his life. To such youth Hebrew is the superlative of their stillness and Zion no longer a symbolic metaphor.

This youth will discard the "Jewish *Erlebnis.*" For since youth could not keep silent or speak, could not see or do, it had living experiences (*Erlebnisse*). In these pages even the Torah has been turned into an *Erlebnis.* The vague mysticism to which Judaism is offered up on the altar of *Erlebnis,* that is the true crown of the youth movement. There is nothing great, from landscape to God and Torah, that in *Erlebnis* has not been connected to chatter. And they even had a living experience of the war when that was still fashionable. For that is the uncanny thing: even if there existed *Erlebnisse,* who today could dare to speak of them? But youth does not know silence. But in truth the *Erlebnis* is, after all, the chimerical, the absolute turned into chatter. It is necessary to recognize that only the false relationship to the community is the ground of this *Erlebnis*. It is the infinite mishmash that is supposed to be the substitute for those orders of the Jewish community that have been crumbled in it. The youth that, pure and chaste in its existence, sets up these orders again is not in need of it. The youth movement, certain of its metaphysical nullity, needed a concept of redemption as a necessary correlate by which it could deceive the movement about its religious meaning: so it proclaimed *Erlebnis*. Pure youth, however, redeems itself in lamentation.

On the basis of these reasons, it is an easy but unpleasant enterprise, whose execution you will spare me, to deduce the whole life of this youth movement down to its particulars. There is no sphere in it that has not been surrendered to those immanent perversions, no disorder that today is not commended to us as order. Look wherever you will! Is there anything more hopeless than this youth since it has become conscious of its importance and significance, of which one has again and again assured it? It saw itself called to a deed in the face of which its standards failed. It was the future of Zionism, about which one prudently concealed that it knows only an eternal present. It was to be history and escaped into development. For the task of restoring Zion threatened its spurious existence, of which strict and ultimately grounded reality was demanded, which it did not, after all, possess. The belief in its existence, that was indeed the axiom in which it sought solace and greatness. And now this axiom was endangered; proof of this existence was demanded, a proof it had no hope of being able to produce. So it perverted its conversion, which was its last and greatest possibility, into flight. A boundless embarrassment in the face of its own phrases: that is the ever-recurring impression received by anyone who wishes to work with it. From this embarrassment all that vocabulary is meant to rescue it by which everyone who expects something serious from it is emphatically refuted.

For in its need the youth movement makes a virtue of its inadequacy in regard to the categories of history. It demands postponement so that it can "develop" itself, continuity so that no one will be lost, and when it is no longer able to help itself at all, it sets upon the "elite," the sectarians who overlook that "we" are a people's movement. The youth that becomes intoxicated in the movement—"drunken ones, and not from wine"—hypostatizes the torments of its unnaturalness to a value. In this world, which truly is not one of ideas, it succeeds in confounding its flight with progress (in line with the truth that what is opposite in chatter is the identically chimerical), and so the perversion of the highest ideas generates that of all others in an uncanny succession. For development is not a historical category to which youth alone is subjected and the only continuity that gains any sense in it is the metaphysical continuity of decision.

Where is the development of youth really headed? The answer is as fearful as the question deserves; indeed, we all know it: from Berlin to Prague. Zion occurs here only metaphorically and is in the best case an outer limit. The orders, however, in which historical existence like that of youth takes place are different. A youth that in its solitude has not reached the point at which it finds its connection to the highest order of Jewish history, and thus embraces history, is excluded from the insight that the true continuity of a peoplehood is generated only in solitude, that the turning away from chatter is not destruction but rather a turning toward our task: that of a peoplehood whose fertility and greatness must unfold in me before I may raise the claim of being a teacher. The education that unfolds immediate religious orders by instruction and tradition requires a vocation and cannot be gained by screaming. That the organization of the wanderers and the students who in the youth movement are the screamers announce this claim: to educate—no matter with what stipulations it occurs—is evidence against them in the court of judgment.

So much is this youth without a vision of history that does not come to pass within the chimerical, that the death of Hermann Cohen found it incapable of lamentation, just as his existence did not arouse its reverence. The coincidence of youth and age in the Torah, in Judaism the metaphysical location of its movement, is when it presents itself in great personalities, the radiant origin of our reverence. Judaism lamented at the grave of Hermann Cohen, but the Jewish youth movement knew only that he was an "enemy."

If, then, everything about the youth movement arouses despair, without there being even the least hope of a conversion within its circle, the thing to do is to take another way. The old way does not lead to Zion but loses itself in innumerable branches of chatter. There can be no doubt as to where this other way leads; which neither is nor needs to be a new one, but an untrodden one. It will not be turned into the object of chatter, and if it has a connection with this youth, it has to be proven by separation. Silence, labor, and knowledge, purity, strictness, and renunciation, and whatever the orders may be that are to unfold themselves in the existence of the Zionists—they all perfect themselves in one thing: responsibility. Responsibility is the relationship of life to death. Our striving must be to be responsible in the face of our task. If we die in the face of history, then our death will be a Jewish one for it will be the teaching we hand down. A life, however, that is related to these basic principles can rightly be called youthful. Zion is the object of this life.

You propose to Jewish youth that it organize itself. I cannot concur with your proposal. The youth that is worthy of a union is not yet here, and if it is here, how can you believe that it will organize itself into anything other than a secret union that presents the one and only possibility of solitary community, which will be realized in concealment? For the power of Jewish youth consists not of its debut and its demands, but rather of the seclusion in which it takes up its task, and of the greatness of the renunciation in which its fullness assumes form.

Shall we then close down our organizations? Yes indeed. Should one no longer write essays about or for us? No. In your circle, rob youth of the possibility of further degrading language, which should be the highest thing to a Jew, into a public vessel for its *Erlebnisse*. Direct the passion of battle against your readers, who threaten your journal with invasion. But I engage in fantasy. For the readers and this, your journal, are, after all, identical: they are the youth movement against which I have here borne witness. The rest is silence.

Against the Myth of the German-Jewish Dialogue[*]

My dear Mr. Schlösser:[**]

Your invitation to contribute to a volume for Margarete Susman[***] honors me to the same extent as it puts me into a position of the most acute embarrassment. I see no other way than to explain the nature of this embarrassment to you, and thereby perhaps to the readers of the *Festschrift* planned by you. For in the announcement of this volume, which you were kind enough to send me, it says the *Festschrift* "is to be understood not only as homage but also as a testimony to a German-Jewish dialogue, the core of which is indestructible." No one could be more dismayed by such an announcement than I. For as ready as I find myself to pay homage to the venerable phenomenon that is Margarete Susman, with whom I have deeper ties than opinions on which we may agree or differ, as decisively must I decline an invitation to provide nourishment to that illusion, unintelligible to me, of "a German-Jewish dialogue, the core of which is indestructible," which this volume, according to your definition, is intended to serve. Permit me to explain myself about this in some detail.

I deny that there has ever been such a German-Jewish dialogue in any genuine sense whatsoever, i.e., *as a historical phenomenon.* It takes two to have a dialogue, who listen to each

[*] "Wider den Mythos vom deutsch-jüdischen 'Gespräch,' " in Gershom Scholem, *Judaica* 2 (Frankfurt-am-Main: Bibliothek Suhrkamp, 1970), pp. 7–11. Translated by Werner J. Dannhauser. Originally published in Manfred Schlösser, editor, *Auf gespaltenem Pfad: Festschrift für Margarete Susman* (Darmstadt, 1964).

[**] A young German writer and anthologist.—Ed.

[***] A German-Jewish poet and essayist (1874–1966) who wrote on many subjects, both general and Jewish. The *Festschrift* in which Scholem's piece appeared contains a bibliography of her writings. It was published in 1964, Susman's ninetieth year, which also saw the publication of her autobiography, *Ich habe viele Leben gelebt.*—Ed.

other, who are prepared to perceive the other as what he is and represents, and to respond to him. Nothing can be more misleading than to apply such a concept to the discussions between Germans and Jews during the last 200 years. This dialogue died at its very start and never took place. It died when the successors of Moses Mendelssohn—who still argued from the perspective of some kind of Jewish totality, even though the latter was determined by the concepts of the Enlightenment— acquiesced in abandoning this wholeness in order to salvage an existence for pitiful pieces of it, whose recently popular designation as German-Jewish symbiosis reveals its whole ambiguity. To be sure, the Jews attempted a dialogue with the Germans, starting from all possible points of view and situations, demandingly, imploringly, and entreatingly, servile and defiant, with a dignity employing all manner of tones and a godforsaken lack of dignity, and today, when the symphony is over, the time may be ripe for studying their motifs and for attempting a critique of their tones. No one, not even one who always grasped the hopelessness of this cry into the void, will belittle the latter's passionate intensity and the tones of hope and grief that were in resonance with it.

The attempt of the Jews to explain themselves to the Germans and to put their own creativity at their disposal, even to the point of complete self-abnegation, is a significant phenomenon, the analysis of which in adequate categories is yet to be accomplished and will perhaps become possible only now that it is at an end. In all this I am unable to perceive anything of a dialogue. Never did anything respond to that cry, and it was this simple and, alas, so far-reaching realization that affected so many of us in our youth and destined us to desist from the illusion of a "German-Judaism." Where Germans ventured on a discussion with Jews in a humane spirit, such a discussion, from Wilhelm von Humboldt to Stefan George, was always based on the expressed or unexpressed self-denial of the Jews, on the progressive atomization of the Jews as a *community* in a state of dissolution, from which in the best case only the *individuals* could be received, be it as bearers of pure humanity, or be it even as bearers of a heritage that had in the meantime become historical. It is that famous slogan from the battles of the

Emancipation—"For the Jews as individuals, everything; for the Jews as a people (that is to say: as Jews) nothing"—which prevented a German-Jewish dialogue from getting started. The one and only partnership of dialogue which took the Jews as such seriously was that of the anti-Semites who, it is true, said something to the Jews in reply, but nothing beneficial. To the infinite intoxication of Jewish enthusiasm there never corresponded a tone that bore any kind of relation to a creative answer to the Jews; that is to say, one that would have addressed them with regard to what they had *to give* as Jews, and not what they had to *give up* as Jews.

To whom, then, did the Jews speak in that much-talked-about German-Jewish dialogue? They spoke to themselves, not to say that they outshouted themselves. Some felt uneasy, perhaps even dismal about it, but many acted as if everything were on the best way to being settled, as if the echo of their own voice would be unexpectedly transmogrified into that voice of the others they so eagerly hoped to hear. The Jews have always been listeners of great intensity, a noble legacy they brought with them from Mount Sinai. They listened to many kinds of voices, and one cannot say that this always served them well. When they thought they were speaking to the Germans, they were speaking to themselves. No one except Jews themselves, for example, was "spoken to" by the Jewish creativity of a thinker like Georg Simmel. And Simmel was indeed a truly symbolic phenomenon for all that of which I speak here, because he was that phenomenon of a man in whom the substance of Judaism still shows most visibly when the latter had arrived at the pure nadir of complete alienation. I will forgo the treatment of that deeply moving chapter that is designated by the great name of Hermann Cohen and the way in which this unhappy lover, who did not shun the step from the sublime to the ridiculous, was answered.

The allegedly indestructible community of the German essence with the Jewish essence consisted, so long as these two essences really lived with each other, only of a chorus of Jewish voices and was, on the level of historical reality, never anything else than a fiction, a fiction of which you will permit me to say that too high a price was paid for it. The Germans were mostly angered by this fiction and at best moved. Shortly before I went to Palestine, there appeared Jakob Wassermann's book, *Mein Weg als Deutscher und Jude* (*My Way as German and Jew*), certainly one of the most gripping documents of that fiction, a true cry into the void that knew itself to be such. The reply to him was in part embarrassment, in part sneer. One will look in vain for an answer on the level of the speaker, one that would thus have been a dialogue. And if once, directly before the onset of the catastrophe, it did indeed come to a dialogue in the form of a discussion, then it looked like that dialogue between the ex-members of the Wandervogel, Hans Joachim Schoeps and Hans Blüher,° the reading of which even today causes the reader's hair to stand on end. But why heap up examples when, after all, the whole of that ghostlike German-Jewish dialogue ran its course in such an empty realm of the fictitious? I could speak of it endlessly, and I would nevertheless always be sticking to the same point.

It is true: the fact that Jewish creativity poured forth here is perceived by the Germans, now that all is over. I would be the last to deny that there is something genuine about that—at once gripping and depressing. But it no longer changes anything about the fact that no dialogue is possible with the dead, and to speak of an "indestructibility of this dialogue" strikes me as blasphemy.

Yours,
GERSHOM SCHOLEM

Jerusalem, December 18, 1962

° Schoeps (b. 1909) is a professor of religious history who has written on the early years of Christianity. Before World War II he articulated a Jewish theology that brought Judaism as close as possible to Christianity. He was also a strong German nationalist who was convinced, even in 1933, that German Jews could get along with the Nazis (though he regretted his failure to recognize the nature of Nazism in his autobiography of 1956).

Blüher (1888–1955) was known for his writings on the Wandervogel and other German youth movements. He published an anti-Semitic tract in 1922 and collaborated with Schoeps in 1933 on a book *Streit um Israel* (*Controversy over Israel*).—Ed.

Once More: The German-Jewish Dialogue*

I

Rudolf Kallner** has raised objections to my statement, "Against the Myth of the German-Jewish Dialogue." By *objections*, one commonly is in the habit of understanding that the theses which have been advanced are attacked. My thesis, that the talk of the German-Jewish dialogue is a myth, obviously presupposed that I clearly define the meaning of the word *dialogue* as in fact I went on to do. Given the sense of this definition, one can agree with or object to my statement. That, for example, is what I would then call a dialogue between Kallner and me. Instead of this, we have here a model example of a dialogue without an object, in which the participants are talking about different things. And not only that, for Kallner expressly declares that a dialogue in the sense that I "seem to" connect with this concept is surely not that which is meant by this concept in modern German linguistic usage. Thus, after having divested the concept of its well-defined meaning in favor of a washed-out and insubstantial journalistic usage, as is common in newspapers, he proceeds to deal with the subject of dialogue in this meaningless sense and therewith to "refute" my statements.

The dialogue in Kallner's sense consists of the completely undeniable fact that there were relations and discussions between Jews and Germans. That historical relations of a passionate and vehement kind existed between the Germans and the Jews,

* "Noch einmal: das deutsch-jüdische Gespräch," *Bulletin des Leo Baeck Instituts*, No. 30 (Tel Aviv, 1965), pp. 167–72. Translated by Werner J. Dannhauser.
** An Israeli attorney, born in Germany.—Ed.

even though in a wholly different manner from both sides, no one, of course, would think of disputing. And whoever will reread my letter to Mr. Schlösser will find out at once that I clearly and distinctly differentiated between a dialogue and discussions of this general kind. The introduction of sublime and solemn-sounding terms like *dialogue* in order to designate wholly trivial states of affairs like the one of historically determined relations and discussions between two groups yields little blessing. I employed the word in that heightened and tolerably precise sense, also used by the addressee of my letter, in which the philosophers of the "dialogue" introduced it for certain spiritual-intellectual (*geistige*) discussions. It was just the pathetic note, the existential factor of the dialogue, and the claim in a certain sense of its "indestructibility," that occasioned my passionate protest. To contradict me by talking of something completely different is as easy as it is unfruitful for a discussion. We are talking past each other. Of a sentence like this: "The dialogue was conducted by the German people in its totality and as well by the totality of the Jewish sector within the territory of the German Reich," I can make no sense whatsoever. And so it goes with all the consequences flowing from such a "definition" of the dialogue, which probably reach their peak in the contention that the historical fact of the legal emancipation of the Jews and their equality of rights is supposedly *de facto* a "decided proof" that "the dialogue actually took place and that the disavowal of this dialogue is a mistake." Since one can presuppose, I take it, that during the composition of my letter I was familiar with these facts and they were present in my mind, these and many other corresponding factual pieces of instruction in Kallner's objection seem to me meaningless.

The salient point of my letter to Mr. Schlösser was that the Germans, where they engaged in a dialogue (in more than a washed-out sense) with the Jews at all, did so under the presupposition that the Jews were prepared to give themselves up *as Jewish* to an ever more progressive extent. One of the most important of the phenomena in the relations between the Jews and the Germans is the fact that the Jews themselves were in large part ready to do this. Nevertheless, not even this readiness, of which all those of us who grew up in Germany received the most overwhelming and shocking proof, led to a true dialogue between the parties. There is nothing in my argument to deny that there were indeed infinite shades and variations in this readiness, and that a really complete analysis and description of the circumstances under which the Jews attempted their—alas so hopeless—dialogue with the Germans would represent the accomplishment of a very great task that has never yet been seriously undertaken, because the standards for it were lacking.

Kallner also speaks of the situation after the catastrophe and the rise of the State of Israel, as it now presents itself, for the continuation of such relations between Germans and Jews or for the resumption of such relations as he calls a dialogue. I am not among those who altogether refuse and oppose the resumption of such relations. In order to render such a resumption fruitful in a serious sense, one requires, however, not only a knowledge of what is, but also of what was. In order to reach that point, a considerable "toil of conceptual reflection" is required. In this generation, in the face of the dead and the murdered, it is very difficult to advance to a level on which not only a critique of the conduct of the Germans but also of that of the Jews would be possible and capable of formulation. We will be unable to circumvent this historical critique in the true sense of the word, if the atmosphere between the Germans and us is indeed to be purified, and I am under no illusions about the difficulties of such an undertaking and about the emotions at stake in it. In recent years a tendency has become visible, which has been seized by many Germans all too enthusiastically, according to which the seizure of power by the Nazis was, in a higher sense, a kind of historical accident without which everything between Germans and Jews would really have been making tolerably good progress; an opinion the echo of which is also still to be found in the letter by Mr. Schlösser. Corresponding to this is now an unlimited and uncritical posthumous enthusiasm for the epoch of Jewish assimilation in Germany, the documents of which often enough cause one's words to fail.

I do not know whether there can once again be a productive dialogue between Germans and Jews, beyond wholly or half-honestly intended "relations" and efforts. I would see in that a significant event, an important new beginning. That, however, presupposes, if it is not to bear in itself the germ of destruction from the start, the will on both sides to the full truth about what has happened and therewith also the will to a fearless critique of prevalent myths about this past. Kallner's warning not to endanger this new beginning through pronouncements of what is and what was seems to me misplaced. If the "dialogue" is possible only under such conditions, it will continue to fail to materialize.

II

With the above I have also, as I would hope, made clear what separates me from Mr. Schlösser, to whom my letter was addressed, beyond all the ties he emphasizes. Before I append some remarks to his letter to me, I would like to clear up some misunderstandings. In contrast to Mr. Kallner, Mr. Schlösser and I are at one about the meaning of the talk of a German-Jewish dialogue. Only I did not deny what would indeed be foolish, that in the last century and a half such dialogues took place between *individual* partners—as Schlösser himself writes restrictively— eye to eye, or letter to letter, more or less passionately. I am familiar with some memorable examples of such a dialogue. What I denied, and deny, was the presence of such a dialogue "as historical phenomenon"; that means, however, no longer as on a purely personal level, no longer as an isolated biographical datum, but rather as a phenomenon of transpersonal significance that could yield a legitimate motto for the whole of the German-Jewish discussions, concerning whose character I had explained myself in my letter to him.

And more than that: I left no doubt, right at the beginning of my letter, of my conviction that the liquidation of the Jewish substance by the Jews themselves must in large part be held responsible for the fact that this dialogue did not come to take place as a historical phenomenon. This liquidation certainly has deep and far-reaching reasons, only a part of which have hitherto been expressed, but the dialectical connection between this liquidation and the fate of the Jews in Germany, for good and for evil, seems evident to me. It is precisely this readiness for self-denial which goes a long way in codetermining the unreal and ghostly element in this "dialogue." They are no longer even Jews, in the full sense of an unbroken historical consciousness, who speak here, but rather Jews in flight from themselves. It is a feeling of panic which these fleeing ones, and often precisely the most significant figures among them, call forth in their partners, which permeates with such destructive dialectic the statements from the German side stemming from goodwill, humane reflections, and liberal dispositions. We will least serve the cause concerning us here by the idealization of both partners. I am a Jew and have a very sharp ear for that "godforsaken lack of dignity" in so many Jewish expressions that Mr. Schlösser finds so offensive in my formulation, and that Schlösser, in a way wholly incomprehensible to me, finds refuted by the passing of the Emancipation laws.

Naturally, my protest against Schlösser's formulation of the "German-Jewish dialogue, the core of which is indestructible" neither could nor should take the place of a still-missing work, which would have to illuminate the situation not only historically-factually but also historically-philosophically. I wholeheartedly agree with Mr. Schlösser that this must be one of the most important tasks of future research. I do not turn against the erection of a future-pointing symbol if it would express a genuine reality. I am against the erection of signposts pointing in the wrong direction. Mr. Schlösser is of the opinion that he has innumerable proofs that the maintenance of an illusion eventually led to a reality and with this device he bestows high praise on those Jews who did not relinquish their illusion. Well, it would be quite difficult to think of a more ironic formulation in this connection, and I must refuse to discuss the unironic and horrible falsity of this sentence when applied to the example of the German Jews that is under discussion here. It then also corresponds to Mr. Schlösser's fascination with the achievements and accomplishments of the Jewish assimilation in Germany—the problematic aspect of which, after all, is precisely what so agitates us Jews—that he ventures the opinion that in spite of all it accomplished for the Jews, Zionism also gave anti-Semitism material for development. What a grandiose perversion of the facts! One might really think that anti-Semitism needed material in order to develop, and it just so happened that it was provided by the utopian retreat of the Jews to Zion from their historical connection with Germany. Here the idyllic view taken of German-Jewish relations leads to a *reductio ad absurdum*.

I did not understand Mr. Schlösser's thesis, according to which, from the invitation of Spinoza to the University of Heidelberg to the appointment of Rathenau as foreign minister, attempts were undertaken at a genuine integration, which for him is "much more" than emancipation and assimilation. Is that not pure fantasy?

The hopes that Mr. Schlösser expresses at the end of his letter are in good faith—but they have nothing to do with what is in dispute between us except, let us be clear, that in this case hopes pregnant with the future can arise only on the basis of a knowledge of the past. Without such knowledge, which is at once commemoration and recollection, this hope will not take wing.

Jews and Germans[*]

I

To speak of Jews and Germans and their relations during the last two centuries is, in the year 1966, a melancholy enterprise. So great, even now, is the burden of emotions, that a dispassionate consideration or analysis of the matter seems almost impossible; we have all been molded too strongly by the experience of our generation to permit any such expectations of detachment. Today there are many Jews who regard the German people as a "hopeless case," or at best as a people with whom, after what has happened, they want nothing to do, for good or for evil. I do not count myself among them, for I do not believe that there ought to be such a thing as a permanent state of war among peoples. I also deem it right—what is more, I deem it important—that Jews, precisely *as* Jews, speak to Germans in full consciousness of what has happened and of what separates them. Upon many of us the German language, our mother tongue, has bestowed the gift of unforgettable experiences; it defined and gave expression to the landscape of our youth. Now there is a kind of appeal from the German side—both from the reaches of history and from a younger generation that is coming to the fore—and precisely because this appeal is so uncertain and irresolute, indeed, embarrassed, something inheres in it that many of us do not wish to shun.

* "Juden und Deutsche," a lecture delivered at plenary session, World Jewish Congress, Brussels, August 2, 1966. Published in Gershom Scholem, *Judaica* 2 (Frankfurt-am-Main: Bibliothek Suhrkamp, 1970), pp. 20–46. An adaptation, in English translation by Werner J. Dannhauser, appeared in *Commentary* (November 1966). The present translation, by Werner J. Dannhauser, is from the original lecture.

To be sure, the difficulties of generalizing, as when we say "the Germans" and "the Jews," intimidate the observer. In times of conflict, however, such all-embracing terms prove easy to manipulate; and the fact that these general categories are vulnerable to questioning has never prevented people from using them vociferously. Many distinctions would be in order here. For not all "Germans" are Germans and not all "Jews" are Jews— with, of course, one appalling exception: when power was in the hands of those Germans who really meant *all* Jews when they referred to the Jews, they used that power to the best of their ability to murder all Jews. Since then, those who survived this murder, or were not exposed to it because of the accidents of history, find it somewhat difficult themselves to make the proper distinctions. The dangerous pitfalls that accompany any generalization are well known: arbitrariness, self-contradiction, and incoherence. The relationships I am discussing are too various and unique to be covered by any blanket assertion that could not be countered by a different and almost equally defensible one. And yet, fully aware as I am of these difficulties, I wish to make clear what it is that moves me about this theme—certainly one of the themes that have most agitated the Jewish world in the past one hundred fifty years and more.

In 1948 Alfred Doeblin, a Jewish writer who had converted to Catholicism in his old age, wrote to another Jew that he should take care, when addressing a German audience, to avoid using the word *Jew*, for in Germany it was still a term of abuse; only anti-Semites would be pleased by its use. According to Doeblin, anti-Semitism was deep-seated among the Germans and more malicious—in the year 1948!—than prior to 1933. Indeed, I myself can testify that even in 1966 many Germans who would like to dissociate themselves from the Nazis (occasionally rather as an afterthought), to a certain extent still confirm the validity of Doeblin's remarks by their evident aversion to calling any Jew a Jew unless he absolutely insists on it. After having been murdered as Jews, the Jews have now been nominated to the status of Germans, in a kind of posthumous triumph; to emphasize their Jewishness would be a concession to anti-Semitism. What a perversion in the name of progress, to do everything possible to avoid facing the realities of the Jewish-German relationship!

But it is precisely the facing of these realities that I consider to be our task, and when we speak of the fate of the Jews among the Germans we cannot speak emphatically enough of Jews *qua* Jews. The atmosphere between Jews and Germans can be cleansed only if we seek to get to the bottom of their relationship, and only if we employ the unrestrained criticism that the case demands. And that is hard: for the Germans, because the mass murder of the Jews has become the greatest nightmare of their moral existence as a people; for the Jews, because such clarification demands a critical distance from crucial phenomena of their own history. Love, insofar as it once existed, has been drowned in blood; its place must now be taken by historical knowledge and conceptual clarity—the preconditions for a discussion that might perhaps bear fruit in the future. If it is to be serious and undemagogic, such a discussion must be approached on a level beyond that of the political and economic factors and interests that have been, or are, under negotiation between the State of Israel and the German Federal Republic. I am lacking in any competence in this area, and at no time will I refer to it. I am not even certain that it can help us at all in posing the right questions or in attempting to answer them. We have all heard a great deal about this matter and, precisely as Jews, we are not always at ease when a false connection is created.

II

Until the latter half of the eighteenth century, and to some extent even beyond that time, the Jews in Germany led essentially the same existence as did Jews everywhere. They were clearly recognizable as a nation; they possessed an unmistakable identity and a millennial history of their own, however they themselves or the peoples around them may have assessed that history. They had a finely honed awareness of themselves and participated in a religious order that forced its way with extreme intensity through their very pores and into their life and culture. To the degree that the influence of the German environment— and such influence was never entirely absent—penetrated into the *Judengasse*, it did so not because the Jews deliberately turned to it and embraced it, but in large part through a barely conscious process of osmosis. To be sure, German cultural values were frequently enough transformed into Jewish values (and, linguistically, into Yiddish). The conscious relations between the two societies were of a delicate nature, however, and especially so during the two centuries preceding the era of emancipation. The religious culture of the dominant strata of Jews was self-contained and remained wholly alien to the German world.

But the economically strongest element—as it was represented in the phenomenon of the *Hofjudentum*—Jewish management of court finances—and the group at the bottom of the social ladder that was in communication with the German underworld, maintained a kind of contact with the Germans that was in both cases perilous. They moved among the Germans in a special manner, and in so doing they were at the mercy of the slightest change in political or social conditions. Nothing would be more foolish than to speak of an intimate attachment between German Jews and Germany during that age, during which not a single precondition existed for it. Everyone knew that the Jews were in exile, and however one might view the meaning of that exile, there was no doubt as to its enduring significance for the social condition of the Jews.

The overwhelming majority of the Jews, which did not belong to these marginal groups and was relatively less affected by their vicissitudes, at that time lived completely within the mold of tradition; a mold cast by their material and spiritual history during the long ages of exile. At the same time there is no mistaking the fact that in the latter half of the eighteenth century a grave weakness at the core of their Jewishness became visible. It was as if they had arrived at the nadir of one phase of their historical existence and were no longer certain where the road would lead. This weakness had already become evident at the time Moses Mendelssohn set out upon his career as a kind of conservative reformer of German Jewry. With him, and above all with the school he inspired, there began among Jews a conscious process of turning toward the Germans; a process subsequently graced and furthered by mighty historical forces. There began a propaganda campaign for the Jews' resolute absorption by German culture and, shortly thereafter, for their absorption by

the German people itself. There also began the struggle of Jews
for civil rights, a struggle which extended over three or four
generations, and which was finally. won because—let us not
deceive ourselves—it was conducted on their behalf by a decisive
and victorious stratum among the non-Jews.

With these struggles, which were furthered no less by the
French Revolution than by the German Enlightenment, a
momentous change commenced in German Jewry. At first the
change was hesitant and most uncertain, just as the Judaism of
those undergoing it was often uncertain and embarrassed. They
still had a strong sense of their peoplehood as Jews, though
frequently not of the meaning of this peoplehood, which had
been or was in the process of becoming lost to them. But, to put
the case explicitly, they also began casting those infinitely
yearning and furtive glances at the realm of German history—as
a possible replacement for the Jewish realm—which became so
characteristic of them in their relations to the Germans for the
next hundred years and more. Those elements of German Jewry
that viewed this process with the greatest reservations—especially the once preponderant and still very strong circles of the
traditionally pious—were marked off from their more enthusiastic fellows by nothing more distinct than an oppressed silence,
broken only rarely among them by direct voices of warning; it is
as if they were recoiling from their own suffering. In any event,
up to about 1820, when the Jews of Germany are mentioned, it is
almost exclusively as the members of the Jewish nation in
Germany. In the next two generations, however, linguistic usage
alters completely; terms such as *Mosaic persuasion,* and similar
phrases favored by Jews and Germans alike, now begin their
career.

The furtive glances cast by the Jews toward the Germans
were from the very outset attended by considerable changes and
dislocations, which at a later stage of the process were to lead to
bitter problems. As a price of Jewish emancipation, the Germans
demanded a resolute disavowal of Jewish nationality—a price the
leading writers and spokesmen of the Jewish avant-garde were
only too happy to pay. What had begun as furtive glances turned
into a passionate involvement with the realm of German history;
and the objects of enlightened toleration not infrequently

became ardent prophets, prepared to speak in the name of the
Germans themselves.

The attentive reader of German reactions to this process and
its acrobatics soon perceives the note of astonishment and a
partly amiable, partly malicious irony that recurs again and again
in these expressions. With the renunciation of a crucial part of
Jewish existence in Germany, the ground was prepared for what
appears to many of us to have been a completely false start in the
history of modern relations between Jews and Germans—even
though, given the conditions of 1800, it possessed a certain
immanent logic of its own. When the Western people emancipated the people of Israel, they did not, to quote Buber (1932),
"accept it as Israel, but rather as a multitude of individuals."
Among the non-Jews, the most stalwart fighters for the cause of
the Jews were precisely those who most consciously and articu-
lately counted on the disappearance of the Jews *qua* Jews—who
indeed, like Wilhelm von Humboldt, considered the disappearance of the Jews as an ethnic group a condition for taking up
their cause. The liberals hoped for a decisively progressive Jewish
self-dissolution. The conservatives, however, with their sense of
history, had reservations about this new phenomenon. They
began to chalk up against the Jews an all-too-great facility for
renouncing their ethnic consciousness. The self-abnegation of the
Jews, although welcomed and indeed demanded, was often seen
as evidence of their lack of moral substance. We have clear
documentation to show that the disdain in which so many
Germans held the Jews fed on the ease with which the upper
cultural stratum of the Jews disavowed its own tradition. For
what could a heritage be worth if the elite of its chosen heirs
were in such a rush to disavow it?

Thus a sinister and dangerous dialectic arose. Broad circles of
the German elite demanded of the Jews that they give up their
heritage, and went so far as to set a premium on defection; at the
same time, however, many despised the Jews for just their
excessive willingness to oblige. As for the socialists, Karl Marx's
grotesque and disgusting invective in *On the Jewish Question*
may be taken as a sign of their total frivolity and ignorance; they
were completely at a loss before the issues involved in this new

turn of events, and could do no more than press for the dissolution of the Jewish people and its historical consciousness, a dissolution to be completed by the advent and victory of the Revolution. They could see no sense whatever in considering the Jews as active participants in any meaningful encounter. For them, as the slogan had it, the Jews were merely "oil for the wheels of the Revolution."

Such, then, was the dangerous dialectic of the whole process. The Jews struggled for emancipation—and this is the tragedy that moves us so much today—not for the sake of their rights as a people, but for the sake of assimilating themselves to the peoples among whom they lived. By their readiness to give up their peoplehood, by their act of disavowal, they did not put an end to their misery; they merely opened up a new source of agony. Assimilation did not, as its advocates had hoped, dispose of the Jewish question in Germany; rather it shifted the locus of the question and rendered it all the more acute. As the area of contact between the two groups widened, the possibilities of friction widened as well. The "adventure" of assimilation, into which the Jews threw themselves so passionately (it is easy to see why) necessarily increased the dangers that grew out of the heightened tension. Added to this was the fact that there was, if I may use Arnold Zweig's expression, something "disordered" about the Jews who were exposed to this new encounter with the Germans—and in a double sense: they were "disordered" by their existence under the undignified conditions they were forced to live in as well as its social and personal consequences; and they were "disordered" by the deep insecurity that began to hound them the moment they left the ghetto in order, as the formula had it, "to become Germans." This double disorder of the Jews was one of the factors that retarded, disturbed, and eventually brought to a gruesome end the process—or trial—that now began in such earnest. The refusal of so many German Jews to recognize the operation of such factors, and the dialectic to which they bear witness, is among the saddest discoveries made by today's reader of the discussions of those times. The emotional confusion of the German Jews between 1820 and 1920 is of considerable importance if one wishes to understand them as a group, a group characterized by that "German-Jewishness" ("*Deutschjudentum*") many of us encountered in our own youth and which stimulated us to resistance.

At the same time, however, and in the very midst of this insecurity, something else happened: the long-buried creativity of the Jews was liberated. It is true that by entering so eagerly into a new world, the Jews relinquished the security their ancient tradition had once bestowed upon them, and would frequently continue to bestow in an impressive way upon those who held fast to it. But in recompense those Jews who threw themselves into this exciting "living experience" (*Erlebnis*) of assimilation found that it awakened something in them that under the old order had long been dormant or forgotten. These factors are deeply connected. Here it is fitting that we briefly examine and clarify those positive aspects of this process that became so meaningful precisely to the Jews, even those living far beyond the borders of Germany.

The intimate passion that the relation to things German assumed for the Jews is connected with the specific historical hour in which it was born. At the moment in time when Jews turned from their medieval state toward the new era of enlightenment and resolution, the overwhelming majority of them—80 percent—lived in Germany, Austria-Hungary, and Eastern Europe. Due to prevailing geographic, political, and linguistic conditions, therefore, it was German culture the Jews first encountered on their road to the West. Moreover—and this is decisive—the encounter occurred precisely at the moment when that culture had reached one of its most fruitful turning points. It was the zenith of Germany's bourgeois era. One can say that it was a happy hour when the newly awakened creativity of the Jews, which was to assume such impressive forms after 1780, impinged precisely on the zenith of a great creative period of the German people, a period producing an image of things German that, up to 1940, and among very broad classes of people, was to remain unshaken, even by many bitter and later most bitter experiences. For the Jews this amalgamation of a great historical hour was defined and symbolized by the names of Lessing and Schiller, and in its intensity and scope it has no parallel in the encounters of the Jews with other European peoples. Due to this encounter, the first on the Jews' way to the West, because of this new image, a high luster fell on all things German. Even today, after so much blood and so many tears, we cannot say that it was *only* a deceptive luster. It was more: it contained elements of great fruitfulness and the stimulus to significant developments.

The significance of Friedrich Schiller for the formation of Jewish attitudes toward Germany is almost incalculable and has seldom been appreciated by the Germans themselves. For to generations of Jews within Germany, and almost to a greater extent to Jews outside Germany, Schiller, spokesman for pure humanity, lofty poet of the highest ideals of mankind, represented everything they thought of, or wished to think of, as being German—even when, in the Germany of the last third of the nineteenth century, his language had already begun to sound hollow. For many Jews the encounter with Friedrich Schiller was more real than their encounter with actual Germans. Here they found what they were most fervently seeking. German romanticism meant something to many Jews, but Schiller meant something to all of them. He was a factor in the Jewish belief in mankind. Schiller provided the most visible, most impressive, and most resounding occasion for the idealistic self-deceptions engendered by the relations of the Jews to the Germans. For the Jew who had lost his self-confidence, Schiller's program seemed to promise everything he sought; the *Jew* heard no false tones in it, for this was music that spoke to his depths. To Schiller, who never addressed them directly, the Jews did indeed respond, and the collapse of this dialogue perhaps contains one of the secrets of the general collapse of relations between Jews and Germans. After all, Schiller, to whom their love clung so passionately, was not just anybody; he was the national poet of Germany, regarded as such by the Germans themselves from 1800 to 1900. In this case, then, the Jews did not, as has happened often enough, "have the wrong address."

In this case a bridge had really been built between the Jews and the Germans, built out of the same boundless passion that induced a number of Russian Jews, who were seeking the road to humanity among the Jewish people itself, literally to adopt the

name of Schiller as their own; one of the noblest figures of the
Zionist movement, Solomon Schiller,° is a notable example of this
practice. Unfortunately, however, the task of building bridges
was pursued by the Jews alone. To Germans of a later day,
Jewish enthusiasm for Schiller seemed merely comic or touching.
Only rarely were other Germans stirred by the feeling that here,
for once, there could have been much common ground.

III

The first half of the nineteenth century was a period in which
Jews and Germans drew remarkably close. During this time an
extraordinary amount of help came from the German side, with
many individual Jews receiving cooperation in their stormy
struggle for culture. There was certainly no lack of goodwill then;
reading the biographies of the Jewish elite of the period, one
again and again finds evidence of the understanding they
encountered, even in decidedly Christian circles like the Moravi-
ans. But in keeping with the inner dynamics of the process we
have been examining, things did not remain at the level of a mere
struggle for culture. The Jews were at a point of radical transition
from the traditional way of life, which still held sway among a
majority of them, to Germanism. In the effecting of this
transition, according to one contemporary source, "the German
national education of the Jews and their participation in the
general interests of human beings and citizens appears as the
most essential task, to which everyone who expects anything of
himself must be dedicated." The formulation is by Moritz
Lazarus, a follower of the philosopher Johann Friedrich Herbart,
and a most pristine representative of the very tendency he
advocated; he himself completed the transition from pure
talmudic Judaism to the new German-Jewish way of life in a
mere five years! The unending Jewish demand for a home was
soon transformed into the ecstatic illusion of being at home.

° Solomon Schiller (1879–1925) changed his name from Blankenstein. Born in Poland,
he was a member of the First Zionist Congress in 1897 and emigrated to Palestine in 1910.
He was a teacher and, later, principal at Jerusalem's prestigious Rehavia Gymnasium.—
Ed.

It is well known and easy to understand that the speed of this transformation, which even today amazes the observer, the haste of this breakup of the Jews, was not paralleled by an equally quick reciprocal act on the part of the Germans. For the Germans did not know they were dealing with such deep processes of decay in the Jewish tradition and in Jewish self-consciousness, and they recoiled from the whole procedure. As much as they would have approved of the eventual result of the process—which accorded at least with the prevailing liberal ideology and to a considerable extent with the prevailing conservative one—they were altogether unprepared for this tempo, which struck them as overheated and whose aggressiveness set them on the defensive. Sooner or later this defensiveness was to combine with those currents of opinion that from the very beginning had reacted to the whole process with antipathy and that, since the whole post-Mendelssohn generation, had never lacked for eloquent spokesmen.

It made good sense to speak of a "host people" whose guests the Jews were. Even in the best of circumstances, it was a matter of a guest being accepted into the family, but subject to dismissal if he did not live up to the requirements. This became especially clear where the liberals were concerned. The talk one occasionally hears today of a fusion that would have made excellent progress had not the advent of Nazism come between the great majority of Jews and the "citizens of a different faith" (the phrase was used in print by a Jew in the Germany of 1965!)—such talk is nothing but a retroactive wish fulfillment. Without doubt, the complete submission to the German people of so many people who in their autobiographies (which are available in abundance) characterized themselves as being "of Jewish descent"—because they no longer had any other inner ties to the Jewish tradition, let alone to the Jewish people—constitutes one of the most shocking phenomena of this whole process of estrangement. The list of Jewish losses to the Germans is infinitely long, a list of great and frequently astonishing Jewish talents and accomplishments that were offered up to the Germans. Who can read without emotion the history of those, like that of Otto Lippmann° from Hamburg,

° A high official of the Senate of Hamburg who wrote an autobiography.—Ed.

who to the point of suicide maintained the claim that they were better Germans than those who were driving them to their deaths?

Today, when all is over, it is no wonder that there are many who wish to recognize this claim as just. These people made their choice, and we should not contest the Germans' right to them. And yet it makes us uneasy, for our feeling points to the inner discord of even these careers. Even in their complete estrangement of their awareness from everything "Jewish," something is evident in many of them that was felt to be substantially Jewish by Jews as well as Germans—by everyone except themselves!—and that is true of a whole galaxy of illustrious minds from Karl Marx and Lassalle to Karl Kraus, Gustav Mahler, and Georg Simmel.

No one has more profoundly characterized this breaking away of the Jews from themselves than Charles Péguy, who had an insight into the Jewish condition rarely attained, let alone surpassed, by non-Jews. To him we owe the sentence: *Être ailleurs, le grand vice de cette race, la grande vertue secrète, la grande vocation de ce peuple.*° This "being elsewhere" combined with the desperate wish to "be at home" in a manner at once intense, fruitful, and destructive. It is the clue to the relationship of the Jews to the Germans. It is at once what makes their symbolic position so alluring and so gripping to today's observer, and what at the time caused them to appear disgusting, to be working under false pretenses, and to be deliberately provocative of opposition. No benefit redounded to the Jews of Germany from what today, under very different circumstances, invests them with positive significance for an important part of the world and brings them special consideration: I am thinking of the widespread current appreciation of Jews as classic representatives of the phenomenon of man's estrangement or alienation from society. The German Jew was held to blame for his own estrangement or alienation from the Jewish ground that had nourished him, from his own history and tradition, and was blamed even more for his alienation from the bourgeois society

° Being elsewhere, the great vice of this race, the great secret virtue, the great vocation of this people.—Ed.

that was then in the process of consolidating itself. The fact that he was not really at home, however much and emphatically he might proclaim himself to be—the "homelessness" that today is sometimes accounted to his glory, in that it is taken as an image of the *condition humaine*—constituted, at a time when alienation was still a term of abuse, a powerful accusation. And it is in keeping with so distorted a state of affairs that the great majority of the Jews, and especially those who had the highest degree of awareness, concurred in this judgment of their situation; this is why, in the very teeth of the skepticism that was a part of their German environment, they aspired to or claimed a deep attachment to things German and a sense of being at home.

Thus the relations between Jews and Germans from the start contained an accumulation of seeds of discontent that was dangerous enough. The Jew's entry into German society was a most multifaceted process. It is, for instance, an important fact that during the generations of entry the Jews to a great extent lost their own elite through baptism and mixed marriages. Yet this fact also points to marked variations in the process, because not all Jews were by any means prepared to go so far. It is true that very broad segments of German Jewry were ready to liquidate their peoplehood, but they also wished—in differing degrees, to be sure—to preserve their Jewishness as a kind of heritage, as a creed, as an element unknowable and indefinable, yet clearly present in their consciousness. Although this is now often forgotten, they were not ready for that total assimilation that the majority of their elite was seeking to purchase at the price of disappearance. Their feelings may have been uncertain and confused, but the flight of their own avant-garde was more than they were willing to accept. These continuous bloodlettings, through which the Jews lost their most advanced elements to the Germans, constitute a crucial—and from a Jewish perspective, most melancholy—aspect of the so-called German-Jewish symbiosis, which is now being discussed with such pleasure and profuse carelessness. It was the petite bourgeoisie, the most ordinary citizens, who made up the main body of the German-Jewish community during the nineteenth century and from whom a wholly new class of leaders had to be brought forth in every generation. Rarely does one find any descendants among twentieth-century Jews of those families that, after 1800, led the "breakup" in favor of things German. On the other hand, the lower classes were almost entirely retained within the boundaries of Judaism, albeit a Judaism now watered down—or rather dried up and emptied—a Judaism composed of a curious mixture of the "religion of reason" with strong, frequently disavowed, strains of feeling. The attitude of these Jews toward the deserters fluctuated greatly, as is indicated by their response to the singular phenomenon of Heinrich Heine. It ranged from sensitive rejection to almost equable indifference. Heine, to be sure, was a borderline case. He could say of himself that he never returned to Judaism because he had never left it.

In all this, we must not fail to consider the inner tensions of Jewish society, which exercised no little influence on the relationship of Jews to the German environment. Germany, after all, was the scene of especially bitter arguments between the pious of the old school: the *Landjuden* and their leaders on the one hand, and the "neologians" or Reformers on the other, with the latter quickly gaining preponderance, if not numerically, then socially and politically. The term *assimilation* was first used by its defenders in the positive sense of an ideal; later the Zionists threw the word back at them in derision and as a form of abuse.

They were doubly indignant at being called "assimilationists." The tendency toward assimilation, which manifested itself in many forms, was certainly significant. Yet one cannot unequivocally say just how far the advocates of assimilation were prepared to go at the time, and not all instances of assimilation can be judged alike. In any case, however, there existed on the Jewish side a strongly critical stance toward Jews and traditional Judaism, and it is well known how often in individual cases this stance was heightened to those extreme forms we have come to recognize as Jewish anti-Semitism. It is, after all, to a German Jew who had left Judaism—though, as he wrote, he of course knew that this was impossible—that we owe what a critic once called "the most naked exposures" of the Berlin Jewish bourgeoisie that exist anywhere and will endure as a sinister document of the German-Jewish reality; I am referring to the monologues of Herr Wendriner, written by Kurt Tucholsky. The anti-Semites took pains to make the Jews look as bad as possible, but their writings are curiously overstrained and hollow. The hatred is there, but there is no knowledge of the subject and no feeling for atmosphere. Small wonder, then, that it remained for one of the most gifted, most convinced, and most offensive Jewish anti-Semites to accomplish on a definitive level what the anti-Semites themselves were unable to bring about.

We often find representatives of extreme possibilities within the same family—for example, the brothers Jacob and Michael Bernays (whose niece became the wife of Sigmund Freud). Jacob, a classical philologist of the highest rank, remained loyal to the strictest form of Jewish Orthodoxy, even to the point of neurosis; Michael left Judaism to venture on an even more illustrious career as a scholar in the field of Germanic studies and as a foremost critical interpreter of Goethe. After their split, the two brothers never spoke to each other again. A similar divergence occurred between two cousins of the Borchardt family. One of them, the writer Georg Hermann, depicted the nineteenth-century Berlin Jewish bourgeoisie in a manner never surpassed—critically, ironically, but at the same time lovingly. The other cousin, the exorbitantly gifted Rudolf Borchardt, convinced he had annihilated everything Jewish within himself, became the most eloquent spokesman for a culturally conservative German traditionalism. He himself was the only person to read his work who was not alarmed by the paradox.

The majority, to repeat, was not prepared to "go all the way," and many searched for a middle way. Only rarely, however, did the Jews benefit from their gifted progeny. The exceptions include such significant and at the same time problematic figures as Leopold Zunz, the founder of "the science of Judaism" (*Wissenschaft vom Judentum*), Solomon Ludwig Steinheim and Hermann Cohen, the two most distinguished German-Jewish theologico-philosophical minds, and Abraham Geiger and Samson Raphael Hirsch, in their stand on tradition the great polar opposites of the German rabbinate. Most of the ablest Jewish minds, however, enhanced *German* society with an astonishingly profuse outpouring in the fields of economics, science, literature, and art.

In a famous essay, the great American sociologist Thorstein Veblen wrote of the intellectual "preeminence" of the Jews in modern Europe. It was precisely this "preeminence" that was to spell the doom of the Jews in Germany. In their economic role, the Jews had served as a progressive force in the development of nineteenth-century Germany, but long after there had ceased to be a need for that, they continued to exercise—especially in the twentieth century—a cultural function that from the very beginning had awakened unrest and resistance and that never did them any good. That the Germans did in fact need the Jews in their spiritual world is now, when they are no longer present, noticed by many, and there is mourning over the loss. But when the Jews were there, they were a source of irritation, whether they wanted to be or not, and their "preeminence" turned into disaster for them. The great majority of Germans displayed great reserve in the face of the increasing prominence of Jewish intelligence and indeed the general phenomenon of the entry of the Jews into German society. They were not prepared, as I have already said, for the turbulent tempo of this process, which struck them as uncanny.

By the middle of the nineteenth century they had at last become reconciled to the political emancipation of the Jews, but there was no corresponding readiness to accept the unrestrained movement of the Jews into the ranks of the culturally active. The Jews, of course, with their long intellectual tradition, considered themselves made to order for such an active role when they now sought to join the German people. But this is precisely what stimulated a resistance that was to become increasingly vigorous and virulent, and was finally to prevent the process of their acceptance from having any chance of fulfillment. By and large, then, the love affair of the Jews and the Germans remained one-sided and unreciprocated; at best it awakened something like compassion (as it did with Theodore Fontane, to name only one famous, but hardly unambiguous, example) or gratitude. The Jews did meet with gratitude not infrequently, but almost never did they find the love they were seeking.

There were misunderstood geniuses among the Jews, prophets without honor, men of mind who stood up for justice, and who also stood up—to an astonishing degree—for the great spirits among the Germans themselves. Thus, almost all the most important critical interpretations of Goethe were written by

Jews! But among the Germans, there was never anyone who stood up for the misunderstood geniuses who were Jews. Nothing in German literature corresponds to those unforgettable pages in which Charles Péguy, the French Catholic, portrayed the Jewish anarchist Bernard Lazare as a true prophet of Israel, and this at a time when the French Jews themselves—out of embarrassment or malice, out of rancor or stupidity—knew no better than to treat one of their greatest men with deadly silence. Here a Frenchman *saw* a Jew in a way the Jews themselves were unable to see him. Nothing corresponds to this in the much-discussed German-Jewish dialogue—a dialogue that in fact never took place. At a time when no one cared a whit about them, no German stood forth to recognize the genius of Kafka, Simmel, Freud, or Walter Benjamin—to say nothing of recognizing them as Jews. The present belated concern with these great figures does nothing to change this fact.

Only very few Germans—some of their noblest spirits, to be sure—possessed that pristine open-mindedness that allowed them to see and accept the Jew as a Jew. One of them was Johann Peter Hebel, who valued the Jew for what he had to give, rather than for what he had to give up. But it was precisely among liberals that unmistakable reservations about Jews were frequently voiced. When Fritz Reuter, a typical member of the North-German liberal intelligentsia, made a speech in 1870 to celebrate the unification of Germany, he could think of nothing better than to level charges against the "miserable Jewish rascals like Heinrich Heine" who were supposedly lacking in patriotism. The feeling was widespread that the liberalism of the Jews was of a radical nature and foreshadowed subversive tendencies. And, indeed, during a century of prominence in journalism the Jews did play a highly visible role in the criticism of public affairs. The situation is completely different from their participation in the opposite direction, which was represented almost exclusively— most impressively to be sure—by converts like Julius Stahl and Rudolf Borchardt. Their main role was deeply grounded in their history as well as their social position and function.

In reaction to this role, the phenomenon of anti-Semitism— to which the Jews responded with peculiar blindness—began to send forth its malignant tendrils. Anti-Semitism now began to assume a sterilizing and destructive significance in the increasingly critical relations between the Jews and the Germans. It is unnecessary here to emphasize the specific social and political conditions under which the most radical forms of anti-Semitism eventually came to rule over Germany. But nothing is more foolish than the opinion that National Socialism came, so to speak, from out of the blue, or that it was exclusively the product of the aftermath of World War I. It belongs to the debit side of Jewish research on this aftermath that the very comfortable theory, according to which National Socialism is a historical accident, was invented by *Jews*—by Jews, to be sure, who have learned nothing and forgotten much. Anti-Semitism could not have become as virulent as it did, or have released all its murderous consequences, without a long prehistory. Not a few of the nineteenth-century tracts against the Jews read today like wholly undisguised documents of twentieth-century Nazism, and perhaps none is more sinister than Bruno Bauer's *Das Judentum in der Fremde (Judaism Abroad)* of 1869. Here one comes upon everything that was later preached in the Thousand-Year Reich, and in formulations no less radical. And this document came from the pen of one of the leaders of the former Hegelian Left. There was, moreover, no lack of the more "sublime" varieties of anti-Semitism—the kind that, shortly after World War I, found expression in works like Hans Blüher's *Secessio Judaica.* Such works, fluctuating between admiration and hatred, and embodying a degenerate metaphysics in the form of genteel anti-Semitism, provided a cue for the more murderous metaphysics to come. Perhaps nothing depresses us more today than the uncertain wavering of many Germans, including some of their finest minds, in the face of this dark swell.

Max Brod has spoken of the ideal of "distant love" as that which should have governed relations between Germans and Jews. The concept is a dialectical one: distance is meant to prevent an all-too-coarse intimacy, but at the same time a desire to bridge the gap. This could certainly have been a solution for the period under discussion, if only both parties would have agreed to it. Yet Brod himself admits that where there is love the feeling of distance disappears—this was true of the Jews; and where there is distance no love can arise—this was true of the main body of Germans. To the love of the Jews for Germany there corresponded the emphatic distance with which the Germans encountered them. We may grant that with "distant love" the two partners could have managed more kindness, open-mindedness, and mutual understanding. But historical subjunctives are always illegitimate. If it is true, as we now perceive, that "distant love" was the right Zionist answer to the mounting crisis in the relations between Jews and Germans, it is also true that the Zionist avant-garde hit upon it too late. For during the generations preceding the catastrophe, the German Jews—whose critical sense was as famous among Germans as it was irritating to them—distinguished themselves by an astounding lack of critical insight into their own situation. An "edifying" and apologetic attitude, a lack of critical candor, taints almost everything they wrote about the position of the Jews in the German world of ideas, literature, politics, and economics.

The readiness of many Jews to invent a theory that would justify the sacrifice of their Jewish existence is a shocking phenomenon, and there are countless variations on it. But nothing, it seems to me, surpasses in sheer self-contradiction, and a credulous demand for self-surrender that could be demanded of no one except just us Jews, the formulation produced as late as 1935 by Margarete Susman, in full awareness of the fact that the time had come of "the most fearful fate ever to strike the Jews." She wrote: "The vocation of Israel as a people is not self-realization, but self-surrender for the sake of a higher, transhistorical goal." In this case the delusion goes so far that we are asked to believe—in the name of the prophets, who indeed did not wish Israel to be a people like all other peoples—that the "original meaning of the Jewish idea is the absorption of this people by other peoples."

What is so terrible about this statement is not that it has been so devastatingly refuted by history, but that it never signified anything except a perversion whereby Christian ideas—rejected by Jews unto their dying breath—now presented themselves as the demand of the greatest Jewish minds. Such solutions have been offered to Jews again and again, and from various sources. They bespeak a great inner demoralization, an enthusiasm for self-sacrifice which has necessarily remained wholly without meaning for the Jewish community itself, and which no one ever took seriously except the anti-Semites, who found in them an especially nefarious trick of the Jews, an especially conspiratorial note. For it was precisely this desire on the part of the Jews to be absorbed by the Germans that hatred understood as a destructive maneuver against the life of the German people—a thesis repeated indefatigably by the metaphysicians of anti-Semitism between 1830 and 1930. Here the Jews are considered, to quote one of these philosophers, as "the dark power of negation which kills what it touches. Whoever yields to it falls into the hands of death."

This, in brief, is an analysis of what from the very beginning was a "false start" in the relations between Jews and Germans, one which brought the elements of crisis inherent in the process itself to an ever riper development.

IV

Where do we stand now, after the unspeakable horror of those twelve years from 1933 to 1945? Jews and Germans took very different roads after the war. The most vital segment of the Jews attempted to build up its own society in its own land. No one can say whether the attempt will succeed, but everyone knows that the cause of Israel is a matter of life and death to the Jews. The dialectic of their undertaking is obvious. They live on a volcano. The great impetus they received from the experience of the Holocaust—let us face it: the experience of the German murder of the Jews, and of the apathy and the hardheartedness of the world—has also been followed by a profound exhaustion whose signs are unmistakable. And yet the incentive, generated by their original insight into their true situation is still operating effectively. The Germans have paid for their catastrophe with the division of their country, but, on the other hand, they have experienced a material upsurge that has placed the past years in shadow. Between these two mountains, produced by a volcanic eruption, can there now be a bridge, however shaky?

The abyss that events have flung open between the two can be neither measured nor fathomed. Unlike many in Israel, I do not believe that the only possible means of overcoming the distance is to admit the abyss into our consciousness in all its dimensions and ramifications. There is little comfort in such a prognosis: it is mere rhetoric. For in truth there is no possibility of comprehending what has happened—incomprehensibility is of its essence—no possibility of understanding it perfectly and thus of incorporating it into our consciousness. This demand by its very nature cannot be fulfilled. Whether or not we can meet in this abyss, I do not know. And whether the abyss, flung open by unspeakable, unthinkable events, can ever be bridged—who would have the presumption to say?

Abysses are flung open by events; bridges are built by goodwill. Bridges are needed to pass over abysses; they are constructed; they are the product of conscious thinking and willing. Moral bridges, I repeat, are the product of goodwill. If they are to endure, they must be firmly anchored on both sides. The people of Israel have suffered fearfully at the hands of almost all the peoples of Europe. The bridges on which we meet peoples other than Germans are shaky enough, even when they are not burdened with the memory of Auschwitz. But—is this memory not an opportunity as well? Is there not a light that burns in this darkness, the light of repentance? To put it differently: fruitful relations between Jews and Germans, relations in which a past that is both meaningful and at the same time so horrible as to cripple communication may be preserved and worked through— such relations must be prepared away from the limelight. But it is only through an effort to bring them about that we can guarantee that official contacts between the two peoples will not be poisoned by counterfeit formulas and demands. Already the worm of hypocrisy is gnawing at the delicate roots! Where love is no longer possible, a new understanding requires other ingredients; distance, respect, openness, and open-mindedness, and, above all, goodwill.

A young German recently wrote to me expressing the hope that Jews, when thinking of Germany, might keep in mind the words of Isaiah: "Remember ye not the former things, neither consider the things of old." I do not know whether the messianic age will bestow forgetfulness upon the Jews. It is a delicate point of theology. But for us, who must live without illusions in an age without a Messiah, such a hope demands the impossible. However sublime it might be to forget, we cannot. Only by remembering a past that we will never completely master can we generate hope in the resumption of communication between Germans and Jews, and in the reconciliation of those who have been separated.

S. Y. Agnon—The Last
Hebrew Classic?*

I

In order to understand the greatness or genius of a contemporary Hebrew writer such as S. Y. Agnon, it is necessary to consider the state of Hebrew and Hebrew literature before Hebrew once again became a language absorbed by infants at their mothers' knees, children playing in the street—before its use again as a natural means of communication and education. Before the present generation, Hebrew enjoyed none of these advantages. It was nourished from another source. Hebrew was the language of a great religious tradition, and almost everything written in it was valuable and significant in the context of that tradition. Even after Hebrew (or, for that matter, Aramaic, so closely related to Hebrew that to the Jewish mind it was something like a younger sibling) was no longer in use as a spoken language by Jewish communities, it could still hold its own as a written language because for generation after generation it occupied a central place in education, in the study of the Bible and the Talmud and all writings connected with them.

Nor did Hebrew remain significant only for a numerically small elite, as was the case with Latin, but for a very considerable part of the community. Everyone was expected to have a working knowledge of Hebrew, and the study of the Bible and

* A lecture in English delivered at University College, London, May 30, 1967. Published as "S. Y. Agnon—der letzte hebräische Klassiker?," in Gershom Scholem, *Judaica* 2 (Frankfurt-am-Main: Bibliothek Suhrkamp, 1970), pp. 87–121. An English adaptation appeared in *Commentary* (December 1967). The present is a revision of the article in *Commentary* based on the text in *Judaica* 2. Translated by Werner J. Dannhauser.

the Talmud was by no means limited to those who intended to become rabbis or judges. In countries where Jewish intellectual and religious life was particularly vigorous—such as Poland, Italy, or Turkey—Hebrew represented the principal means of expressing the spiritual life of an important segment of the male community.

It is true that the spark of vitality which comes to language from women was lacking, and this lack was indeed very much in evidence. What remained, however, was of overwhelming richness. Hebrew became the language of literary tradition insofar as the latter claimed higher significance. Books for womenfolk were composed in the vernacular, but almost everything else—not only scholarly literature, but also chronicles, poetry, and even parodies—was written in Hebrew. Biblical and talmudic associations were employed up to the hilt; the works contained a never-ending stream of witty and surprising uses of old phrases or of playful variations upon them. Quite often, the measure of a Jew's education was not only his command of Bible and Talmud, but his ability to use these sources ingeniously for secular purposes as well.

When modern Hebrew literature began to develop, especially in the nineteenth century and the early part of the twentieth, it was built on a paradox from the start: it fed on a language of predominantly religious tradition but strove for secular goals. Writers of considerable talent and some, indeed, of genius did their best to achieve this metamorphosis of Hebrew into a language of secular literature. In its earlier stages this new literature was directed mainly against the petrified state of Jewish tradition and came to criticize the many shortcomings and basic defects of East European Jewish society.

Later, however, with the emergence of the Zionist movement, the renascence of Hebrew gravitated toward a more positive purpose. A new life was springing up in the old land of Israel, and Hebrew literature undertook to serve as the connecting link between the disintegrating life of the Diaspora, with all its contradictions, and the new society being erected in Palestine. Still, even this renascence and such outstanding representatives of it as Bialik, Tchernichowsky, and Shneur were as yet limited in the means of expression at their disposal. Hebrew remained a language of literary tradition, and though the great writers I have just mentioned spent their later years in Israel, the spoken Hebrew of the new generation had no formative influence on their language.

Agnon occupies a position at the crossroads of Hebrew. That is a position enabling a writer of genius to attain the rank of a classic. He can be heir to the totality of Jewish tradition and have the chance to give the highest artistic form to the life of the Jewish people under the reign of tradition and under the impact of the historic forces that make for its disintegration. If he is a great artist, he will remain incomparable. He can become a classical master—but he will be the last of his line.

Agnon, who has spent most of his creative years in Israel, has witnessed the development of Hebrew as a "natural" language, as a language spoken at first in consequence of a moral decision made by a small number of Utopians, and later by an ever-increasing number of youngsters who have grown up in Israel and know no other language. He was fully aware of this process, and he knew that this metamorphosis of Hebrew involved a decisive loss of form. When a language is no longer forged by the study of ancient texts and conscious reflection, but rather by unconscious processes in which the power of tradition is a minor factor, that language is bound to become chaotic. This chaotic quality of present-day Hebrew, which was already becoming apparent about forty years ago, when Agnon settled permanently in Israel, may one day become the vehicle of expression for a new genius, but by then that language will be essentially different in its means and potentialities.

Agnon, with his highly developed sense of form, was obviously alarmed by this prospect of a Hebrew language liberated from the fetters of tradition. He, too, strove for the renascence of Hebrew, but he worked for it in the quarries of tradition and through the potential of great forms contained in it. Being a writer of supreme gifts, he achieved the form for which he labored. But, to repeat, he may well be the last great author in this medium. It is, after all, the most obvious result of the regeneration of Hebrew as a natural language, that the words have sloughed off the heavy ballast of historical tones and overtones accumulated through 3,000 years of sacred literature.

They have acquired a new virginity; they are now ready to be molded into new contexts from which the old and sometimes oppressive odor of sanctity has evaporated.

Of course, this is precisely what the writers of the last two generations have tried to accomplish, but in the last analysis the burdens of history were in their bones and asserted themselves even in their revolt. In this respect, the new "innocents," for whom the Bible is no longer a holy book but a national saga, and for whom rabbinical and medieval literature is a book with seven seals, are in a happier situation than Agnon and his contemporaries. They are free to wrestle with the words in a completely new emotional setting, and on a level of freedom unheard of hitherto. They are confronted, it is true, with dangers of rebirth which are in no way less than those of birth. Nobody can foretell what will come of this sweep and whirl in terms of literature. For the time being, nothing is audible but stammering. Much of Agnon's work is contemporary with these first stammerings, and one can speak of a secret and mutual fascination between the two: the occupant of the most advanced outpost of the Hebrew language in its old sense, and the pioneers of the unbroken land that stretches beyond. The anarchic vitality, the lawlessness and roughness of the new language has alarmed Agnon and appears as an object of scorn and irony in quite a few of his stories. But the reader of Agnon cannot escape the feeling that more and more of the master's work was produced as a kind of desperate incantation, an appeal to those who would come after him. It is as though he were saying, "Since you no longer accept the continuity of tradition and its language in their true context, at least take them in the transformation they have undergone in my work; take them from someone who stands at the crossroads and can see in both directions."

II

I have tried to explain the condition of Hebrew and Hebrew literature insofar as it is relevant to the task of placing Agnon's work in our time. But to understand the work we must also take a look at its author. Both, to say the least, are somewhat enigmatic.

It is small wonder that over the last forty years a considerable literature of interpretation on the meaning of Agnon's writings has sprung up in which widely differing and even contradictory points of view have been argued. A number of the commentators have indulged in much overinterpretation and have read much into Agnon that is their own point of view.

To be sure, the manifest contradictions in his writings amount to an open invitation to such excesses. These interpretations concentrate upon one point: Agnon's position on the historical, indeed the religious tradition of Judaism. Is he to be considered a spokesman for this tradition, a messenger delivering its message in a highly artistic and articulate form, or should we regard him rather as an accomplished artist who uses tradition to express all the intricacies of the life of a Jew in our time, but who proffers no easy answer to the old question of where we are going? Is he a great defender of the faith, as the Orthodox have acclaimed him? Or is he some kind of existentialist genius, showing the emptiness of all fullness and the fullness of emptiness? Is he, perhaps, like the king of the Moors who filled his palace with portraits of white men, setting up an ideal which he is fully conscious can never be attained in our times?

Agnon himself, for all his great gifts as a conversationalist, has been very reticent when it comes to these questions. He is not a man to commit himself. He has delivered his work and left his readers the task of coming to terms with it, his commentators the task of fighting it out among themselves; and, I should say, he rather enjoys the spectacle. As a matter of fact, having known Agnon for fifty years, I can testify to great changes in Agnon's own outlook over the years, and I doubt whether a harmonizing view would do him justice. He was anything but what one could call an observant Jew when I first knew him, but even then he gave the impression of being a bearer of spiritual tradition. And now, in his later years, when he has become an observant Jew, he still gives the impression of being a man of complete intellectual freedom and of utterly unorthodox mind.

This is confirmed by the story of his life. He began writing as a youth, more than sixty years ago. He grew up in Buczacz in Eastern Galicia (now Western Ukraine), an old and settled community of no more than 8,000 Jews and a center of Rabbinic scholarship. He came from a family of scholars, some of whom strictly opposed Hasidism and all it represented, but some of whom embraced it. The experience of his childhood reflected both these worlds, which combined to determine the physiognomy of Jewish piety in nineteenth-century Galicia. He had hardly any schooling outside traditional talmudic education; his father was his main teacher in the study of the Talmud.

He spent the years of adolescence in the local *bet hamidrash* (house of study), which boasted a tremendous Hebrew library; there he became an ardent and omnivorous reader. He was a bookworm at a very early age, but the old books fired his imagination. He wrote notes and glosses to the old talmudic tomes, but at the same time he started producing stories and poems in the style of the writers of the Haskalah, the rationalist movement that was attempting to introduce enlightenment and European culture into Hebrew. Galicia was then one of the centers of neo-Hebrew literature, and its writers enjoyed a great reputation as masters of Hebrew style. Still a lad, Agnon joined the ranks of the Zionists.

In local Hebrew and Yiddish journals that have long since disappeared, Agnon began his literary career in 1904. An older friend, Eliezer Meir Lipschitz, to whom he remained intimately attached to the end, used to say to him, "Make up your mind what you propose to be, a writer of talmudic notes, *hiddushim* and *pilpulim,* or a writer of stories and a poet." Agnon made his choice early. But Yiddish soon lost its hold on him, and after going to Palestine in 1907 (not in 1909, as is often erroneously stated) he never again resorted to it as a vehicle of literary expression.

His lifelong struggle with Hebrew as both the matter and the form of his inspiration took shape in those first supreme efforts of his literary genius as a storyteller, which were published in Palestine in the years preceding World War I. Their impact was instantaneous.

The first story by him to be published in Palestine, a most lyrical and melancholy tale called *Agunot* ("Deserted Souls"), remains a classical piece of imaginative Hebrew writing to this day. Those with an ear for Hebrew prose—and there were quite a few of them in Palestine in those days—realized at once that they were faced with a novel phenomenon. In 1913 the Hebrew critic Shalom Streit said of *Agunot*: "An electric current ran through our community at its reading." No Hebrew writer before had dared to begin a short story with a long quotation from one of the old and forgotten books, presumably a kabbalistic one, or to use that citation as a leitmotif.

And what greater paradox could there be than the fact that the weekly of the socialist group Hapoel Hatzair, a group strongly influenced by Tolstoyan and *narodniki* ideas, published in a long series of installments Agnon's first book, *Vehayah he-akov le-mishor* (*And the Crooked Shall Be Made Straight*)? The story develops an Enoch Arden theme in a strictly traditional Hasidic framework; it is written not so much in the style of the old devotional books as in the style their authors would have used had they been great artists. Joseph Haim Brenner, a convinced atheist who was the first to recognize Agnon's literary genius, scraped together his last shillings to publish the story in book form (1912); incidentally, the man who set it in print was a convinced follower of Rabbi Nahman of Bratzlav, one of the great saints of Hasidism. It is on record that both these men took the greatest delight in the book, thereby anticipating, so to speak, all the later contradictory attitudes of Agnon's admirers. For Brenner, it represented the first work of secular Hebrew literature in which tradition had become the medium of pure art, untouched by extraneous factors such as criticism of, or apologetics for, Jewish society. For the typesetter, whom I have known for many years, it was a true embodiment of Hasidic lore and spirit.

In those formative years of his first stay in Palestine, Agnon indeed felt at home in both camps. He lived with ease among the first pioneers of the Second Aliyah, who wished to revitalize the Jewish people through the Tolstoyan religion of work and a humanistic renewal of hearts, rather than through social revolution. He accepted their vision of Zionism as the only hope for a Jewish future, even if that Zionism always appears with a peculiar paleness in his writings.

At the same time, however, he could establish close relations with the representatives of traditional piety. There was, no doubt, a difference of nuance in his attitude toward the two camps. He had consciously left the world of tradition as he had known it in his youth, but he was saturated with, and fascinated by, that world. From the vantage point of a great movement which attempted to transform this life, tradition and its representatives seemed to clamor for artistic shaping. The charmed world of the old *yishuv*, the pre-Zionist settlers, in those years certainly held no message for the young Agnon, so far as his own vision of the renascence of the Jewish people was concerned; but it provided him with a great store of strange figures and with the excitement this atmosphere was capable of evoking. The life of centuries seemed to have been arrested here in a curious mixture of immortality and decay. And this encounter challenged the young artist who here, too, recognized a submerged part of himself.

In those years before the war, Agnon had absorbed the life of Jewish Palestine, and he longed to dissociate himself from both the centers, Galicia and Palestine, which had determined his life so far. He sought a place for further development and for the crystalization of his artistic experiences. Thus he went to Germany in 1912, intending to stay only a few years, but the war overtook him and it was not until 1924 that he returned to settle permanently in Jerusalem.

Agnon's years in Germany were of the greatest importance to his work. There he met a new kind of Jew who left him forever baffled. Curious as he was about them, he was not involved with them in any deeper sense, as he was with Galicia. Nothing prevented him from truly feeling in exile, and at the same time savoring the exhilaration of a man who knows where he belongs. He was still an inveterate reader, and when I first saw him, it was in the excellent library of the Jewish community in Berlin, where, as he told me, he was looking for books he had not yet read.

At this time, too, he made his main contact with European literature; he was, in particular, an avid reader of Hamsun. Even at that time his natural inclination to perfectionism was quite pronounced; he wrote and rewrote his stories six or seven times, a trait which was to become the bane of his publishers, since he would indefatigably rewrite even during proofreading. He published very little during those years, but he worked persistently both at revising his older stories and at writing new ones. He also wrote a great amount of poetry at that time and a long autobiographical novel in which he took critical stock of his earlier years and the movements which had shaped them. The only chapter which has been preserved and published paints one of the most bitter and devastating pictures we have of Galician Zionism during Agnon's youth.

I have referred to the "only chapter," for in June 1924 all his manuscripts and other papers, together with his invaluable Hebrew library, were completely destroyed by a fire that broke out in his house in Homburg (near Frankfurt). This catastrophe constituted a turning point in Agnon's life. He was never again the same and, indeed, who can fathom the impact of such a blow on the personality of a great artist? Agnon had to start once more from scratch. He gave up writing poetry and never tried to reconstruct his lost novel. He surrendered what was lost and started again from what he had, prepared a semifinal version of his published writings, and turned to new beginnings out of the depths of his creative imagination.

A few months after the fire, Agnon returned to Jerusalem. He developed an ever deeper and more indissoluble bond to the city and he adopted a conservative way of life within the framework of the Jewish tradition. In the ensuing quarter century he returned to the Diaspora only once, and then only after another shock, after his house in a suburb of Jerusalem had been pillaged by Arabs during the riots of 1929. This time he went for a short visit to his home town, and for a longer stay of nearly a year in Germany to see through the press the first four volumes of his collected works, which had taken five years to prepare.

This trip was his last encounter with Europe and European Jews, an encounter leaving an imprint on his mind and constituting a ferment for some of his most significant later writings. In fact there was no further need for him to seek out the Diaspora—the Diaspora was coming to Palestine, in ever larger waves of *aliyah*. In these years his work took on ever wider dimensions.

It is relevant in this connection to mention Agnon's peculiar gifts as an anthologist. This activity represented much more than a mere sideline in his creative work as a writer. To be sure, Agnon was never a scholar in the sense of a person dedicated to historical and critical analysis and to the study of phenomena within a conceptual framework. Nevertheless, he had a penchant for scholarship, enamored as he was of the study of primary sources. He had a genuine feel for the significant and the curious in the vast realm of Hebrew literature, and a talent for synthesis.

Already during his first years in Germany, he had edited, in German, two anthologies, *The Book of the Polish Jew* and *The Book of Hanukkah*. In Jerusalem, he devoted a considerable amount of work and time to three anthologies into which he inserted a great deal of himself. They represent a perfect intermingling of his propensities for scholarship and connoisseurship with his ambitions as a writer and master of form. In their way, they, too, are outstanding examples of creative work. The first of them is *Days of Awe, A Treasury of Traditions, Legends and Learned Commentaries Concerning Rosh Ha-Shanah, Yom Kippur, and the Days Between*, culled from 300 volumes, ancient and new; an abridged edition of this work exists in English. Agnon well knew the value of this book and it was clear to him that he would be widely plagiarized, as indeed he was. With his caustic sense of humor he included a number of highly imaginative (and imaginary) passages, culled from his own vineyard, a nonexistent book, *Kol Dodi* ("The Voice of My Beloved"), innocently mentioned in the bibliography as a "manuscript in possession of the author."

The second anthology is comprised of stories and anecdotes about books and their authors and reflects Agnon's unquenchable thirst for the anecdotal side of Jewish bibliography. It is a wonderful book that for some unfathomable reason has never been published except in a private edition. The last of these anthologies is a great collection of sayings about the Ten Commandments.

Agnon has given years of his life to the preparation of these works, and they must have meant a great deal to him. In them he turned himself into an instrument through which the pure voice of tradition could be heard to speak with a voice of laconic refinement, and frequently his own voice is mingled indistinguishably with that of the primary sources. Many years ago Agnon had also planned a thesaurus of Hasidic stories on which he had agreed to cooperate with Martin Buber. He had commenced the work, but the first batches of the manuscript fell victim to the flames in Homburg, and he never returned to it.

These scholarly propensities of Agnon show his genius in the service of craftsmanship. It is unobtrusive but nevertheless effective. It is noteworthy that the only great Hebrew writer with whom Agnon felt perfectly at ease was the poet Haim Nahman Bialik, who in this respect had the same inclination for creative anthologizing.

As a matter of fact, Agnon never felt as comfortable in the company of writers as he did in that of scholars, who surprisingly enough appear in some of his strangest stories set against a contemporary background. The calling of the writer or artist as such seems to have held no mysteries for him, in contradistinction to that of the scholar, whose utter and largely hopeless concentration on his subject matter excited a sinister fascination in him—as, for example, it comes to the fore in *Edo and Enam*, an enigmatic story about the greatness and failure of scholarship.

III

Agnon's work over the last sixty years ranges from short stories, some of extraordinarily small compass, to great chronicles and novels reflecting Jewish life during many generations, particularly the last four or five. Many critics have rightly observed the obvious tension between the artist and the traditionalist in Agnon. It is of his essence. He started from tradition, but only in the sense that he used it as his material. From there he set off on a double track: on the one hand, he penetrated ever deeper into this tradition, its grandeur and its intricacies; on the other hand, he exposed its ambiguities and, as it were, left it in limbo, starting instead from the insecurity, the *Verlorenheit* (forlornness) and alienation of the modern Jew who must—or fails to—come to terms with himself without the guiding lights of a tradition that has ceased to be meaningful.

The ellipse of Agnon's work moves between two poles essentially, the world of Buczacz and Polish Jewry as a whole, and the world of the new life in the old center, the land of Israel. Both of these worlds are portrayed on the two levels mentioned above, a circumstance that has proved confusing to many of his readers.

The world of established Jewish values and the world of utter confusion often seem to be separated by two or three genera-tions, but this first impression is somewhat misleading. For there are great tensions even within the world of tradition, notwith-standing its seeming simplicity; and the duality of harmony and disintegration is visible as well in the struggles of the writer's own times. Now confusion seems to be predominant, but a delicately balanced equilibrium exists even now. A forlorn corner like the little town of Buczacz could still contain the entire world of human passions and ambitions, of infinite richness and abysmal tragedy, just as the struggle for a new life in the old land would have comprised the infinite ambiguities and inner problems of Zionism, had Agnon carried out his intention and given us the promised continuation of his novel on the Second Aliyah, called *Tmol Shilshom* (*Not Long Ago*).

Agnon began by writing short stories and in this mode he almost at once achieved a perfection leaving the reader breath-less. More than twenty years of intense productivity passed before he published his first long book, a chronicle of Jewish life in Hasidic Galicia nearly 150 years ago which in many ways stands on the borderline between a story and a novel, being itself full of what the author calls "stories within a story."

Many of these first stories, which gained Agnon a wide reputation and which must be considered classics of their kind, are legends of the Jewish past. The secret of their perfection lies in the fact that they succeeded in expressing an infinite wealth of content in infinitesimal space. Unsurpassed in this respect are his masterpieces in the third volume of his collected writings, many of which are suffused by a spirit of immense sadness and at the same time hold out a great promise of consolation.

This intermingling of consolation and sadness is a profoundly Jewish feature of Agnon's creativity. There is, for example, the story of Azriel Moshe the Porter, an ignoramus who grows enamored of the books in the great library of the *bet hamidrash* and teaches himself the titles of all the books whose contents he will never be able to grasp; he becomes the keeper of the library, dying a martyr's death while shielding the books with his body during the hour of persecution. Then there is the story of the messenger from the Holy Land who, while delivering a talmudic discourse before the congregation, is put to shame by its learned members who confuse him with their objections until he leaves the town in tears; the synagogue building, witness to his shame, sets out after him.

A number of these legends are inspired by some colorful talmudic saying. Another story concerns an impoverished vinegar maker, all alone in this world, who saves up penny after penny in order to make his way to the Holy Land; uncertain as to where he should hide his money for safekeeping, he places it in an almsbox under a crucifix at the crossroads. Upon finally coming to fetch his money, he is arrested for robbing sacred funds. However, "that man," as Jesus is called in Hebrew, comes to his prison cell and takes him to Jerusalem, where he is found dead by his compatriots. Agnon, who was attacked by fools (of which there is no lack even in Israel) for having glorified Christ in this case, later maintained that this story was a bitter allegory about the failure of political Zionism, which clung to the coattails of empty English promises, by which one at best arrives in the Holy Land but thereby loses one's life by crashing into the hard ground of reality. I do not believe this cunning interpretation.

Through the years Agnon has produced a great number of these stories of very short or medium length. Some relate a single episode, while in others an entire drama is condensed into a dense narrative. I have mentioned some examples of the former. Among the more dramatic stories, it is difficult to say which of their great number deserves the greatest praise. I will mention only three, which in my opinion are of the highest possible merit. They are "The Tale of the Scribe," "The Doctor's Divorce," and "Two Scholars Who Lived in Our Town."

The first story tells of a Torah scribe whose wife craves a child and asks her husband, a man of irreproachable piety, to intercede with Heaven on her behalf. But she dies young, before her wish is granted. The scribe, whose craft is described with much Hasidic and kabbalistic detail, writes a Torah scroll in her memory and, having finished it, dies on the night of Simhat Torah in an ecstatic-erotic vision of his wife. The story is told without any psychological instrumentation, but with a full account of the

dramatic tension in the life of Raphael the Scribe. It is one of
Agnon's few stories written in a highly solemn style and one
would almost expect to read it on a scroll in the ceremonial
letters used by scribes. I vividly recall the evening of the Hebrew
Club of Berlin, in the spring of 1917, when Agnon read this story
in manuscript. It made a tremendous impression, and I can still
hear the mournful and monotonous intonation of his voice,
reminiscent of that used in the synagogue by the reader who
recites the *haftarah*.

The other two stories are quite different; in each, one act
determines the course of a whole life. A Viennese doctor marries
a nurse who has told him that before meeting him she has had an
affair with another man. But this knowledge destroys the
marriage from the start. He cannot live with such knowledge and
thus a deep and genuine love is wrecked from within.

In contradistinction to the utter laconism of these pages
is—in "Two Scholars Who Lived in Our Town"—the full
description of the lives of two friends that develop under an
ever-darkening shadow, caused by a slight, unkind remark made
quite inadvertently by one of them in the course of a casual
conversation. One of the friends, Rabbi Shlomo, goes on, as it
seems, from one success to another, and tries in vain to placate
the silent but inexorable enmity of his friend Rabbi Moshe
Pinhas, whose heart has been hurt beyond repair, and whose
bitterness grows with every new step taken by his friend toward
reconciliation. Both are first-rank talmudists, but they cannot live
together in the same world. The story is told with uncanny logic
and magnificent psychological insight. The light of the Torah is
not enough to warm a frozen heart. This bitter truth, however, is
brought home not with the polemical passion that any earlier
Hebrew writer would have employed, but with a depth of
understanding and a superior serenity and objectivity that makes
it one of the greatest stories of all Hebrew literature.

I have referred to the human passions which have their
natural place in Agnon's work. Yet, with some rare and
remarkable exceptions, Agnon's writing is distinguished by a
singular stillness, by an absence of pathos and exultation. He
hardly ever raises his voice, and his writings are free from even a

trace of expressionistic hysteria. Not infrequently he describes situations which could do with a bit of the latter, but he never despairs of conveying them in a still, small voice.

Without doubt, he was greatly helped in this respect by the extraordinary sobriety of rabbinic prose, of the style of the Midrash and Mishnah, which have had such a profound influence on his manner of writing. This prose dislikes exuberance and emotionalism and makes its restraining force felt even when Agnon deals with situations of high emotional tension.

That is particularly true of his Hasidic stories, a genre in which the depiction of the impact of mysticism on Jewish life has led almost every other Hebrew writer who attempted to portray it into sentimentality. Agnon, however, deeply steeped in the unemotional prose of kabbalistic literature, found a different way to respond to the challenge of such situations. A long road leads from the highstrung sentimentality characterizing the famous Hasidic stories of I. L. Peretz to Agnon's descriptions of the world of Hasidism. Even in this, part of his work is dominated by a kind of perfect bonhomie and urbanity. The miraculous is closely interwoven with stark reality; indeed, the former is part of the latter. Moreover, it is not the saints and their ecstatic raptures who are the authentic objects of his interest—they appear mostly in quotations or in what other people tell of them—but the little man, the faithful member of the Hasidic community for whom all aspects of life are at the same time real and full of unfathomable mystery. It is he who is the true "hero" of these tales.

Withal, the ground on which even the pious Jew treads is thin enough. Dark powers lurk everywhere, and the magic of the Law barely suffices to keep them at bay. It takes very little for the ground of belief to crack, leaving man, be he within the domain of the Law or without it, prey to the demons that may or may not be mere extensions of his own uncertainties and confusions. Agnon, who has given great attention to this side of human experience, takes no stand as to the true character of the arena in which these strange happenings occur. His stories about such uncanny experiences, told with utmost lucidity and realistic simplicity, are collected in his *Book of Deeds* or *Book of*

Happenings, which has aroused much controversy because of the obviously Kafkaesque nature of the experiences described.°

Some see these stories as a direct counterpart to Agnon's other writings, which stray far from the world of tradition, the ambiguities of which he so often puts into sharp relief. Others regard them, rather, as merely a complement to his earlier *oeuvre,* and many simply prefer to look the other way and to take no notice at all of the existence of this disturbing book. But that it is meant to express something of the greatest relevance to Agnon's purpose is clear. The paradox inhering in every step a man undertakes is already expressed in the utter incongruity of the title—the Hebrew word *maasim* means at one and the same time "deeds," "stories," and "happenings"—for what this book stresses is precisely the impossibility of performing even the smallest deed without becoming enmeshed in an inexorable jumble and confusion from which there is no escape, except through some kind of *deus ex machina,* or by waking up as from an oppressive dream.

In fact, some of these stories seem to me to be simply that: descriptions of dreams. But this dreamlike quality also applies to the simplest happening in life. The storyteller wants, say, to mail a letter or to go and meet a friend, but these prove to be hopeless undertakings. What determines this hopelessness cannot be unequivocally determined. It may be the simplest obstacles and obstructions which stand in the hero's way, or something like what Friedrich Theodor Vischer calls "the malignity of the objects"; but it can just as well be a nightmare of surrealistic proportions. In any case, it always becomes perfectly clear that there is not the slightest security in even the smallest step of real life, let alone the sphere of transcendence.

That all this should be said by a writer who is in full command of the heritage of that tradition, the absence or inaccessibility of which has frequently been noted as the determining characteristic of Kafka's universe, should certainly

---

° I wish only to refer to one of the many characteristic traits that Kafka and Agnon have in common. Max Brod says of Kafka, "It was almost impossible to talk to Kafka about abstractions. He thought in images and spoke in images. He tried to express what he felt simply and in the most direct manner possible, but nevertheless the result was usually very complicated and led to endless speculation without any real decision." This is precisely true of Agnon as well, as I have seen over and over again.

set us thinking. Agnon, to be sure, was in no way the first to recognize or to be shocked by, the permeability, the loosened state of tradition. He could, and possibly did, learn much about this state of things from the teachings and famous tales of Rabbi Nahman of Bratzlav, which have that same intrinsic quality. If the "Story of the Seven Beggars" had not already been told by Rabbi Nahman, it could have become an Agnon story and would have taken on a perfectly Kafkaesque aura.

IV

After his return to Jerusalem Agnon produced a number of full-length novels, the most outstanding of which might perhaps more aptly be described as chronicles. As chronicles of Jewish life in the century between 1830 and 1930, three of them in a way constitute a trilogy which, for all the diversity of its parts, is bound together by the unity of historical dynamics. I refer to his three novels *The Bridal Canopy* (1931), *A Guest for the Night* (1940), and *Not Long Ago* (1946). In terms of historical continuity, the third novel should be considered the second, if incomplete, part of the trilogy. It is a pity that as of now only the first is available in English translation.

The Bridal Canopy depicts the wanderings and adventures in Eastern Galicia of Rabbi Judel Hasid, who has set out to collect a dowry for his daughters. Without earthly goods, he has undertaken the journey with a letter of recommendation of the rabbi of Apta, one of the great figures of Hasidism. Rabbi Judel is a perfect embodiment of Hasidism in its prime, when, around 1830, it had conquered a very large segment of Galician Jewry. He is at home in the Holy Books and in the sayings and tales of the great *tzaddikim;* these constitute for him the true face of reality which whatever happens to him on his travels can serve only to confirm. His is a serenity of mind that can never be perturbed because everything fits into the sacred scheme explained in the Holy Books. The most incredible things befall him and his coachman, his down-to-earth Sancho Panza, and the prospects of his success seem less than dim. But all this fails to touch him. The assurance of the holy Rabbi of Apta, who has sent him on his way, means much more to him than all the vicissitudes and adversities of life.

I noted before that Agnon's stories, especially those of his early years, are suffused with an atmosphere of great sadness. In *The Bridal Canopy*, however, Agnon's delicate humor comes to the fore. He never offers the slightest criticism of his hero's conduct, which involves him in such an unending chain of absurdities. In telling the story, he plays it straight and lets dialogue and situation speak for themselves. The first stories of Agnon's *Book of Deeds* were composed at about the same time as *The Bridal Canopy*. They are, as it were, two sides of the same coin, but if Rabbi Judel had been the central figure of Kafka's trial, he would have waited patiently for the repeal of the verdict. Much of the naked absurdity of *The Book of Deeds* is already present in *The Bridal Canopy*, but it is resolved by humor and, finally, by a miracle at which Kafka himself would have been the last to be surprised.

Moreover, the canvas of Jewish life, before it was affected by the impact of modern times, is painted in precise and colorful detail. Agnon belongs to the category of craftsmen who take details seriously. Rabbi Judel will never take a step that is not vouchsafed by the Holy Books, and each and every ceremony or superstitious hocus-pocus is in strict conformity to the literary sources. The great rabbis who are quoted are flesh and blood and have lived and their books exist. (This precision characterizes the whole of Agnon's work, and even the most minute details concerning Berlin streetcars are accurate.)

Eighty years later, however, the scene—and much more than the scene—has changed. Yitzhak Kummer, the hero of *Not Long Ago*, is the grandson of Rabbi Judel. Hasidism and, for that matter, Jewish tradition have broken up. The magnificent impulse has been exhausted and a new ideal, the rebirth of the Jewish people in its old homeland, now arouses the enthusiasm of the young. It is a revolutionary beginning although it purports to be, at the same time, a continuation of the past, albeit in a transformed shape. It is never made completely clear what the place of religious tradition in all this is or will be. Tradition, too, has been worn out and is manifestly in a state of crisis. Where it still lingers on—and it certainly does in no small measure—it keeps within closed boundaries and its attraction as a living force for the outsider is negligible. After all, Hasidism was the last great social reality in which, under the guidance of a great idea, Judaism as a living form was powered from within. At the beginning of the twentieth century, Zionism was to be the new driving force, born out of the crisis of Jewish life in the Diaspora and calling for a new metamorphosis. I say it *called* for such a metamorphosis, but it had obviously not yet produced it, and the birth pangs of the new Jewish society were to be cruel and perilous indeed.

This is the atmosphere that is brought to life in Agnon's masterpiece. Like Agnon himself, Kummer goes as a very young man to Palestine, where everything is in transition. He cannot find his place, even though he is prepared to take upon himself any chore required of him in the life of the new *yishuv*. Thus he moves between two societies, the old one in Jerusalem and the new one in recently founded Tel Aviv and in the agricultural settlements. The positive side of the new life, even in its most problematic aspects, is visible more or less only as background; it is barely sketched.

Agnon planned to make the life of these young pioneers who clung to labor in the new settlements and the kibbutzim just then arising the center of another novel, as promised at the end of *Not Long Ago*. But it has not appeared to this day. Thus we are left only with the tribulations of a lost soul, described in loving detail with a mixture of melancholy and humor.

Agnon possesses a keen sense of the melancholy emptiness that shows through the busy bustle of the new life. His hero is forever seeking some fulfillment whose substance he is unable to define. In time he comes to Jerusalem and is strangely attracted by its haunting atmosphere. His adventures there—adventures of a restless seeker after redemption in a stagnant life—constitute the core of the book. He strives to reestablish a genuine relation to the world of tradition, which increasingly seems to hold out to him some great promise that he can find himself at home. But it is all in vain. Something is wrong from the beginning. This "something" is made symbolically clear in the surrealistic goings-on between Kummer and a stray dog. It all begins with an incidental joke and it ends as tragedy. Kummer is utterly unaware of what he has done to the dog on whose back he (working as a painter at the time) jokingly wrote, with the remaining paint in his brush, the words *kelev meshugah* ("mad dog"). In a piece of perfect art, using the modern technique of stream of consciousness, the author relates how this inscription, unknown to the dog, becomes the instrument by which the hero's life, as well as that of the dog, is destroyed. The researches of this dog, if I may be permitted to refer to his musings in that way, are a counterpart to the experiences and quest of Kummer, which also come to no good end.

Zionism, to be sure, has proclaimed a new life, but it would be too much to say that anywhere in Agnon's work has it been seen to be attained. It would be much better to say that in Agnon's writing Zionism appears basically as a noble failure, while everything else is even worse, namely a sham. As for the old life, notwithstanding all its past glory, there is, in our time, no way back. To the extent that Agnon's stories and novels take place in our time, they move between these two impossibilities. Nostalgia is no solution. To be conscious of the greatness of our past is still to be far from having a key to our own problems. A key may exist somewhere, but it is not ready for use, and the locksmith who could forge a proper fit has yet to be found.

Nowhere is this forlornness between past and future depicted with greater precision than in the last novel of Agnon's trilogy, the novel *A Guest for the Night*, the excellent translation of which into German undoubtedly played a great part in the decision of the Nobel Prize Committee. Whereas *Not Long Ago* is placed in the years before World War I, this book chronicles a visit which the narrator, after an absence of twenty years, pays to his home town.

Among the melancholy works abounding in Agnon's *oeuvre*, this book is by far the most melancholy. The Hebrew original appeared in 1939, two years before the German murder of the Jews, which physically destroyed the community portrayed in this book. But what we see here is the death of a Jewish town before it was drowned in actual blood. The narrator comes for a visit from the land of Israel. That he had followed the message of the new life and left his home town was in its time itself a sign of Jewish life in its positive aspects, for the struggle and polemics of that time had an object and a meaning. Now, however, life in Szybuscz—a thin disguise for Buczacz—becomes empty, idle, and miserable; it is perishing in resignation and resentment and even the promises of Zionism have become doubtful and questionable.

It is the year 1930, and the narrator himself has suffered during the Arab riots of 1929. There is no ultimate purpose to his visit, and his coming is but that of a wayfarer stopped for the night. Clearly the image of his home town has never left him, and during a break in his life in the new land he wishes to see again the city in which so much of himself is rooted. But he no longer finds what he came to seek. He encounters instead the horror of decline and decay, a horror no less sinister for its ignorance of the murder yet to come. The narrator arrives full of the vivid images of his town as it was in his youth.

It is the utter incongruity of the old and the new experience of life in its fullness and life in its full decline that is at the center of the novel. At every step, remembrance of things past intertwines with the present experience of the visitor. The sad reality of the town confronts him, but he tries to establish a continuity with a past that has vanished forever. If, as I have said, Kummer's efforts in Jerusalem failed, all the more so is the narrator's attempt in Szybuscz bound to fail. There he begins a life whose perfectly illusionary character becomes ironically visible in the course of the narrative.

Irony permeates the book from beginning to end. His nostalgia focuses upon the old house of study, whose key is delivered to him with a disdainful shrug by its last keepers when they set out to emigrate into the wide world, presumably to America. The only people he can attract to fill it again are those who are too poor to heat their own homes during the long winter and who come to warm themselves in the old place where the heating is paid for by the narrator. The key to the old house of study gets—not wholly unsymbolically—lost, and the narrator must have a new one made; upon his departure it finally passes to a Communist who had gone to Palestine ten years before as an ardent Zionist but after enduring much suffering and disappointment had returned to his old town. The debit side of Zionism finds its spokesman in him.

What, then, is this debit side, according to Agnon? It is the reign of empty phrases and bombastic oratory not followed by action; it is held up to scorn in very many of Agnon's writings about the Jews of our time. The new key to the old house of study that Agnon has left with the disappointed-Zionist-turned-Communist is in itself an ironical symbol; and it is small wonder that the old key, deemed lost, turns up rather surprisingly, but perhaps not all that surprisingly, in the narrator's bag upon his return to Jerusalem. In contradistinction to *Not Long Ago*, there is a key in this novel, but it fits nowhere in the new land. But there is a secret hint, however slight, of messianic restoration and integration, as is indicated in the old talmudic saying: "Even the houses of study and the synagogues in exile are destined to be transplanted to the land of Israel."

As I have noted, the efforts of the narrator to establish a genuine and living relationship to his town, especially those he has known in his youth or their relatives, are in the main unsuccessful. The reason may be that there is no longer any true reality in Sczybucz and that life there has a somewhat ghostlike quality. But another factor may also be involved: most surprisingly, the narrator's mind is set on the restoration of the past. He comes as a visitor from the sphere of the new life, but he brings no message along that would make him efficacious. It is not only the people he encounters who are slow and inflexible; he himself succumbs to this atmosphere. Although he befriends a group of *halutzim* who are preparing themselves for their *aliyah* to Palestine, his visit to them remains a romantic interlude. The silence and inability to respond of most of the other people he meets exerts a much greater attraction for him, and his heart goes out to them. Thus there unfolds a picture of Polish Jewry in a little town on the eve of the Holocaust, written with great love but at the same time with perfect sincerity. Somewhere in his tale the narrator says, "When I was young I could see in my mind all I wished to see; nowadays I do not see either what I wished to see or what I am shown." What then does he see? That is what the book is about.

V

These are some highlights of Agnon's work before he fully realized the impact and significance of the destruction of European Jewry. The main body of his later work has not yet been collected, but is scattered through various journals and daily newspapers. Moreover, much of what he has written is apparently still unpublished.

Here I should like only to stress two tendencies that stand out in many of these later writings.

There is first of all the predominant wish to emphasize the ritual aspects of Jewish life. Formerly, Agnon took them largely for granted. Now, however, there is an almost morbid effort on his part to stress each and every detail of ritual in his narrative, an effort that scarcely favors the progress of the particular story being told. For all their breathtaking perfection of language, much in these writings seems to be of greater relevance to students of folklore and Hebrew style than to readers of literature. We observe a frenzied endeavor to save for posterity the forms of a life doomed to extinction. It is a somewhat sad spectacle, for one notices the intention and becomes annoyed.

The second tendency now coming to the fore has to do with a curious widening of Agnon's retrospection. He no longer tells the story of the last four or five generations, but goes back much farther. Thus he may pretend to be editing the family papers of his ancestors and thereby covering important episodes in Jewish history over the last 400 years; or he may even undertake to tell the story of his own soul in its transmigrations since the days of Creation, a most peculiar autobiography. He sees himself as being present at all stages of Biblical and post-Biblical history and provides, as it were, eyewitness accounts of the most arresting events over thousands of years, out of a deep sense of identification with the Jewish people. This metahistorical autobiography is contained in a book, *Hadom Ve-kisse* (*Stool and Throne*), of which large fragments have been published during recent years. Whereas it may be said with regard to all his preceding work that there was never a total identification of the author with the narrator, this tension, arising from nonidentification, is now gone. Gone, too, is the novelistic element and the narrative is transformed into a plain chronicle of what has happened to the author's own self. There is no longer the unfolding of a story, but rather the undialectical juxtaposition of events told in separate paragraphs, each under its own heading.

It seems to me a most peculiar work, but I would not venture to judge it on its literary merits before it is published as a whole. The author's dialectical attitude toward his own experience and toward his tradition, which was so predominant in his other writings, has been abandoned, and that, I would almost say, is a great pity. For, if I were to reduce to one formula what I think is the core of Agnon's genius, I would say: *it is the dialectics of simplicity.*

Agnon in Germany: Recollections*

I came to know Agnon in the days of our youth, during and after World War I, and our friendly and close relations stem from this time.

By that time a great reputation preceded Agnon in the circle of Zionist youth, insofar as they sought to become intimate with the Hebrew language and literature. To be sure, the hunger for Hebrew and for knowledge of the sources of our literature was limited to a fairly narrow group. Agnon, however, obliged these rare birds with great affection. We first read about him in a small literary collection, published by the Zionist Association of Germany in 1916, and meant for those young Zionists who served in the war. This book was called *Loyalty (Treue)* and contained several stories by Agnon and a big section from the German translation of his first book *And the Crooked Shall Be Made Straight (Und das Krumme wird grade)*, together with introductory remarks about Agnon written by Martin Buber and in Buber's characteristic, slightly elevated style. It said there of Agnon that he had "dedication to Jewish things." Dedication (*Weihe*) was, coming from Buber, a word of the highest appreciation, though it was not completely clear to us what he really meant by it.

Even before I came to know Agnon personally, I had often seen him in the reading room of the library of the Jewish

* A speech in Hebrew delivered in the house of the President of Israel, November 16, 1966, in celebration of Agnon's receiving the Nobel Prize. Expanded and published as "Agnon in Deutschland: Errinerungen," in Gershom Scholem, *Judaica 2* (Frankfurt-am-Main: Bibliothek Suhrkamp, 1970), pp. 122–32. Translated from the German by Werner J. Dannhauser.

community in Berlin, where he indefatigably leafed through the card index of the Hebrew catalog. I asked him later what he sought so intently there. He answered with a guileless-ironic wide-eyedness, "Books that I have not yet read." For he came from a city in Galicia in whose *bet hamidrash* (house of study) many thousands of Hebrew volumes were to be found that he had devoured in his youth, and he knew how to tell some story or other about each book and its author. At that time, he was a very slender, almost emaciated young man with sharp features. Only somewhat later, about the time we came to know each other, did his face and figure round out. I met him at his first translator's, the lawyer Max Strauss (the brother of the poet Ludwig Strauss), an unusually gifted, very sensitive, and magnificent-looking young man. He was of the same age as Agnon but treated him with great politeness and respect, like a rare example of the species man. Strauss had a very fine feeling for language, but was not wholly secure in his knowledge of Hebrew and consulted a number of acquaintances, among them also me (who had written a wild article against a translation from Yiddish that had just been published) about questions of Hebrew style and Hebrew usage.

Agnon was surrounded by an aura of solitude and not a little *Weltschmerz*, a delicate melancholy, as was becoming to sensitive young persons. At that time he wrote many poems, over which hovered a spirit of infinite isolation. When, some years later, after the end of World War I, we were living in Munich, he read a number of them to me. They have all been burned. Only one of them, which I transcribed into German verse, is still among my papers in the original text and in translation.

On the other hand, one could often find Agnon in the company of young men and girls. He attempted to step out of himself. Not always did he succeed in this, and then he often sat there silently, but when he did engage in a conversation, he overflowed with old stories, anecdotes and words of the old sages, and we, young Jews with a German upbringing, were enchanted by him. Naturally, at the time we spoke German with him, even though Agnon's German was quite peculiar, with its Galician accent, half-Yiddish syntax, and with its cadence of Hasidic anecdotes. Sometimes he spoke with the greatest shyness and reticence, but sometimes also with a certain firmness. All this very much raised him in our esteem. This, after all was the time when a kind of veritable cult of the Eastern Jews (*Ostjuden*) reigned in Germany, which represented a backlash against the arrogance and presumption against them, which at the time were accepted attitudes in the circle of assimilated Jews from which we were descended. For us, by contrast, every Eastern Jew was a carrier of all the mysteries of Jewish existence, but the young Agnon appeared to us as one of its most perfect incarnations.

I recall an evening in May 1917 in Berlin's Hebrew Club, which was frequented almost exclusively by Russian, Polish, and Palestinian Jews. A born Berliner like myself stood out like a sore thumb there. On this evening Agnon read one of his most perfect stories, "The Tale of the Scribe," which at the time was not yet in print. Even now the deep impression made by Agnon's story is present in me, and I still hear the reverberation of Agnon's delicate and plaintive voice as he read his story in a kind of inward-turned, monotonous singsong. It was like an illustration of the word of the poetess about the "languages which are notched like harps."

At that time he set great value on sharply distinguishing between Agnon the artist and Agnon the human being. It is characteristic of this that he protested at once when I addressed him by his Hebrew *nom de plume,* "Agnon." "My name is Czaczkes," he used to correct me. When I asked him what he had against being called Agnon, he explained to me that Agnon was, no doubt, a very beautiful literary name, but how much could there be to a name he had invented himself and which did not occur in the Holy Books, while the name Czaczkes could be found expressly among the mystical names of angels in the Book of Raziel (an ancient Hebrew book about angelology). Even at that time I was unable to take this argument really seriously. Indeed, eventually, when he returned to Palestine at the end of 1924, he let—at my urging—his civil name be exchanged for his literary one and came once and for all to be called Agnon. I was at that time a librarian of the Jewish National Library in Jerusalem and said that with us he would be listed by the name of Agnon and that no remonstrations would be accepted.

As far as I know, during World War I he lived mainly from his work as literary adviser of the "Jewish Publication House" of

Dr. Aron Eliasberg, who was particularly fond of Agnon even though the former was a pronounced "Litvak," which is to say, a Lithuanian Jew, and Litvaks and Galicians in general could not stand each other. (Today, when all have fallen under the hand of the same murderer, these controversies are forgotten.) Agnon edited at least two books which at that time were published in German by the "Jewish Publication House," *The Book of the Polish Jew* and *The Book of Hanukkah* (I already collaborated on the last one as translator). I remember that my first familiarity with one of the most famous works of kabbalistic literature, the book *Hemdat Yamim* (*The Adornment of Days*), which describes exactly how a Jew must comport himself if he wishes to lead his life according to kabbalistic principles, stemmed from a discussion with Agnon about the depiction of the Hanukkah festival in that book.

At that time, Agnon spent every morning writing in his room. Many of his later writings date back to this period, even though what was written at that time, insofar as it was not already published, perished in the great fire in his house in Homburg. At first I could still quite well decipher the handwriting of his letters and the stories he gave me to read and also to translate. But even at that time he already showed a marked tendency to transform his handwriting into a kind of secret writing that puts the eyes of the reader at a loss. In the course of time things went so far that if his wife Esther wished to do one a favor, she simultaneously enclosed a transcription of his letters in order to facilitate the work of deciphering his secret writing, which resembled fly-spots rather than Hebrew letters. It also happened that Agnon wished to honor his friends. Then he would send his things to them in a form that was a joy to behold, and one could notice that his heart was drawn to the calling of the Torah-scribe, the Jewish calligrapher. I still see before me the complete copy of *And the Crooked Shall Be Made Straight*, in one of its innumerable versions, which Agnon had made for his friend and patron Salman Schocken in Zwickau, later his publisher, and which he showed me before he sent it. Whoever wants to see an example of the author's beautiful handwriting can presumably still admire it in the Schocken Library in Jerusalem, where it ought to be lying among many other papers of Agnon's.

I said that in the morning Agnon remained alone with his work. But during the afternoon and evening he already at that time indulged his sense for conversations and going for walks. Many hours have I spent walking with him through the streets of Munich, Frankfurt, and Homburg and have listened to his torrent of speech, and presumably also talked quite a bit myself. If I have won his heart it ought to be owing to three things. I was about ten years younger than he and his personality made a deep impression on me, and I very much admired him, just as at the time I was full of admiration for several Russian Jews with whom I was living in the same boardinghouse in Berlin, when my father threw me out of the house because of my Zionism. But these Russian Jews—like the deceased Dr. Zvi Kitain and Zalman Rubashoff-Shazar, the current President of the state of Israel who is hopefully destined for a long life to come among us—were, in accordance with their disposition and character, enlighteners and "enlightened men." Agnon, however, came, as it were, from very far away; he was no intellectual but rather a man from the world of creativity in which the fountains of imagination bubbled most richly. His conversations had a thoroughly profane character and content, but he spoke in the style of the heroes of his stories, and there was something infinitely attractive about his manner of speaking.

I gave expression to my admiration for him in two sonnets which I wrote in German in praise of Menashe Chayim, the hero of *And the Crooked Shall Be Made Straight*. One of them read:

Menashe Chayim*

Du, der das Leben sich vergessen macht
unsterblich ist es in Dir auferstanden.
Da Du in Not vergingst, in Schmach und Schanden,
bist Du zur höchsten Ordnung aufgewacht.

Dein Dasein ward dem Schweigen dargebracht,
in das nur klagend unsre Worte fanden,
doch nicht wie unsre Klagen Deine branden,
denn des Siloah Wasser fliessen sacht.

* *Menashe Chayim* literally means "who makes life forget."

Dein Leben steht im Licht der letzten Zeit,
aus deiner Stille Offenbarung spricht.
Unendlich gross erstrahlt in Dir das Leid,
Du aber bist das Medium das es bricht.

Und heisst solch Armut Leid und Irrsal nicht
Unschuld vor dem verborgenen Gericht?

(You, who makes himself forget life,
immortally it has been resurrected in you.
Because you perished in need, in disgrace and shame,
You have awakened to the Highest Order.

Your existence was offered to silence
into which our words could only enter when lamenting,
but not like our laments did yours surge,
for the waters of Shiloam flow softly.

Your life stands in the light of the final days
Out of your stillness revelation speaks.
Infinitely greatly does grief radiate from you
But you are the medium that breaks it.

And is the name of such poverty, grief, and erring
Not innocence before the hidden Judgment?)

I sent them to Agnon and thereby earned a place in his heart—evidently I was the first to write poems about his books. But perhaps a contributing factor was the youthful enthusiasm which caused me to return to the primary sources and which was bound to awaken his sympathy. We agreed in our judgment of many phenomena of Jewish life in Germany and poured out our hearts to each other in critical speeches about our surroundings, about people, and about literary conditions. At that time Agnon had formed a friendship with some Germans, men with heads on their shoulders, and was accustomed to deliver speeches of praise to me about them. To tell the truth, Agnon, who came from a foreign place, had by virtue of his intuition a better and deeper understanding for many a German than I did.

Toward the end of World War I and afterward, I lived in Switzerland for one and a half years. After my return, I met

Agnon in Berlin and he took me to Moses Marx, the brother of Esther Marx, who became Agnon's wife. Moses Marx, who at the time was a textile merchant in Berlin, had one of the most wonderful Hebrew libraries existing in Berlin, and Agnon (as I myself later on) was enthused by it. For already at that time he began to collect Hebrew books to a great extent, which passion enslaved him for several years. At that time Germany was dominated by inflation, and everyone who had his income in "hard currency" could be considered rich. At that time Agnon's star rose visibly in the sky of Hebrew literature, and the publisher Abraham Josef Stiebel in Copenhagen, who made his name as a patron of Hebrew literature, courted him very much and acquired his stories for good money.

After his marriage Agnon settled first in Wiesbaden and later in Homburg von der Höhe, a place to which he found himself drawn not only because of its scenic beauty, but also, as he liked to maintain, because of the old Hebrew prints that appeared there 250 years earlier. To be sure, one of the main attractions of these cities was their closeness to Frankfurt, a true metropolis of Jewish life, though in Agnon's eyes not so much because of the Jews living there, but rather on account of the secondhand Hebrew bookstores of which the Old City was full and the excellent Hebrew collection of the City Library (which burned down in World War II). With the librarian, a figure who seemed to have stepped directly out of the works of Anatole France, Agnon got along famously.

During the summer of 1923, before I went to Palestine, I taught at the "Free House of Study" in Frankfurt, which Franz Rosenzweig had established, and there I read a number of Agnon's stories with a group of students who already knew Hebrew to some extent. This gave great pleasure not only to my pupils but to Agnon himself. At that time he was not yet used to having his books read in schools.

During these years after World War I, I took a stab at a few translations of Agnon stories into German, of which several appeared at the time in Buber's monthly *Der Jude* (*The Jew*). That was an uncommonly difficult undertaking, and I acquired a precise concept of the enormous difficulties encountering anyone who undertakes to translate his great Hebrew prose, who not only wishes to reproduce the content of what has been narrated but to give expression in a foreign language to something of the particular tone and rhythm of the original. I would not like to make the claim of having been successful in my undertaking, but perhaps I can say of myself that since then I have been entitled to a judgment of the work of other translators. If we now praise the genius and greatness of Agnon, it also behooves us to praise the powerful achievement of his most recent translators, above all that of Karl Steinschneider and Tuvia Rübner, who have contributed significantly to making Agnon's *oeuvre* familiar in German-speaking circles.

During the three years Agnon resided in Homburg, three things were granted to him which, according to a saying by the sages in the Talmud, enlarge the sense of a human being: a beautiful residence, beautiful tools (that is to say, books, which after all are the tools of the writer), and a beautiful wife, who in all ways stood by his side. If I am not mistaken, she began already at that time to copy his ever-increasingly unreadable manuscripts in her calligraphic handwriting. In short, at that time he was really well off. He was happy and engulfed by his work, and one story followed on the heels of another. At that time he told me much about his great novel *In the Bond of Life*, his autobiography transformed into the medium of art, in which he looked back on and came to terms with his youth. Never again have I seen him so open of heart, so radiant and overflowing with genius, as in those days.

Undoubtedly the special atmosphere of Homburg also contributed to his well-being. For at that time many of the most significant writers, poets, and thinkers of Israel congregated there, as for example Haim Nahman Bialik, Ahad Ha-am, and Nathan Birnbaum, and around them a circle of excellent minds from Russian Jewry such as Yehoshua Ravnitsky, Shoshanah Persitz, and that legendary Semititzki,° of whom the initiate whispered that he was the only one of that generation who really had a perfect command of Hebrew grammar down to its ultimate subtleties, and whom all writers considered the court of last

° A proofreader for some of the most distinguished publishing houses, first in Russia and later in Israel.—Ed.

resort in ticklish questions. Agnon found great pleasure in these friendly relations, and became especially attracted to the great poet Haim Nahman Bialik, the poet of the Jewish Renaissance in Russia sixty to seventy years ago, and who, like Agnon himself, was a conversationalist of genius. Their discussions were memorable and it paid to listen to them. Ofttimes Agnon took me along on his walks with Bialik when I came to Homburg, and it is easy to understand how much I, a young German Jew, was impressed by these discussions. Naturally, at that time one already spoke in Hebrew. Agnon used to say, "Scholem, don't forget to write in your notebook what you heard." Well, I had open ears, but no notebook, and wrote down nothing.

This splendid period of Agnon's life came to an end in a tragic manner when the house in which he lived, together with his books and manuscripts, went up in flames on a summer night of the year 1924. Walter Benjamin, who esteemed Agnon most highly, wrote to me at the time: "I am not even in the least able in my imagination to reach the situation of a man who has to go through that, not to say anything of one who has to overcome it." Indeed, when Agnon returned to Palestine in the autumn of that year, he came as one whose world had grown dark and who had to begin everything anew. Which one of us could have put himself into his situation? So he returned from the depths of misfortune. The Agnon of before 1924 was completely different from the later Agnon. He kept on creating ever more splendidly and deeply, but he was locked into himself, and the many conversations he conducted were now but walls by which he shielded his isolation. So he entered on the way that has led him to the Nobel Prize, the way of a great artist who has mastered his torments.

Martin Buber's Conception
of Judaism*

I

At a conference the focus of which is the theme "Creation and Formation," I hardly know of a better way to introduce this difficult problem, to orchestrate it, as it were, with a great phenomenon of the spiritual world, than by reflection on the figure and work of Martin Buber, who left us in 1965 as a very old man and, throughout his whole life until his most advanced age, was centrally concerned with the question posed here. What is more, I will not deal with the abstract element of this question, as, for example, it was expressed in Buber's writings on philosophy, sociology, and education, but with what most persistently moved the man himself, throughout almost seventy years: namely his conception of Judaism.

Another speaker could perhaps develop this conception without entering into Buber's personality and intellectual biography. I confess that I am unable to do so. Buber, who put such emphasis on the unmistakably personal in the relationships of spiritual life, can be considered without inclusion of this personal element only at a very high cost, and one injurious to the subject matter itself. His achievement and its problematic aspect are inextricably linked with his life and the decisions of that life. Here it behooves me, who for a period of fifty years, from my student days to his death, was in alternately casual and intensive contact with him, to extend my gratitude, albeit not uncritically,

* "Martin Bubers Auffassung des Judentums," *Eranos Jahrbuch*, XXV (Zurich, 1967), 9–55. Translated by Werner J. Dannhauser.

to Buber, who for my generation meant so much in terms of challenge and reflection—even at those times when he became thoroughly opaque, questionable, or unacceptable to us.

No one who knew Buber could avoid the strong radiance emanating from him and making an intellectual engagement with him doubly passionate. To engage Buber intellectually meant to be tossed hither and yon between admiration and rejection, between readiness to listen to his message and disappointment with that message and the impossibility of realizing it. When I came to know him, he stood at the zenith of his influence on Jewish youth in German-speaking circles, during the years of World War I and shortly thereafter, when his words reached and moved a large audience. Buber *sought* this influence, even as he once more attained it among another group of young people (The League of "Comrades") in the years directly preceding Hitler and the onset of National Socialism in Germany.

It was among Buber's most bitter experiences that in both cases this encounter with a Jewish youth that was ready to depart and expected Buber to go along with it ended in deep estrangement. To be sure, one could just as well say that it was among the most bitter experiences of these youths that Buber did not draw the consequences they expected from his own message. Buber, a most multifaceted and complicated human being, had summoned these youths to go to the land of Israel and out of a creative impulse to undertake the formation of the new life that was to grow there. They never forgave him for not coming along when the chips were down. They did not understand that the man, who for so many years and with such eloquence had diagnosed and combated the "illness, distortion, and tyranny" of a disfigured Judaism in exile, was not in their midst when what mattered, during the turmoil following World War I, was to draw vital consequences from his message. Buber, whose conversations, speeches, and summons were centered on the word *realization* had refused to accept the latter—or so it seemed to the disappointed. From Buber's perspective, things looked different: he had come to a different personal decision, chosen a different medium of realization.

Here I have touched on a delicate, not to say tragic, point of Buber's manifestation and influence, one which is intimately

connected with a fact which has struck all those who have
written about Buber in recent years, without their really being
able to explain it to themselves: the almost total lack of influence
of Buber in the Jewish world, which contrasts strangely with his
recognition among non-Jews. It is notable that Gustav Landauer,
one of the few intimate friends of Buber, already saw this point,
in a highly positive manner, to be sure, in 1913, when Buber was
thirty-five years old. From him derives the prophetic sentence
that it was already noticeable but would soon become much
more evident that Buber was "the apostle of Judaism to
humanity." At the same time Landauer saw in him an "awakener
and advocate of that feminine thinking without which no renewal
and rejuvenation will come to our ruined and fallen culture." [1]
These assertions, with whose precision little bears comparison,
already express in a splendid and positive formulation the
dialectical tension and the factor of criticism that are inseparable
from a true insight into Buber's achievement. For the apostle of
Israel spoke a language that was more comprehensible to
everybody else than to the Jews themselves, and his tragedy is
based on this apostleship, even, indeed, on its overwhelming
success in its time.

At the same time, another man of considerable intelligence,
Frederik van Eeden,° said of Buber:

> If circumstances had ordained it, then Buber could certainly have
> developed into a teacher of his people, to one of the recipients of
> the legacy of traditions from Moses and Elijah. Then his life would
> have run its course quietly and obscurely in some house of prayer
> or other, or in some Polish village or other. Now, instead, he felt a
> calling for another task, for the one of spreading the knowledge of
> the ecstatic spirit of his people among others. He had to wander
> on the way of publicity and fame.

It remains a serious and legitimate question why Buber, one
of the most eloquent and mighty rhetoricians of Judaism, failed in
general to catch the ear of the Jews. The personal factor of which
I had occasion to speak before, and that has for the most part
been shrouded in silence in the literature about Buber, consti-

---

1. Gustav Landauer in the "Buber issue" of *Neue Blätter* (Hellerau, 1913), p. 96.
° A Dutch novelist and poet (1860–1932) of a strong mystical bent.—Ed.

tutes only *one*—an important one, to be sure—element of the understanding of this situation. It is surpassed in significance by another factual one with which I will have to deal thoroughly: Buber sought the creative transformation of Judaism; he sought *those* moments in the latter's history and present in which the creative bursts forms asunder and seeks a new formation, and in the course of his emphasis he abstracted extensively from the given historical forms of Judaism. From the moment when as a twenty-year-old he joined the newly arisen Zionist movement, to the end of his days, he indefatigably sharpened, preserved, and developed his sense for the creative transformation of the phenomenon closest to his heart.

The provocative element in his conception of Judaism and its history, with which we will have to deal here analytically and interpretatively, was unmistakable, and Buber, who cannot be denied either self-assurance or courage, was ready to pay the price for this reinterpretation, this new view. From the start, he placed himself emphatically among the heretics in Judaism, not among the representatives of what in many of his early writings he called "official Judaism" in opposition to the "underground." The paradox of his appearance and renown in the great world, shored up by a significant *oeuvre*, consists of the fact that the world considered just this individual to be the great representative of Judaism in our time: this man who even denied having a teaching that might be transmitted—indeed, in general whenever he appeared for a considerable time in a teaching capacity, success as a teacher was mostly denied him—this man who with complete radicalism stood aloof from the institutions of Judaism as a cult, and whom nobody ever saw in a synagogue during the almost thirty years he lived in Israel. Seen from a distance, and perhaps reinforced through the medium of his extraordinary stylistic capacities, the features connecting him with the great historical phenomenon of Judaism emerged more strongly than they did to those who had to assume a position vis-à-vis Buber from the perspective of a concrete closeness to Judaism and its tradition.

In the sixty years up to 1963, when he terminated the collection of his writings, Buber's conception of Judaism changed greatly in its formulations, especially if one compares the work of his early period up to about 1923 with his later one; but it is to be grasped by way of a central principle which he progressively undertakes to interpret himself: by way of his search for what is living and creative in this phenomenon and the wish to lend it words. In this last point, to be sure, also lies the reason for the great difficulty of analyzing Buber's intuitive views, a difficulty that has all along greatly impeded a coming to terms with him. His language is infinitely colorful, poetic, rich in images, suggestive, and at the same time of a singular vagueness and impenetrability. The lack of specificity in many of his writings and his inclination for the abstract, which as a philosopher of the concrete he again and again denied passionately, stood—to use Gustav Landauer's description—"in indissoluble connection with his love for feelingful expression and his preference for the latter over a precise, logically determined terminology." The reader is always aware that every translation into other words runs the danger of being denounced as a misunderstanding by Buber, and this was, in fact, the ever-recurring note of his answer to critics who wished to suggest concepts for his poetic metaphors. Yet Buber's capacity to grasp nuances of the inexpressible in words was extraordinary, even though it makes his writings well-nigh untranslatable, because in the case of translation the slippery and indefinite had to yield to a decision for a definite content and context of meaning.

II

Let us picture Buber's origin and his starting point. Buber, who was a Polish Jew and identified himself as such to the end of his life, had received an upbringing in which strict Jewish tradition and German enlightenment were intermingled. He grew up multilingually with Hebrew, German, Yiddish, and Polish (a whole string of his earliest pieces are written in Polish, and I recall having heard him give a lecture in Polish as late as 1943). Here Judaism encountered him as a historical form. For most of his contemporaries it was a firmly circumscribed phenomenon in which impulses and aspirations *capable of formulation* had actualized themselves, a historical continuum in which the life of a people had been forged by certain decisive ideas: by monotheism, by the Law and the prophetic exhortation to justice, by a theology centered on the concepts of creation, revelation, and redemption. As a youth, he broke with the institutions of that tradition, to which he never again returned. For years he imbibed the atmosphere of the European *fin de siècle*. The air of Vienna and the *Jugendstil* entered into a competition, having the most important consequences, with the heritage, so completely different, of his grandfather's house where he grew up. In this confusion, his encounter with the Zionist movement arising at the time became decisive, the latter carrying away Buber as a twenty-year-old student and in manifold metamorphoses determining his life and thought.

What did the watchword of Zionism mean for a modern young Jew of those years? I would formulate that meaning in three points that became important for Buber's attitude: (1) the awareness of the deadly crisis of the Rabbinic tradition of Judaism, of the senselessness and weightlessness of a religion that has become petrified in social institutions; (2) the awareness of a Jewish identity and loyalty, of a life unfolding beyond those institutions, in which the Jew is at home and rooted and which may make demands on him; (3) the Utopia of a living future and a rebirth of this people in its land, to be accomplished in a creative metamorphosis of the old form, but also, perhaps, in a revolutionary new beginning.

The wavering between these two poles rendered the features of the Zionist movement quite uncertain, and not only for Buber. In any case one can say that the "yes" and the "no" of Zionism to the present and the future of the Jews and their Judaism were resolved in these three points. They forge Buber's early reflections on the subject. His attitude, as articulate as it was from the start, was not based on a theoretical conception he had thought through, it was based on the raging feeling of a young romantic and revolutionary who sought to further the rebirth of his people, decayed and become unreal in exile, and therefore sought ways to substantiate his yearnings for a "new Judaism" a "Jewish modernity," or a "Jewish Renaissance."

Buber belonged to the generation that around 1900 was deeply influenced by Nietzsche and his slogans. Nietzsche's talk of the "creators" pervades all his earliest writings. The creative, as opposed to the unproductive and the idly persistent, is once more to come to the fore in Judaism. In 1901 Buber writes:

> To create! The Zionist who feels the whole holiness of this word and lives up to it seems to me [in contrast to other types of Zionists, from whom he differentiates himself, G.S.] to be of the highest rank. To create new works from out of the depth of one's primeval unique individuality, out of that uniquely individual, incomparable strength of one's blood that has been for so fearfully long cast in the irons of unproductivity . . . that is an ideal for the Jewish people. To create the monuments of one's essence! To let one's way burst forth into a new intuitive view of life! To set forth a new form, a new configuration of possibilities before the eyes of infinity! To let a new beauty glow, to let a new star ascend in the enchanted night sky of eternities! First, however, to penetrate to one's self, with bloody hands and undaunted heart to struggle through to one's essence itself, from which all these wonders will rise to the surface. To discover oneself! To find oneself! To gain oneself by struggle! [2]

This breakthrough of the Jew to himself recurs as a slogan in all of Buber's writings, albeit in less romantic formulations. He writes in 1919:

> In testing ourselves, we recognize that we Jews are altogether apostates. Not because the life and soul of other peoples have penetrated our landscape, language, culture; if our own land- scape, our own language, our own culture were given us again, we would not regain that innermost Judaism to which we have become untrue. Nor is it because many of us have renounced the norms of the Jewish tradition and the forms of life enjoined by it; those who have preserved them inviolate in all their Yes and No have no more preserved that innermost Judaism than the others. All this so-called assimilation is superficial compared to that fatal appropriation of which I am thinking: the appropriation of Western dualism, which sanctions the split of human being into two spheres, each existing by its own right and independent of the other, the appropriation of the cast of mind that thinks in terms of the compromise. [3]

2. Buber, *Die jüdische Bewegung*, 1916, p. 42.
3. Buber, *Der Jude und sein Judentum* (Cologne, 1963), p. 89. (*On Judaism*, edited by Nahum N. Glatzer [New York: Schocken Books, 1967], pp. 108–109.) (All translations

Here, then, there is an "innermost Judaism" that is to be resuscitated but which he finds expressed in the documents of "classical Judaism." What Buber understood by this, we still have to investigate.

There is a "genuine Judaism" [4] that is opposed to the spurious one. And from here too starts the talk of "primordial Judaism" that pervades the *Drei Reden über das Judentum* (1911) ("Three Addresses on Judaism"), so very influential in their time, a primordial Judaism that surmounts all forms and norms that count as Jewish. This talk about the primordially Jewish, the definition of which concerned Buber, again recurs in his last speeches about Judaism which appeared in 1951 under the title *An der Wende* (*At the Turning*). The basic impulse in all this was a critical one: the rejection of all the historical phenomena—capable of formulation—of Judaism in fixed formations. The slogan of the young Buber was, and basically remained, "Not the forms but the forces." [5] The demolition of the forms, the distrust of every structure and formation that has become historical, is turned into the index of something positive. It is the as yet unformed forces that attract the revolutionary and the romantic in Buber. It is the forces that in historical Judaism "never gained dominion, which at all times have been oppressed by official Judaism, which is to say by the impotence that has dominated at all times" and without which "no renewal of Jewish peoplehood can succeed." The early Buber developed a deep aversion to the Law, to *halakhah* in all its forms. Not only does he fail to accord it a legitimate position in genuine or primordial Judaism, but in his early and passionate years as a romantic he sees in it a power that is hostile to life and which one must combat or in any case desert.

The young Buber, in whom religious and aesthetic motives are still at least equally strong, is indefatigable in his polemic against the Law. He is of the opinion that before the era of the Emancipation

---

throughout this article of Buber's writings have been made directly from the original even where English translations are available and are cited in parenthesis for the reader's convenience.—Ed.)

4. Ibid., p. 91.

5. Ibid., p. 77. (*On Judaism*, p. 93. The "Three Addresses on Judaism" and *At the Turning* appear as part of the volume *On Judaism*.—Ed.)

the strength of Judaism was not only held down from without, by dread and torment, . . . but also from within, by the despotism of the "Law," which is to say by a mistaken, disfigured, distorted, religious tradition, by the constraint of a harsh, unmoved system of obligations which was alien to reality, but which accused of heresy and annihilated all that was instinctively bright and joyous, all that thirsted after beauty and was winged, which dislocated feeling and cast thought in irons. And the Law attained a power such as no law ever possessed among a people at any time. . . . There was no personal action born of feeling: only action according to the Law could exist. There was no independent, creative thinking: only the brooding over the books of the Law and the thousands of books interpreting those books of interpretation was allowed to express itself. There were, it is true, heretics again and again; but what could a heretic do against the Law? [6]

The systematic rigor of the *halakhah* and rabbinical dialectics enrage the romantic and artist in Buber, whose heart goes out to all manifestations of a struggling of the life forces not determined by the Law. When Buber speaks of the rebirth of Judaism, as he does so often, it never means to him "a return to the old traditions of feeling rooted in peoplehood and to their expression in language, customs, thoughts." [7] Rather such talk means to him the liberation from an "unliberated spirituality and the compulsion of a tradition divested of its meaning. . . . Only by a struggle against these powers can the Jewish people be reborn."

At that time, Buber's attitude toward *halakhah* was connected with a further point, namely his negation of exile, the Diaspora, as a legitimate Jewish form of life and his identification, to a great extent at least, of *halakhah* with everything he rejects about exile—the "slavery of unproductive economy" and the "hollow-eyed homelessness"—as unproductive and barren. The negation of that which was Judaism in exile and the actualization of "latent energies" and characteristics which since Biblical times "are grown dumb in the torments of the Diaspora" are close to his heart. The old characteristics are to be "presented again to our modern life in the latter's forms. Here, too, no return; a new beginning out of age-old material." [8]

6. Ibid., p. 272.
7. *Die Jüdische Bewegung*, p. 11.
8. Ibid., pp. 11–13.

Here something surprising comes to the fore, which in this form was given up by Buber thirty years later, without, however, having lost its significance for his conception of Judaism. At that time Buber, probably under the strong influence of the Hebrew writer, Micha Joseph Berdyczewski, was among those who saw salvation in the leap over the period of exile, in the denial of its productivity, and among whom the demand for, or expectation of, a reunion with Biblical times constituted the watchword. Here, as so often, revolutionary Utopianism expresses itself by appealing back to something very archaic, to a creative primordial time. This tendency, which from the beginning entered into competition and conflict with the restorative strivings of the conservative elements in the Zionist movement, belongs even now, in the newly arisen life in Israel, to the most important factors operating there.

For Buber, this interpretation of a great (and as it seems to me extremely problematical and in reality impossible) leap looked like this: the undivided, unbroken feeling for life of the Jews was to be enthroned again in a revolt against the "pure spirituality" which alone had counted as the highest ideal in exile. Buber recognizes this Jewish spirituality as "an enormous fact, perhaps the most striking one in the whole great pathology of the Jewish people," [9] whose transformation into the undisguised creative is the great challenge which for him coincides with the slogan "renewal of Judaism." This summons to the leap refers, to be sure, to the liberation of the creative forces of the Jewish people, not to the identification, always assessed positively by Buber, of the Jew with his tragic history.

> But whoever receives his Judaism into his life in order to live it, broadens his own martyrdom by the martyrdom of a hundred generations of his people, he links the history of his life to the history of innumerable bodies who once had suffered. He becomes the son of millennia and their master. He elevates the tone, meaning, and value of his existence. He creates for himself new possibilities and forms of life. Magic fountains open themselves up to his creativity and the elements of the future are placed into his hands.[10]

9. Ibid., p. 84.
10. Ibid., p. 74.

The youthful pathos of these sentences later became alien to the old Buber, but the intuitive view behind them remained the same. Even the latest writings of Buber contain something of this theory of the leap, even though he had in the meantime made discoveries which necessarily led to a complete transformation of the bleak, negative picture of Judaism in Exile. Even the discovery of Hasidism is from the beginning effected by him as that of a phenomenon which represents a relinking to the Biblical era, "the classical time of Judaism," a renewal, not, say, a mere repetition of the primordially Jewish.[11] His late writings on the Bible also contain many overtones of this kind, which resonate silently, though, to be sure, they were often most strongly stressed by Buber in private conversation.

The most penetrating formulation of these views of Buber's in his earlier period is to be found in a speech he gave impromptu in 1912 during a discussion and which he entitled "The Formative" (*Das Gestaltende*). Here he explains Judaism as a peculiar, "peculiarly predetermined, special case of the eternal process" that takes place in each individual human being but also in the life of each historical community. Everywhere two principles are at work: the formless and the formative, undifferentiated matter which is subject to the creative act, and [as he says, using a concept from the writings of Paracelsus, G.S.] the "Archeus" who strives to shape the former into spiritual life and who yet is never completely successful in this work. In the community of men that which has been formed (*das Geformte*) never remains pure form (*Gestalt*), and again and again the formless (*Gestaltlose*) breaks in and breaks up the form (*Form*).

> What once was created as a victory of the formative over the formless, the structure of the community, norm, and order, the institution, all the creation of the spirit, is at all times exposed to the disfiguring influence of the formless and under it becomes rigid and deaf and senseless, and yet does not want to die, but rather persists in its rigidity and deafness and senselessness, for it is preserved in life by the power of the opposing principle. Hence formation is transformation and hence the battle of forming [*formende Kampf*] is a process that begins ever anew. He who

11, Ibid., p. 100.

gives form (*Der Gestaltende*) [12] conducts his battle not against the formless alone, but also against the latter's monstrous allies, against the realm of the decomposing form.[13]

Buber opposes attempts to find the "essence of Judaism" in a purely qualitative definition. Rather, the process described here only takes place in Judaism "more purely, strongly, clearly than in any other group of human beings. . . . For as in the individual Jew, so in Judaism there is more visible than elsewhere in the world a struggle between the formative and the formless." It is this view that Judaism displays the polarity residing in each human being, but in an especially concentrated and elucidated manner, which completely determines the first of his "Addresses on Judaism." Here the Jews' innate striving for unity, which is the striving for form, for the overcoming of that duality which breaks forth in all things, was designated and glorified as the core of the Jewish, as the primordially Jewish. Buber explained Jewish monotheism and Jewish messianism from this perspective. The God of the Bible himself

> issued from the striving for unity, from a dark, passionate striving for unity. . . . He was not disclosed by nature but by the subjective self. Man had created him not out of reality but out of yearning because he had not *beheld* him in heaven and earth but *built* him up for himself as the unity above his own duality, as the salvation above his own suffering. . . . The striving after unity is what made the Jew creative. Striving for unity, for oneness from out of the dualization of his ego, he created the idea of the One God. Striving for unity out of the dualization of the human community, he created the idea of universal justice. Striving for unity from out of the duality of all that is living, he created the idea of universal love. Striving for unity out of the duality of the world, he created the messianic ideal, which a later time, again with the leading collaboration of the Jew, has diminished and been rendered finite and called socialism.[14]

According to Buber, this was true of the human beings of Jewish antiquity and was to become true again of the human

12. *He* who gives form, not a printer's error, as follows from the context.
13. *Der Jude und sein Judentum*, p. 240. ("Addresses on Judaism" forms part of the volume by Buber, *On Judaism*, op. cit.—Ed.)
14. Ibid., pp. 22–24. (*On Judaism*, p. 28.—Ed.)

beings of the Jewish Renaissance, which he summoned forth in his "Addresses on Judaism." In between stood the world of *galut*, of exile, which had brought on a deep social illness in Judaism.

> For that contrast and conflict between the formative and the formless, that was, no matter how fearfully it might sometimes present itself, the *health* of Judaism. Its sickness in the *galut* consists of the impotence and the estrangement of those who can give form. It happened that that eternal process of Judaism could no longer achieve productivity . . . and the realm of the formative spirit was expelled by the realm of the decomposing form. . . . The destiny of Judaism can take no turn ere the conflict in its old purity is resurrected, ere the fruitful battle between the formative and the formless begins anew.[15]

I am among those who in their youth, when these speeches appeared, was deeply moved by them and who—even as happened to the author himself—many years later can now read these pages only with a feeling of deep estrangement. They no longer contain anything convincing for our historical conscious-ness; their psychology no longer convinces us, and the connection between the psychology and the theology strikes us as merely rhetorical. The distinction between an official Judaism, which was disposed of as the realm of decomposing form, and an underground one in which the true sources can be heard to murmur, was naïve and could not bear the scrutiny of historical observation. Buber himself later disavowed this distinction. And nevertheless, these words exuded a considerable magic in their time. I would be unable to mention any other book about Judaism of these years, which even came close to having such an effect—not among the men of learning, who scarcely read these speeches, but among a youth that here heard the summons to a new departure that many of them took seriously enough to act on it.

It is precisely the concepts that were especially influential in these speeches that in the later writings of Buber do not recur, or only in a changed form. Among these is, above all, his distinction, based on a widespread linguistic usage of the time, between religion and religiosity, through which Buber could give expres-

15. Ibid., p. 244.

sion to his aversion to the Law as the form of the Jewish religion, and his advocacy of the truly formative forces. Renewal of Judaism, always a revolutionary and not an evolutionary concept for Buber, always meant to him "renewal of Jewish religiosity." He explains this as follows:

> Religiosity is the feeling of man—ever coming to be anew, ever expressing and shaping [ausformen] itself anew, astonished and worshiping—that there exists above his conditioned condition [Bedingtheit], and yet breaking forth from the midst of it, something Unconditional; it is his demand to institute a living communion with the latter, his will to realize it by his action and to install it in the human world. Religion is the sum of customs and doctrines in which the religiosity of a given epoch of a peoplehood has expressed and shaped itself. . . . Religion is true as long as it is fruitful; that, however, is as long as religiosity, when it takes up the yoke of commandments and articles of faith, is nevertheless capable—often without knowing it—of impregnating and transforming them most intimately with a new, glowing meaning, so that they appear to every generation as though they had been revealed to it personally on that very day to fill its own needs, alien to the fathers. If, however, the rites and dogmas of a religion have become so rigid that religiosity is incapable of moving them, or no longer wishes to submit to them, then religion becomes unfruitful and thereby untrue. Thus religiosity is the creative and religion the organizing principle; religiosity begins anew with every young person deeply moved by mystery; religion wants to force him into its structure, stabilized once and for all. Religiosity means activity—an elementary placing of the self into relationship [Sichinverhältnissetzen] with the absolute—religion means passivity—the self's taking upon itself [Aufsichnehmen] the traditional commands. Religiosity has only its own goal; religion has purposes; due to religiosity the sons rise up against the fathers, in order to find the God of their very own self; due to religion, the fathers curse the sons for not permitting them to impose their God on them. Religion signifies preservation; religiosity signifies renewal.[16]

It is not hard to see that in the first half of this quotation so characteristic of his conception of Judaism, Buber—no matter

16. Ibid., pp. 66–67; the following pages should also be consulted. (On Judaism, pp. 80–81. The whole speech, "Jewish Religiosity," appears on pp. 79–94.—Ed.)

what one may think of the terminology used here—puts his finger
on a state of affairs that is highly significant and fruitful for the
understanding of the history of religion. It is equally clear that in
the final sentences he slips into a pathetic rhetoric that sets up
dubious antitheses, which, to be sure, is one of the main
weaknesses of Buber's writings in general.

Buber's concern in this period was, as he said, "to extract and
salvage the special essence of Judaism from the refuse with which
the rabbinical and the rational have covered it." Buber considered the essential ground of Jewish religiosity to be "the act of
decision as the realization of divine freedom and absoluteness on
earth" and in the conception of this realization he found three
strata in which "the coming to be of that underground Judaism
announces itself . . . in opposition to official pseudo-Judaism,
which rules without appointment and represents without legitimacy." [17] The earliest one deals with the realization of God by
imitation in the sense of the Biblical phrase of "the image of
God." It determines the basic demand of the Torah (Lev. 20:26):
"Become holy, for holy am I." The second stratum deals with a
realization of God by the intensification of His reality. Buber is of
the opinion that the more God is realized by human beings in the
world, the more real He is. For this second stratum, and even
more for the third, in which the realization of God by man
becomes an influence of human action on God's destiny on earth,
Buber refers essentially to kabbalistic trains of thought. The basis
is always the conception that an infinity of things flow into a
human deed, but that also an infinity of things flow from it.

Here emerges Buber's view that, when all is said and done, he
never abandoned, no matter how many variations he gave to it in
the course of fifty years. The truth about the relationship of
human beings to God

is not a What but a How. Not the content of the deed turns it into
truth, but whether it occurs in human conditionality or in divine
absoluteness. Not matter determines [its position and its value],
. . . but the power of the decision causing it to emerge, and the
dedication of the intention inhering in it.[18]

17. Ibid., p. 69. (*On Judaism*, p. 83.—Ed.)
18. Ibid., pp. 71–72. (*On Judaism*, p. 87.—Ed.)

The historical aspects in which the primal Jewish religiosity becomes most clearly visible are, according to Buber, Prophecy and many movements tendentiously distorted in our Bible, like the one of the Rechabites depicted in the Book of Jeremiah, as well as the Essenes and the primordially Jewish phenomenon of Jesus, whose Sermon on the Mount Buber claims with great emphasis as a "Jewish avowal in the most intimate possible sense," [19] and finally the *kabbalah* and Hasidism. These are also the phenomena which determined the further development of Buber's conception of Judaism and his attempts at further clarification.

Here Judaism is ever a battle between the priests and the prophets, between the rabbis and the heretics who undermine their authority, between the law of the *halakhah* and the popular *aggadah* and the world of mysticism. With growing insight, Buber disavowed the radicalism of these antitheses, in which he reveled twenty years, and here and there he ventured on a more just distribution of emphasis.

Notwithstanding all this, however, it remains crucial that already at this time Buber considered Judaism not as something static, standing before us in fixed form, but rather, as he often says, as a "spiritual process" which in accordance with its historical nature is *unfinished*, in which great ideas are at work—he gives as examples those of unity, deed, and future[20]— which, however, again and again demand a creative reformulation from out of the spirit of the times. Buber never abandoned this line and in this, I would say, he was right.

III

This is the place to speak of two elements which become of surpassing significance for Buber's conception, be it that he was carried away by them and unreservedly sold his soul to them and glorified them, or be it that he tried to differentiate himself from them and in his relation to them stated more or less convincing

19. Ibid., p. 38. (*On Judaism*, pp. 45–46.—Ed.)
20. Ibid., pp. 33–43. (*On Judaism*, pp. 35–55.—Ed.)

reservations about them. I mean the role of mysticism and myth in Buber, and thus the two elements which in the nineteenth century were most lacking in the emancipated Jew's consciousness of his Judaism or, to put it more exactly, which were excluded and repudiated by this very consciousness. No one deserves more credit for first causing these features of Judaism to come to view again than Buber, who did not approach them with the methods of science and historical research, sociology, and psychology, but with all the passion of a heart overwhelmed by a new discovery.

There was something fascinating about the imperturbable and self-assured subjectivity and sovereignty with which he proceeded in this case. He followed a hidden inner compass which led him to places where, in the treasure house of time, there could be found unrecognized jewels, seeming dull and counterfeit to eyes not prepared for them. Or, in order to put it more clearly perhaps: Buber was a listener of great intensity. Many voices came through to him, and among them soft ones which had become completely unclear and incomprehensible to the generations before him, and whose call moved him deeply. In his quest for a living Judaism which, as we saw, Zionism had awakened in him, he penetrated to the sources by resuming the Hebraic studies of his boyhood. He read the aggadic texts edited by his grandfather, Solomon Buber, the Midrash scholar,[21] "at first repelled again and again by obstinate, stiff, unformed matter, gradually overcoming the strangeness, discovering one's own, intuiting the self with growing devotion." [22] The first fruits of his reading that he reaped on his way to the sources can be found in the old volumes of the weekly edited at one time by Buber and published by Theodor Herzl, *Die Welt*, the central organ of Zionism. From this point he turned one day, in 1902 or 1903, to Hasidic literature.

To be sure, Buber brought along his inclination toward mysticism to this reading. It arose in him as a student, and years

21. The author's copies of Solomon Buber's Midrash editions, which he preserved from the latter's literary remains, stood behind Buber's desk to the very end.

22. Buber, *Mein Weg zum Chassidismus* (Vienna, 1918), p. 18. ("My Way to Hasidism," in Buber's *Hasidism and Modern Man*, edited and translated by Maurice Friedman [New York: Harper Torchbooks, 1958], pp. 58–59.—Ed.)

before he ever picked up Hasidic or kabbalistic writings he had already, in 1899, given lectures on Jacob Boehme.[23] German mysticism had attracted him even before he sought and came to know Jewish mysticism. As is readily apparent from his writings, Buber himself was no stranger to mystical experiences. In fact they occupy the center of his first philosophical book, which appeared in 1913 under the title of *Daniel, Gespräche von der Verwirklichung (Daniel)*, and amounts to a philosophical interpretation of such experiences. So his intense listening to the voices which came through to him from Hasidic literature stemmed from a kindred spirit in which these voices now awakened an enormous echo. To put it another way, Buber sought out the mysticism in Judaism, and that is why he was in a position to find it, to perceive it, when he hit upon it. What moved him about the Hasidic world for many years was its mysticism, and when he later attempted to reinterpret, or interpret away, this mysticism in line with his own later development, it always remained—even under the cover of a new terminology—nothing other than mysticism.

The deep impression made by Buber's first writings about Hasidism, which appeared sixty years ago, was evidently due to the fact that here a man of great culture and sensitivity undertook to point out a living dimension of Judaism, of which up to that time there had scarcely been any talk among the scholars, indeed, whose existence was denied point-blank in favor of a widespread prejudice. When at that time Buber and his friend Berthold Feiwel established the *Jüdischer Verlag* in Berlin as the organ of the "Jewish Renaissance," it was no accident that its first publication of a nonliterary or artistic character was a booklet by Professor Solomon Schechter, *Die Chassidim, eine Studie über jüdische Mystik* ("The Hasidim, A Study of Jewish Mysticism) (1904), in which a scholar coming from a Hasidic milieu—who had, to be sure, moved far away from it—undertook to sketch the first picture of this movement that was not distorted by polemics. Buber's own efforts, however, went far beyond this. He wrote not as an observer but as one deeply affected. For all that, his first pronouncement on Hasidism that we possess in

23. Hans Kohn, *Martin Buber, sein Werk und seine Zeit* (Cologne, 1961), p. 23.

print (from the year 1903) is still characterized by unpathetic objectivity, and can lay claim to validity even today:

> The Hasidic view of life dispenses with all sentimentality; it is a mysticism as forceful as it is full of profound feeling, which brings the beyond completely into this world and lets the latter be formed by the former as the body is formed by the soul: a completely original, popular, and warm-blooded renewal of neo-Platonism, at the same time a highly God-filled and highly realistic guide to ecstasy. It is the doctrine of active feeling as the bond between man and God. Creativity endures eternally; the Creation continues today and forever and ever, and man takes part in Creation in power and love. All that comes from a pure heart is worship. The goal of the law is that man become his own law. Thereby despotism's hold is broken. But the founders of Hasidism were not negators. They did not negate the old forms; they put a new meaning into them, and thereby liberated them. Hasidism, or rather the deep outpouring of the soul that generated and bore it aloft, created the emotionally regenerated Jew.[24]

To the extent, however, to which Buber became engrossed in Hasidic doctrine and legends during the following years, he became, as he wrote, "aware of the vocation to preach them to the world." [25] His own meaning and his concept of adequate literary communication intermingle with the meaning and style of the old books and pamphlets. The reporter and transmitter turns into the interpreter and herald. There begins in him the process, never again discontinued, of projecting his own system into the interpretation of historical phenomena.[26]

> In Hasidism underground Judaism was victorious for a while over the official kind—over the notorious, clearly arranged Judaism whose history one narrates and whose essence one grasps in easily understood formulas. Only for a while. In our time there are still hundreds of thousands of Hasidim; Hasidism has rotted. But the Hasidic writings have delivered its doctrine and its legends to us. The Hasidic doctrine is the strangest and most characteristic thing the Diaspora has created. It is the proclamation of rebirth. No

24. *Der Jude und sein Judentum*, p. 273.
25. *Schriften*, III, p. 968. (*Hasidism and Modern Man*, op. cit., p. 59.—Ed.)
26. Hans Kohn already formulated it this way, op. cit., p. 304.

renewal of Judaism will be possible that will not contain its elements.[27]

Buber was the first Jewish thinker who saw in mysticism a basic feature and continuously operating tendency of Judaism. He goes very far in the formulation of this thesis, but the stimulus he provided by it is effective to this day, albeit in other perspectives.

The mystical predisposition is characteristic of Jews since primal time, and its expression is not, as is frequently the case, to be conceived of as a temporarily appearing conscious reaction to the domination of intellect. It is a significant characteristic of the Jew, which seems hardly to have changed in millennia, that the extremes in him quickly and powerfully ignite each other. So it happens that in the midst of an unspeakably narrow existence, indeed, precisely out of its narrowness, the boundless breaks forth with primordial suddenness and now rules the soul surrendering to it. . . . If, accordingly, the strength of Jewish mysticism comes from an original characteristic of the people, which has generated it, then it has also gone on to put its stamp on the destiny of this people. The wandering and the martyrdom of the Jews have again and again transported their souls into those waves of despair from which now and then the lightning of ecstasy awakens. At the same time that wandering and martyrdom have prevented them from completing the pure expression of ecstasy and have misled them into throwing together necessary, deeply experienced things with superfluous, randomly gathered ones, and—feeling unable to say one's own because of pain—into chattering about alien things. Thus arose writings like the Zohar, the Book of Splendor, which are a delight and an abomination.[28]

Along with the contact with mysticism as a creative element of Judaism, a no less passionate interest in the mythical element of Judaism had its way with Buber, one which, connected with the positive revaluation of myth by him as by so many of his

27. "Introduction" to *Legende des Baalschem* (Frankfurt, 1907), p. 6. This introduction has been omitted in Buber's *Schriften zum Chassidismus* (Vol. III of *Schriften*) along with many other of his early pronouncements. (*The Legend of the Baal-Shem* [New York: Schocken Books, 1969], pp. 11–13.—Ed.)

28. *Die Geschichten des Rabbi Nachman* (Frankfurt, 1906), pp. 6, 8. The reprint of these pages in *Schriften*, III, pp. 11–12 is greatly changed. (*Tales of Rabbi Nachman*, translated by Maurice Friedman [New York: Horizon, 1968], pp. 32–34.—Ed.)

contemporaries—the writings of Arthur Bonus, forgotten today, played a great role at the time—flows from the influence of Nietzsche.

> The Jews are perhaps the only people that has never ceased to generate myth. At the beginning of their great document stands the purest of all mythical symbols, the plural-singular Elohim. In that primordial time there springs up the stream of myth-bearing strength that—provisionally—flows into Hasidism: from which the religion of Israel at all times felt itself to be endangered, from which, however, in truth Jewish religiosity . . . received its inner life. . . . The personal religiosity of the individual soul has its birth in myth, its death in religion. As long as the soul is rooted in the rich ground of myth, religion has no power over it. Therefore religion sees in myth its sworn enemy and . . . combats it where it is . . . incapable of absorbing it. The history of the Jewish religion is the history of its struggle against myth.[29]

Buber dedicated one of his "Addresses on Judaism" to this "Myth of the Jews." [30] There he attempted to recognize the essence of monotheistic myth in the sense of the Platonic definition of myth as a report of divine doings as a sensual reality. For Buber, "every living monotheism [is] full of the mythical element, and only as long as it is, is it living." The great mystics of Judaism have "renewed the personality of the people from the roots of its myth." Buber sees two basic forms of Jewish myth which traverse the Biblical and post-Biblical literature of the Jews: the saga of the deeds of God and the legend of the life of the "central" man. For him, the first represents eternal continuity, the second eternal renewal. Buber never tired of pointing to the mythical element in living Judaism, even when he later began to deny his own ties to mysticism.

Buber's work on the Hasidic tradition moves between these two poles of mysticism and myth, whose relation to each other never became wholly clear in Buber (which is connected with his radical widening of the historical sphere of mysticism's impact). That work appears at first in extremely pathetic, indeed precious language, in which metaphors chase each other and language

29. "Introduction" to Legende des Baalschem, pp. iii–iv. (An English translation of a revised version appears in The Legend of the Baal-Shem, op. cit., p. 11.—Ed.)

30. Der Jude und sein Judentum, pp. 78–88. (Translated under the title of "Myth in Judaism" in On Judaism, op. cit., pp. 95–107.—Ed.)

walks on stilts; later in a much simpler and therefore also much more impressive language of the terse anecdote in which a dictum of the Hasidic *tzaddikim*, presented in the shortest form and even the smallest compass, with a renunciation of all the trimmings, presents a whole. In the beginning, the Hasidic sources seemed to Buber too awkward and clumsy, and he helped their intention along by rhetorical embellishment, indeed by complete re-creation; which he himself later found so alarming that he no longer included them in the final collection of his *Schriften zum Chassidismus* (*Writings on Hasidism*).

A peculiar contrast exists between the precisely translated quotations from Hasidic writings in his introductions and prefaces, and the overly elevated language of the stories and legends following them. The interpretation he gives to the Hasidic phenomenon most emphatically stresses its mystical aspects and the life of the Hasidim is still understood from the perspective of their thoroughly mystical doctrine. Rabbi Nachman of Bratslav, the great-grandson of the Baal-Shem who died in 1810, and to whom Buber dedicated his first book, is to him "perhaps the last Jewish mystic." He was the first in a long series of *tzaddikim*, a veritable galaxy of saints, whose figures Buber sought to comprehend in a progressive effort at clarification, and in whom he glimpsed the representatives of the most authentic Judaism. His conception of the significance of these men, however, changed profoundly. It is the meaning of this change, which at the same time characterizes the change of his conception of Judaism, that we will have to discuss, among other things, in what follows.

IV

There are two periods in Buber's preoccupation with Judaism that correspond to his efforts as a thinker in general. In both, creation and formation constitute a pivot on which Buber's thinking turns. He sought out the creative moments in which the great forms are born and he made himself the advocate of the living force breaking through in these moments, over against the gradually decaying forms and figures which, as relics of great hours, lay claim to our awe or veneration. Basically this always remained Buber's attitude; but the way he broached the subject changed considerably, and from Buber's perspective even decisively. Throughout, however, the key word in which his thinking is summed up remains "realization" (*Verwirklichung*), though the way to the latter is now substantiated in another manner.

"Realization" was the slogan of his "Three Addresses on Judaism"; "realization" was the theme of his philosophical book *Daniel* in 1913, which constituted a philosophical justification of a cult of living experience, *Erlebnis*, completely under the sway of mysticism. It was this unrestrained cult of *Erlebnis* that already at that time evoked opposition to Buber, and it was the emphatic disavowal of this cult of *Erlebnis* that characterized Buber's later period, and certainly its philosophical formulations. He turned vehemently (not exactly convincingly, to be sure) against interpretations of his thought that found even in the latter's new form only a metamorphosis of the old cult.

In *Daniel* he speaks of a twofold stance by a person toward his *Erlebnis:* that of orienting or adjusting and that of actualizing or realizing. *Orientation* manipulates the world by yoking it in coordinates according to its forms and laws. It classifies things and practical experiences and seeks chains of connections. By it man finds his way about reality, a reality to which Buber denies that title. *Actualization,* however, represents submersion in pure *Erlebnis,* not in one manufactured, connected with what comes before and after, absorbed by cause and effect. Only actualization, which is nothing other than the practical experience of the unity above all polarities and tensions, creates reality out of *Erlebnis.*[31] The attitude of actualization is that of the directness of *Erlebnis,* while orientation "adjusts it to the ancestrally accustomed connection of indirectness." The realizing person is whole and united and none other than what we call the creative person. In the creative person, the hours of actualization link themselves "into a series of summits of the eternal which shines out of the transitory sequences of ups and downs of his human life," and which also fills the mass of hours of mere orientation with a reflection of meaning.[32]

31. *Schriften*, I, pp. 22–23. (*Daniel* [New York: Holt, Rinehart and Winston, 1964], pp. 64–65.—Ed.)

32. Ibid., p. 27. (*Daniel*, pp. 70–71.—Ed.)

Both attitudes are necessary and make up human life. It matters only which one of them the choosing person grants power over himself. In orientation he has a security radically denied him by actualization, which rather demands of him that he descend into the abyss of *Erlebnis*, to surrender to the abyss and thereby to close it. Orientation incorporates all events into useful connections which, however, remain fruitless beyond their range; actualization, by contrast, "relates each occurrence to nothing but its own content and precisely thereby fashions it into a signum of the eternal." [33] The world is manifold, torn by infinite dualities, and only in the act of realization does it become a unity. The act of realization is the establishment of a true and immediate relation to things or to that which the realizing person takes from things and inserts into the relation.[34] The *Erlebnis* of which there is such rapturous and metaphor-rich talk here is basically nothing other than the one of mysticism, a mysticism, to be sure, which can appear without any theological foundation, and even as atheistic mysticism. No wonder that Fritz Mauthner, the great skeptic and critic of language, who saw in atheistic mysticism the only answer to the questions formulated by philosophy, wrote to a lady friend of his after he had met the young Buber: "Exceptionally valuable person. Polish Jew. Friend of [Gustav] Landauer. Atheistic Zionist." [35]

In Buber's later years, this mystical philosophy of *Erlebnis* turned into the one of "the life of dialogue," the key words of which are developed in *I and Thou*, which appeared ten years after *Daniel*. The categories of orientation and actualization have in no way ceased to carry weight with Buber, but they have been transformed and now have other names. Actualization, at least, has assumed a slightly different function, without, however, being able to deny its descent from its older form. Now Buber's talk is of the two "basic words," that is to say basic relationships of man to things: I-Thou and I-It. The I-Thou is the world of living and direct relations; the I-It is the world of reified things in which the one I sense to be a person who addresses me and is addressed by me as "Thou," decays into an impersonal "It."

33. Ibid., p. 42. (*Daniel*, p. 94.—Ed.)
34. Ibid., p. 74. (*Daniel*, pp. 141–42.—Ed.)
35. *Yearbook of the Leo Baeck Institute*, VIII (London, 1963), 147.

According to Buber all real life is an encounter between "I" and "Thou." "Between them stands no abstraction, no foreknowledge, and no fantasy." Between them there exists pure relation, for Buber a basic category beyond which one cannot go. "I" and "Thou" become "I" and "Thou" only through their relation to each other, and Buber betrays—notwithstanding all protests—the mystical origin of these new categories in many passages, but never more clearly than when he says "the 'Thou' encounters me through grace—it is not found by seeking. But that I speak the basic word to him is a deed of my essential being." [36] Exactly as was the case with actualization in *Daniel*, the new basic word "I-Thou" can also "only be spoken with one's whole essential being. The ingathering and coalescence to the whole essential being can never happen through me, can never happen without me." What had previously been said of orientation and actualization is now carried over to the "It world" and the "Thou world."

The It-world is the one of cohesion in space and time, in which man knows his way, in which it is possible to live. The Thou-world has no cohesion in space and time; it shakes up all security, is dangerous, uncanny, and indispensable to the true life of man. Where things enter into a living relation, the It can become a Thou. But his Thou, too, must, after the expiration of the relation, which is an isolated occurrence without dimension, become an It.[37]

The breakthrough to religion, or to religiosity, to God, to whom Buber will now testify constantly and emphatically, becomes clear: Every individual Thou is a glimpse of the "eternal Thou." The inborn Thou of a human being cannot realize or perfect itself in any single individual relation between I and Thou. This perfection—and according to Buber that is obviously the religious act—is achieved "only in the direct relation to *the* Thou that according to its essence cannot become an It." [38] Buber's philosophy of culture and religion turns on these philosophical-anthropological definitions, which he brought to fruition in many applications.

36. *Schriften*, I, p. 85. (*I and Thou*, translation, prologue, notes by Walter Kaufmann [New York: Charles Scribner's Sons, 1970], p. 62.—Ed.)

37. Ibid., pp. 100–101. (*I and Thou*, pp. 84–85.—Ed.)

38. Ibid., p. 128. (*I and Thou*, p. 123.—Ed.)

There is no mistaking that the definitions themselves—which render the so called "lived reality" and the "concrete" prominent for the sake of a victorious opposition to the abstractions of a conceptualization that tears asunder direct relations—admit of more than a few doubts. The immediate evidence for, and validity of, words like "direct relation," "eternal Thou," the "interhuman" (*Zwischenmenschliche*) and their like, on which Buber builds, are in no way clear. They continue to terminate in a hypostatization of the old concept of *Erlebnis* unto the ontological realm. Corresponding to this is the ambiguity and indeterminateness of very many, often highly poetic passages of Buber's, concerning which fairly arid discussions between him and his critics have been conducted.[39]

For the understanding of Buber's world of ideas, precisely in connection with what concerns us here, we must, however, start from these basic concepts, which dominate all the writings of his whole later period. In this, Buber's pronounced turning away from mysticism—emphatically proclaimed by him—plays a great role. While realization in *Daniel* is admittedly of a mystical nature—not for nothing is the motto of the first edition of the book taken from Scotus Erigena's *De Divisione Naturae*, a highly mystical statement, and not by accident has it been omitted from the reprint in the *Schriften*—the realization that emanates from the I-Thou relation as its fulfillment is, according to Buber, no longer of a mystical nature.[40] As to the objection that the I-Thou relationship, established by him and in principle capable of infinite extension, involves (in the form of a suppressed *petitio principii*) a mystical relationship of man with the world or with God—Buber persistently dismissed it indignantly, without thereby being able to convince his critics. His "empirical" descriptions of his own concrete I-Thou experiences, such as his contemplation of a tree or his gazing into the eyes of his pet cat, are, it seems to me, to be understood as nothing other than descriptions of mystical experiences.[41]

It is, however, indisputable that Buber, who now speaks of

39. That is true above all of the extensive volume, *The Philosophy of Martin Buber*, edited by Paul Arthur Schlipp and Maurice Friedman (La Salle, Ill.: Open Court, 1967), the philosophical pieces of which leave at least this reader particularly perplexed.
40. *Schriften*, I, p. 166. (*I and Thou*, pp. 177–79.—Ed.)
41. Cf., for example, ibid., I, p. 144. (*I and Thou*, p. 145.—Ed.)

God as, one might say, a "Biblical Jew" (as he often referred to himself) has definitely repudiated the talk of "the God who comes to be" that seems to lie behind many of his earlier pronouncements.[42] So, too, he has now devalued the *Erlebnis*, previously raised so high by him, in favor of the "encounter." But this devaluation, and the critique connected with it, is purely verbal, and exactly that is now transferred to the moment of encounter which had previously made it an actualized *Erlebnis*, but which is now to be absent from the *Erlebnis* in the devalued sense of the word.

> The moment of encounter is not an *Erlebnis* that stirs in the receptive soul and blissfully rounds itself out: in an encounter something happens to a person. It is at times like an afflation, at times like a wrestling match; no matter: it happens. The person who steps forth from the essential act that is pure relation has in his essence something More, something grown into him, of which he did not know before and to the origin of which he is incapable of doing justice by description. However the scientific world-orientation, in its legitimate striving for unbroken causality, may classify the descent of the New. For us, who are concerned with the real consideration of the real, no subconsciousness and no other apparatus of the soul can be worth anything.[43]

In other words, Buber's terminology, from the misuse of which he often dissociated himself, did, to be sure, change at a decisive point—but the matter on which it was based did not. It is only that *Erlebnis* is no longer that of polar unity, but that of the I and Thou in a state of relation, that of the finite and infinite person.

The I-and-Thou relationship is the basis of everything that is creative; it gives birth to the word that is speech and reply, the dialogical relation in which life is no longer a mere biological fact but is pervaded by spirit. In this relation there also originates, in a "timeless moment," the form [*Gestalt*] which only becomes a realized form when it seeks to prevail among the process of formation in the world of the It—a world out of which it is chiseled—and in which therefore, as Buber says, there is always a "mixture of Thou and It."

---

42. *Der Jude und sein Judentum,* pp. 7–8. (See *On Judaism,* op. cit., pp. 4–10.—Ed.)
43. *Schriften,* I, p. 152. (*I and Thou,* pp. 157–58.—Ed.)

This holds as true of art[44] as it does of religion.

Thus in the course of history, in the changes of the human element, ever new regions of the world and the spirit are elevated into form, called to divine form. . . . The spirit answers [to revelation] also by a viewing, a *constituting* viewing. Though we earthly ones never view God without the world, only the world in God, in this act of viewing we eternally constitute God's form. Form is a mixture also of Thou and It. In faith and cult it can harden into an object: but out of the essence of relation that survives in it, it again and again becomes the present. God is close to his forms as long as human beings do not remove them from Him. . . . When, however, the expanding movement of religion suppresses the contracting movement and form displaces God, then the countenance of the form is darkened, its lips are dead, its hands hang limp, it no longer knows God, and the world-house that is built around its altar, the cosmos grasped by spirit, crumbles, . . . [and] man, in the destruction of his truth, no longer sees what has happened there.[45]

Buber's talk of the cosmos grasped by spirit is to be understood as follows:

Every great culture, embracing a whole people, is based on an original event of encounter, on an answer to the Thou that once ensued at the point of its origin, on an essential act of the spirit. The latter, strengthened by forces directed to the same end in the following generations, creates a unique comprehension of the cosmos by the spirit—only through it does the cosmos of man become possible again and again; only now can man, with comforted soul, build houses for God's worship and human habitations out of a unique comprehension of space, only now can he fill the whirling time with new hymns and songs and fashion into form the community of man itself. But just so long as in his own life of action and passion he possesses that essential act [that is to say, the dialogue of I and Thou]; so long as he enters into this relation: that long he is free and thereby creative. If a culture no longer centers on a living, unceasingly renewed process of relation it hardens into an It-world, which is broken through eruptively only from time to time by the glowing deeds of isolated spirits.[46]

44. Ibid., pp. 104–105. (*I and Thou*, pp. 89–92.—Ed.)
45. Ibid., pp. 158–59. (*I and Thou*, pp. 166–67.—Ed.)
46. Ibid., p. 114. (*I and Thou*, p. 103.—Ed.)

The rapidly growing It-world, continually spreading itself out in the course of history, therewith also turns into the tyranny of rules and laws, against which the breakthrough of a new relation, a new dialogue, is directed in protest and in revolution. Again and again must the Thou-world be opened up in order to renew the decomposing form of the It-world. Here it becomes clear how intimately and firmly even the thoughts of the later Buber are linked to those of his earlier period. Buber still seeks to understand the creative, the process of the generation of configurations and forms [Formen und Gestalten] and has now, he is convinced, found in the doctrine of I and Thou and of the life of dialogue, the "Open Sesame" that grants him a new understanding of the phenomenon of the life of the spirit, and above all precisely of Judaism and its position in the world. After all, three of the four very comprehensive volumes, in which at the end of his life he collected his writings, are dedicated to his conception of Judaism: Volume Two of his Works, called the Writings on the Bible and Volume Three, Writings on Hasidism, and the volume The Jew and His Judaism, in which he put his fundamental insight to the test of a great example.

V

According to Buber, it must be said, the life of dialogue is the great discovery of Israel. "Israel understood—or, rather, lived—life as being-spoken-to and answering, speaking-to and receiving answers." [47] From the perspective of this basic insight, it is also possible to understand his conception of Jewish monotheism. He turns against the saying of Lagarde, one of the most profoundly learned and embittered anti-Semites, that the monotheism of the Jews stands "at the same level as that of the report of an NCO commanded to appear before the Commissariat, who reports the existence of only one item of some object or other." [48] According to Buber, monotheism bases itself on the fact

that the relationship of belief in accordance with its essence wishes to hold good for a whole lifetime and be effective during it.

47. Ibid., III, p. 742.
48. Paul de Lagarde, Mitteilungen, II (1887), p. 330.

. . . The uniqueness of monotheism . . . is that of the Thou and
the I-Thou relation, as long as the totality of the lived life does not
repudiate it. "Polytheism" turns every divine appearance—that is
to say every mystery of the world and of existence with which it
has to deal—into a divine being; the "Monotheist" recognizes in
everything once more the God he experienced by way of
confrontation.[49]

In other words:

Israel's Thou-experience of direct relation, the perfectly singular
experience, is so forceful that the idea of a multiplicity of
principles can no longer arise . . . the basic stance of the Jew can
be designated by the concept *yihud* (the unifying act), which is
frequently misunderstood. It concerns the incessantly renewed
confirmation of divine unity in the multiplicity of appearances,
and grasped quite practically at that: through human perception
and confirmation it happens again and again—in the face of the
enormous contradictoriness of life and especially in the face of
that primordial contradiction which announces itself in such
manifold fashion and which we call the duality of good and evil;
not with spite toward this contradictoriness but with love and
reconciliation—the unifying act [*Einung*] happens, which is to
say, the cognition, the recognition, the recognizing again of divine
unity. Not only in a credo but in the fulfillment of knowledge.
Therefore, not at all in pantheistic theorems, but in the actuality
of the impossible, in the realization of the image, in the *imitatio
Dei*. The mystery of this reality completes itself in martyrdom, in
dying with the call of unity "Hear O Israel" on one's lips, which
here serves as witness in the most living sense.[50]

For Buber, the Bible is the classic document of the situation
of dialogue and the life of dialogue. While before 1925 his
concern with the Bible had obviously not yet assumed any
productive forms, it stands at the center of his work for forty
years thereafter. From the perspective of his new vision, as he
presented it in *I and Thou*, he began in 1924—supported and
stimulated by Franz Rosenzweig's collaboration for five years—
to translate the Bible anew.[51] At the same time he undertook—in

49. *Schriften*, I, p. 629. (*Good and Evil: Two Interpretations* [New York: Charles
Scribner's Sons, 1953], pp. 103–104.—Ed.)
50. *Der Jude und sein Judentum*, pp. 188–89.
51. See my speech on Buber's translation of the Bible, in *The Messianic Idea in*

a never-ending stream of lectures, pieces, and larger works on the central clusters of the Biblical world of belief and ideas—to give an interpretative account of what he read; or, to say it better, of what came to him from the ancient words.

I have already said that Buber was a listener of great intensity. His attitude to the Bible was that to a document of revelation, but in saying that we must be clear as to the meaning of revelation in his usage. Buber does, to be sure—above all under the lasting influence of Rosenzweig's *Star of Redemption*— use the terminology of the theologians, when they speak of creation, revelation, and redemption as fundamental categories of Judaism. But as with so many religious thinkers, in his case the meaning of the old concepts shifts, and never more clearly than when he speaks of revelation, or, what amounts to the same thing with him, the word of God. Nor does he make a distinction, as, for example, recent Catholic theologians are wont to propose, between inspiration—in which human authors, even without being clearly conscious of it, are stimulated in their expression by God—and revelation, in which God Himself can be perceived to speak. For him the two spheres merge.

For Buber, revelation is an "affair of the Here and Now"—we must add: potentially in each and every Here and Now—"a present primordial phenomenon," namely that of the creative encounter between the I and the eternal Thou in calling and responding. And, in fact, the person receives in it not something like a "content," but a "presence as power." He does not receive a fullness of meaning but rather the guarantee that there is meaning, "the inexpressible confirmation of meaning." This meaning is not that of a different life, as for example, the life of God, but that of this, our life, "not that of an 'over there' but of this, our world." Thus revelation is the pure encounter in which nothing can be expressed, nothing formulated and defined. The meaning rooted in it can, according to Buber, find expression only in the deeds of man. The meaning cannot be transferred, cannot be distinctly expressed or impressed as generally valid knowledge; it cannot even

> become a valid imperative, is not inscribed on any tablets which might be set up above all human minds. Each man is able to

Judaism and Other Essays on Jewish Spirituality (New York: Schocken Books, 1971), pp. 314–19.

confirm only the received meaning with the uniqueness of his being and with the uniqueness of his life. Just as there is no precept that can lead us *to* the encounter, there is also none coming *out* of it.

This definition by Buber is, as must be stated candidly, a purely mystical definition of revelation. It is among Buber's most astonishing illusions that he believed to have left the sphere of mysticism with such words, indeed to have rejected it. Some years ago[52] I attempted to define in detail the kabbalistic concept of revelation and the word of God. In the decisive respect, Buber's statements belong to this sphere, with, however, the big difference that for the mystics historical revelation implies mystical revelation, in that the former is articulated and developed by the latter. There is, to be sure, no longer any talk of that in Buber. He knows only one revelation, and that is the mystical one, though he denies it this designation. At the end of the passage excerpted here, one reads:

That is the eternal revelation, the one present in the Here and Now. I know of none that in its basic phenomenon would not be the same; I believe in none. I do not believe in a revelation understood as God's naming Himself in a self-determination of God vis-à-vis man. . . . That which exists is and nothing more. The eternal wellspring of strength flows, the eternal contact tarries, the eternal voice resounds, and nothing more.[53]

In Buber's writings on the Bible, this concept is more or less loosely connected by way of interpretation with the historical phenomena, above all with the Sinaitic revelation as presented by the Bible, and with prophetic revelation, which is always held by Buber to be at once a mission and a summons to decision. Inadvertently his talk of the true dialogue between the I and the Thou turns into talk of true revelation. This becomes especially clear in the very remarkable exposition he dedicates to the revelation on Mount Sinai, or the "covenant at Sinai," between God and Israel in his book, *Königtum Gottes (Kingship of God)* (1932), which in general sticks fairly closely to the Biblical text.

52. See *The Messianic Idea*, pp. 292–98.
53. See *Schriften*, I, pp. 152–54. (*I and Thou*, pp. 157–60.—Ed.) On the eternal sounding of the voice that goes forth from Sinai, see the quotation from the kabbalist Meir ben Gabbai in *The Messianic Idea*, pp. 299–303.

In the reports of the Torah, which he considers unhistorical, he seeks the "core" of an original event, namely that "encounter" in the highest sense, and he finds the latter by the application of a purely pneumatic exegesis, the subjectivity of which bewilders the reader. In place of analysis, as it is often applied most fruitfully in his writings on the Bible, there appears, precisely in the most decisive pages of the book—dedicated to the religious origin of the Israelite theocracy in the covenant at Sinai—a pneumatic construction according to which the league of half-nomadic tribes who had wandered out of Egypt did not elevate its human leader to the position of king, but rather "erected theocracy on the anarchic ground of the soul." [54]

Buber's general mystical concept of revelation, as set forth here, is projected on what the religious tradition asserts to be specific and historical occurrences of revelation. Thereby Buber attains not only an extraordinary loosening of the texts which are the basis of historical Judaism as a religious society, but also the identification, defended by him, of revelations accepted by religious tradition and considered authoritative by it, with those revelations which at any time and place can fall to the lot of the intense listener.

> The mighty revelations by which religions take their bearings are
> in essence the same as the silent one which proceeds everywhere

54. *Schriften*, II, pp. 686 and 721 (*Kingship of God*, translated by Richard Scheimann [New York: Harper & Row, 1967], pp. 138, 161.—Ed.), as also in an only slightly more subdued tone in the exposition presented in the chapter "Holy Event" of his book *Der Glaube der Propheten* in *Schriften*, II, pp. 281–97. (*Prophetic Faith* [New York: Harper Torchbooks, 1960], pp. 43–59.—Ed.) By contrast the formulation is even sharper in *Schriften*, II, p. 856 (*On the Bible: Eighteen Studies*, edited by Nahum N. Glatzer [New York: Schocken Books, 1968], p. 9.—Ed.), where one reads about the Sinai revelation that it was

> the trace remaining in words of a natural event—which is to say an event that happened in the common world of the senses of human beings and adapted into it and its context—which the group experiencing it expressed as God's revelation to it and thus preserved as an enthusiastic, formative memory of generations that was free of caprice; this way of experiencing, however, is not a self-deception of the group, but its vision and its perceiving reason, for natural events are the bearers of revelation and revelation has occurred where the witness of the event, steadfast in the face of the latter, experienced the content as revelation, and where one could thus state what in such an event the voice speaking in it wished to say to the witness regarding his condition, his life, his duty.

Such a quotation shows clearly how Buber pneumatically loosens up the historical assertions of the Bible he can no longer accept, and inserts a thoroughly mystical concept of revelation—albeit in modern formulation—into the historical one.

and always. The mighty revelations which stand at the beginning of great communities, at the turning points of human time, are nothing other than the eternal revelation. But, after all, revelation does not pour into the world by using its recipient like a funnel [*it is, to be sure, precisely this that historical revelations do!* G.S.]; it lays its hands on him, it seizes his whole element of current being and fuses with it. Even the person who is the "mouth," is just that, and not a megaphone—not an instrument, but an organ, relating what has been heard in accordance with its own inner necessity; and to relate (*lauten*) means to translate (*umlauten*).[55]

Buber is a long way from asserting that the experience and grasp of the dialogical situation is a peculiarity of Judaism. He is, however, quite sure "that no other group of human beings has sacrificed as much energy and fervor to this experience as the Jews." [56] He could find the classical, and in the history of religion, unsurpassed exposition of this situation at its most convincing in the phenomenon of Biblical prophecy, and in his book, *Prophetic Faith* he seems to me to have reached the high point of his efforts to understand the Bible as a great dialogue. The prophet is the one who hearkens and to whom at the same time God's decrees and demands are clarified in symbols. He is, however, just as much the one who, in the certainty of his instructions and mission, summons up his people—in concrete historical situations—to a decision for the demands of God and their realization. He demands a conversion (*Umkehr*) of Israel, which in Hebrew is identical with the word for answer or response, as Buber often pointed out.

With great energy Buber depicted the significance of the call to conversion that succeeded in finding its expression in prophecy—a call not to the individual but to the community—for the latter's constitution as the religious society of Judaism. He depicted the failure of the call, the unfinished state of the never-completed dialogue as a constitutive element of Judaism. For the dialogical is in no way secure from a convulsive shift into the violent and destructive. Buber could have pointed out—I often wonder why he never did—that the first dialogue among human beings mentioned in the Bible, the one between Cain and Abel, also leads to the first murder.

55. *Schriften*, I, p. 158. (*I and Thou*, pp. 165–66.—Ed.)
56. *Der Jude und sein Judentum*, p. 190.

Next to the conception of dialogue in a mightily expanded sense, Buber was most concerned with the problem of messianism and redemption. Again and again he emphasized its central character for the understanding of Judaism in all its phases, down to its metamorphosis into the purely secular. In his writings on the Bible, he traced its origins; in his other writings, its effects and transformation in Judaism. In it he finds the strongest expression of Israel's tie to history as the arena of the decisive dialogical relationship and its realization. According to Buber, the eschatological hope of a future in which the deepest expectations between the I and the Thou would be actualized always contains a historical hope, which only becomes "eschatology" proper—a projection unto the end of days—through the growing disappointment in history. This disappointment has ever been, throughout almost 3,000 years, Israel's most bitter experience, precisely because of its ties to the historical. For faith, the messianic future becomes a radical historical turning point, indeed a radical overcoming of history. Later a new mythologization of this expectation breaks forth in messianic Utopianism. For faith mythologizes its object, and even if myth is not its substance, it is nevertheless "the language of expecting faith as well as remembering faith." [57]

In some notable pages about the Book of Isaiah, Buber attempts to show that originally the messianic expectation existed "in the full concreteness of the lived hour and its potential" and becomes strongly eschatological only when one reaches the great speeches of Deutero-Isaiah, a tranformation which for Buber coincides with a transformation of God that is decisive for the entire history of Judaism, from the Lord of history to the God of the suffering and the oppressed. Justice and love-in-action—the Hebrew word hesed can hardly be translated briefly in a different way—are as much the demand of the hour that supports the sufferer as they are the hope of the future in which they will be actualized on earth.

For Buber, however, the messianic idea is not a revolutionary idea, and that is certainly peculiar. The Messiah is, according to him, the one who fulfills "the person who finally fulfills the

---

57. *Schriften*, II, p. 490. (*Kingship of God*, op. cit., p. 14.—Ed.)

magnificent mandate, who in a human community with human forces and human responsibility sets up the divine order, which is to say the order of justice and love demanded by God." [58] For Buber in his later years, the call to that which is coming and to the new no longer represents a call to revolution—in strict contrast to his earlier years.[59] What is new is only the unfolding of the human into God's image, the human being who does not, say, "come over to the side of God but remains standing before his countenance in irrevocable dialogue." [60] Therefore Buber sees in the *imitatio Dei* the core of the Jewish ethic, which draws its life from the messianic tension, from the certitude of the eventual dominion of the good.

The messianic idea conjointly brings together creation and redemption, primordial beginning and end of time, as Buber sought to show, particularly in the cases of Deutero-Isaiah and Hasidism. God's creating is something that happens again and again, indeed something historical. "In the historical hour, for which the prophet speaks, He creates something new, for the sake of the work of redemption He creates a change of nature, which, however, is at the same time a symbol of spiritual change. . . . For the Deutero-Isaiah no theological demarcation exists between creation and history." [61]

Buber once more finds exactly this conception in the teachings of Hasidism. The foundation of Jewish messianism can be summarized, according to Buber, in the following sentence: "God wants to make use of man for the work of completing his creation." [62] Or, to formulate it in greater detail: "The lived moment of man stands in truth between creation and redemption, linked to creation in its *being* effected and to redemption in its *power* to effect; rather it does not stand between both but in both at once. For just as creation does not exist just for once at the beginning but constantly in the whole of time, so too redemption exists not just for once at the end but constantly in the whole of time." Just as God, according to the words of the

58. Ibid., pp. 349, 395. (*Prophetic Faith*, op. cit., p. 150, pp. 107–108.—Ed.)
59. Ibid., p. 468. (*Prophetic Faith*, p. 220.—Ed.)
60. Ibid., p. 399. (*Prophetic Faith*, p. 153.—Ed.)
61. Ibid., II, p. 461. (*Prophetic Faith*, p. 213.—Ed.)
62. *Schriften*, III, p. 752.

ancient Jewish prayer, renews the work of creation each day, so, according to Buber, does God permit and demand that in the sphere of redemption also, "his efficacy is joined incomprehensibly by the efficacy of the human person. The redemptive moment is real, not only for the sake of completion and perfection but also in itself." [63]

That these statements about creation and redemption in their Biblical as well as Hasidic aspects are most problematic and can be disputed with good reason need not be shown in detail here, where our task is to understand Buber. Suffice it to say that his points of emphasis and association betray an immense subjectivity, because for the texts to which Buber refers creation and redemption are, to be sure, complementary but not really parallel. Moreover, as true as it is that the constant renewal of creation corresponds to later Jewish doctrine, as little does the latter know of the redemptive moment of which Buber likes to speak so much and so completely in the spirit of religious existentialism. But for Buber this is a crucial point. "Only out of the redemption of complete everydayness can come the complete day of redemption." He considers it an error to see messianic Judaism as exhausted "by the belief in a unique event at the end of time and in a unique human figure as mediator of this event. The certitude of the collaborating force which is accorded to man connected the end of time with present life." We do, it is true, live in an unredeemed world, "but out of every human life connected to the world more than capriciously a seed of redemption falls into it and the harvest is God's." [64]

Buber's sharp turn against the revolutionary element in Jewish messianism is connected with another important point, his striking aversion to the apocalyptic. Buber is among those—no less than Franz Rosenzweig and a long line of liberal Jewish thinkers—who, at least in his later period, represent a tendency to remove the apocalyptic sting from Judaism. I have discussed this tendency in detail in my lecture, "Toward the Understanding of the Messianic Idea in Judaism." [65] It represents a legitimate tendency, opposed, to be sure, by one no less legitimate, bitterly rejected by Buber but extremely effective.

63. Ibid., p. 753.
64. Ibid., pp. 755, 757.
65. *The Messianic Idea*, pp. 1–36.

For Buber, the apocalyptic is a distortion and falsification of the prophetic impulse which arose under Iranian influence and about which he now has to say as many bad things as he did in his earlier period about the Law. An excellent expression of this attitude, which runs through all his later writings, can be found in his essay *Prophetie und Apokalyptik*.[66] Prophecy and Apocalypse represent two basic attitudes for him, and he takes a passionate position on them. The prophet who is addressed by God belongs himself in the midst of events, in which he wants to take a hand with his summons to conversion, and in which he participates by staking his whole self. For the task of the prophet is not to be a soothsayer but to confront people with alternative decisions. The apocalyptic man, by contrast, stands over against the midst of events; he sees in them an unalterable course which has now, when the end of time is dawning, become visible and which leads not to a fulfillment of history but to its annihilation; only then will arise the new eon, the world of Utopia, which follows the great catastrophe.

"For the seer the future is not something that comes into being; it has, as it were, been ever-present in heaven. That is why it can be 'unveiled' to the visionary and he can then unveil it to others." "A small measure of bad seed was sown in Adam's heart at the beginning" as is said in the apocalypse of the so-called fourth book of Ezra. Now the whole harvest must sprout, and only when it has been cut in the final catastrophe can the soil of the good appear. In place of decision in the sense of the prophets there is only the separation of the chosen from a fallen creation destined to doom. "The human being can accomplish nothing, but then there is no longer anything for him to accomplish." Buber sees an optimistic modern transformation of the originally pessimistic Jewish apocalyptic element in Karl Marx's vision of the future, whose "primordial prophetic ground" he denies because he sees in him an apocalyptic in secular form, who is indifferent to the inner change of human beings which precedes the change of the world, being only concerned with the unalterable course of events that will swallow up previous history

---

66. *Schriften*, II, pp. 925–42. The quotations in the following paragraph come from these pages. (The essay appears as "Prophecy, Apocalyptic, and the Historical Hour" in *On the Bible*, op. cit., pp. 172–87.—Ed.)

in a revolutionary way—and who thinks that the coming catastrophe of these events ought, if anything, to be hastened. In the modern version of the apocalyptic, which he finds not only in Marx but rediscovers among the Protestant theologians of Karl Barth's school, Buber sees a codification of all that which is most calculated to trigger his objections. He attempts to the best of his ability to minimize the significance of this factor in the history of Judaism.

Therewith, however, he was driven to a revision—albeit not a very decisive one—of his attitude toward the Law, in which the steadfastness of the conservative element as an antiapocalyptic factor now appears to him in a more positive light. This change of position stands out above all in *Pharisäertum*,[67] his 1925 essay against Oskar H. Schmitz. Now he no longer finds rigid legalism in the position of the Pharisees toward the Law. He acknowledges that a "living tradition" existed there

> which basically, it is true, wished to be nothing other than the taking over of something handed over, something orally preserved, but which in its reality nevertheless in every new generation gave new expression to every new situation: an expression, which to be sure, had to legitimize itself by its link with tradition, but in this process broadened and modified its stock and indeed changed matters.[68]

Buber goes so far as to say that "the Pharisees, when they ventured to interpret Scripture, projected it into the area of worldly events." This amounts to a new tone, of which little could be heard in Buber's earlier period. But Buber is still very far from according normative Judaism, *halakhah*, a central position, in his conception of Judaism. In his discussion of Christianity, which he undertook in his weakest book, *Two Types of Faith* (1950), and tied to a discussion—an extremely dubious one, to be sure—of the allegedly different meaning of faith, *emunah*, in Judaism and of *pistis* in the New Testament, the Law, and the attitude of Judaism and Christianity toward it, decidedly takes second place. In his other writings of this period as well, which proceed under the slogan of I and Thou, he distinguishes

67. *Der Jude und sein Judentum*, pp. 221–30.
68. Ibid., p. 222.

between the Commandment, which is the demanding address of revelation to man, and the Law, in which the summons is objectified and all too soon deteriorates and dies off in the It-World.[69] His pronouncements about the Law become more measured, but for what is close to his heart in his reflections on Judaism, the Law still means nothing.

VI

Buber's principal work in the grasp and interpretation of the great phenomena of Judaism concentrated on the Bible and Hasidim, which in his view coincided completely and in different forms proclaimed the same message of authentic Judaism, the realization of the genuine—maintained by him to be unmediated —relation of I and Thou in the lived moment, the relation lending life and meaning to all times and forms. But one may point to a difference in his attitude to these two areas which is most visible in his work and which ought to have set the reader thinking—had it ever been noticed. Buber's writings on the Bible present themselves, at least in their literary structure and manner of execution, as scientific analysis. They fit into the traditional framework of scientific questioning; they are circumscribed—by precise indications of sources and—compared to his other writings—a downright strikingly rich and seemingly ostentatious discussion of scholarly literature on the subject. His exegeses are, to be sure, as I have already said, pneumatic exegeses when it comes to the crunch. But it is pneumatic exegesis with learned notes, which cause its pneumatic character to recede a bit or even blot it out. His Hasidic writings, however, avoid all these accessories. They represent *ex cathedra* pronouncements which offer no encouragement of help or verification by their sources.

Here I may perhaps be permitted to mention something personal by way of illustration. Only once, in 1921, when I was still very young did I succeed, with great pressure, to bring Buber to the point of accompanying a book of his—*Der Grosse Maggid und seine Nachfolge* (*The Great Maggid and His Succesors*) with

69. *Schriften*, II, p. 1080.

references to his sources. I talked to him about the impetus such an inclusion would necessarily give to serious readers with a good knowledge of Hebrew to compare his stories with the originals and that, indeed, they were entitled to such a comparison. He promised to ponder the matter and as a compromise he finally added to the book a list of references that was, as he wrote to me, to be "printed separately in a small edition and sent free of charge to anyone interested." In this case there was at least a reference to the title and edition of the book that served as a source for each of the stories, though there still was no indication of exact page numbers. Even this concession, which so obviously went against his grain, disappeared from his later Hasidic books and editions and only in 1957 did he permit himself to be persuaded at least to include the titles of his source books for the Hebrew version of his *Tales of the Hasidim.* For him that was the utmost limit of his accommodation to historical and scientific discussion. He held too closely to the completely personal note he had lent to Hasidism to wish to expose it to the cold light of confrontation with traditional critical methods.

It was inconvenient for Buber to accentuate this difference between his attitude and that of pure research, and I myself only gradually became aware of the severity of that difference. When I visited him in Germany in 1932, I said to him, "Why don't you at long last write an expository work on the theology of Hasidism?" He replied, "I intend to do that, but only after you have written a book about the *kabbalah.*" I said, "Is that a deal?" He said, "Maybe." At the time I did not yet understand that he was unable to maintain a scholarly attitude toward this topic. It was a shattering experience for me to learn as much when, in 1943—two years after the publication of the book of mine he had been awaiting—I went to him so that, as I told him in advance, we could have a talk, in which I could explain to him my fundamental doubts about his interpretation of Hasidism; doubts which had grown during long years of continuous study of the texts and which I have aired elsewhere.[70]

Buber listened with great seriousness and with great tension.

70. "Martin Buber's Interpretation of Hasidism," in *The Messianic Idea of Judaism* (New York: Schocken Books, 1971), pp. 227–50.

When I was done he was silent for a very long time. Then he said slowly and stressing every word, "If what you are now saying were right, my dear Scholem, then I would have worked on Hasidism for forty years absolutely in vain, because in that case, Hasidism does not *interest* me at all." It was the last conversation I ever had with Buber about substantive problems of Hasidism. Words failed me. I understood that there was nothing more to be said.

Just as Buber's work on the Bible exhibits itself in the presentation of the Biblical text itself in the medium of his new translation and in the interpretive discussion of that text, so do his efforts on behalf of the Hasidic world of ideas resolve themselves in his collection of Hasidic anecdotes of didactic content, as represented most impressively in the *Tales of the Hasidim* and in the interpretive works in which he presents what he calls the "Hasidic message." Buber was aware of the paradox of his enterprise when he "directly expressed as message, the message to humanity which Hasidism did not wish to be, but was and is. Thus I express it as such against its will, because the world is in such great need of it today." [71] At the same time, however, he emphasizes that he has not "transposed" this message into "impenetrable abstraction," and has thus also tried to preserve the mythic forms in which the Hasidic essence expressed itself. In this he disassociated himself from the contemporary postulate of the demythologization of religion, for "myth is not the subsequent investiture of a truth of faith, it is the instinctual product of the creative vision and creative memory of what is overwhelming, and nothing abstract can be extracted in this case." [72] One must, however, say that, his own protests notwithstanding, he does not fail to engage in very far-reaching attempts in just that direction. The emphasis on those tendencies in Hasidism that according to him contain its message to the world and at the same time its innermost Jewish meaning is based in large part on a fusion of those tendencies through concepts forged by himself. His own contribution to the understanding of Judaism appears to the same extent in that act of forging as its analysis would render

71. *Schriften*, III, p. 741. (*The Origin and Meaning of Hasidism*, edited and translated by Maurice Friedman [New York: Harper Torchbooks, 1960], p. 22.—Ed.)
72. Ibid., p. 946.

visible what is problematic, that is to say questionable, about it.

While previously Hasidism appeared to Buber as a paradigm of "activist mysticism," he later finds in it a summons to an actualization of the I-Thou relation, which is realized in the concreteness of the world without any mystical transports. The characteristic mystical features, which he had previously accentuated, are now cast aside, or else they are reinterpreted. Remaining crucial to him are the transcendence of the separation between the sacred and the profane, the consecration and sanctification of *every* concrete deed, no matter of what it consists, a pansacramentalism which is to be "open toward the world, pious toward the world, in love with the world." [73]

The tendency toward the overcoming of the separation between the sacred and the profane which, according to Buber, attains to a "highly realistic perfection" in Hasidism, is also set off sharply for him against the background of an opposite tendency that meets the eye, a situation leading to a strict demarcation of the two spheres.[74] It is, after all, precisely the opposite tendency which fundamentally characterizes the world of *halakhah*, the Jewish order of life under the Law. Buber, however, looks at it this way: the separation of the two spheres is only provisional, for even according to older views the Law stakes out only that area which "has *already* been claimed for sanctification," while in the messianic world everything will be sacred. Thus the profane "can be seen as a preliminary stage of the sacred; it is that which has not yet been sanctified." [75]

It is in this sense that Buber interprets a famous saying by one of the great *tzadikkim*, Rabbi Menahem Mendel of Kotzk—a saying that, to be sure, had a completely different meaning in its original context—"God dwells wherever he is admitted." What matters, in other words, is the sanctification of everyday life. "What is necessary is not the attaining of deeds that consist of the sacramental or the mystical, what is necessary is the doing of what one is assigned to do, the habitual and obvious in its truth and pure aspect." [76]

73. Ibid., p. 844.
74. Ibid., p. 939.
75. Ibid.
76. Ibid., p. 812.

For Buber, that is the meaning of Hasidic pansacramentalism. Man has to fulfill his calling in the concrete world itself, not by way of mystical transports out of it or by way of esoteric or even magical performances in it. Buber contrasts the principle of the selection of sacramental materials and actions in the movement of the Protestant Reformation with the Hasidic attitude which, according to him, "knows that the sacramental substance is not to be found or maintained in the totality of things and functions but believes that it can be awakened and redeemed in every object and action," namely "through the fulfilling presentness of the whole, wholly dedicated person, through sacramental existence." [77]

What gives Buber's conception its specific tone is this acute stress of a tendency for which there is undoubtedly ample evidence in Jewish literature, and certainly in Hasidic literature especially. He has, to be sure, bought this particular conception at a high price, namely by a resolute disregard of those features in which the encounter with the concrete is interpreted as its transcendence, because in the true encounter—and that is the tenor of the decisive Hasidic texts—the concrete loses the character of its concreteness and is taken up into the divine. Upon closer inspection, Hasidism's "love affair" with the world turns out to be Buber's love affair with the world. The Hasidic attitude was much more dialectical than it appears in Buber. In Buber's later writings his heated polemic against all gnosis contributed to this unequivocal glorification of the "concrete." He considered Jewish *kabbalah* to be gnosis; with good reason, to be sure. While previously, in an excellent formulation, he had defined Hasidism as "*kabbalah* become ethos" [78] he now sees Hasidim—precisely when it is most characteristic—as the opposite of *kabbalah*. What he had previously seen, in a no less felicitous expression, as the "deschematization of mystery" [79] is now polemically overstated in antitheses.

Buber's predilection for exaggerated antitheses, which no longer pinpoint the real phenomena of faith, though they always contain a grain of truth, is a fundamental weakness of his work.

77. Ibid., p. 841.
78. Ibid., p. 15.
79. Ibid., p. 810.

His theses thereby more than once run the danger of flipping over into the absurd. The most radical formulations of what Buber's slogan of the sanctification of everyday life declares to be the basic tendency of a Hasidism that has left the kabbalistic element behind are to be found precisely in kabbalistic writings. For Buber, however, there is an eternal opposition between what he calls *Devotio* and gnosis. In his interpretation of Judaism he feels himself to be the spokesman of *Devotio* against gnosis, which he designates as a "great power in the history of the human spirit." [80] Gnosis is for him the presumption of a knowledge of God that does not behove us while *Devotio* signifies service to the divine, the presupposition of which is that the servant never understands his own self as *the* Self.

Though ever so little is gained by such antitheses for the understanding of historical phenomena, they all give an exact picture of Buber's conception. Even in his later phases he takes the side, as he did at the beginning, of that which cannot be formulated, the creative beginning and doing against all forms of the great religious traditions, which if one takes a closer look, are gnosis in Buber's sense, or corroded by it. He concedes that the gnostic element determines the mythical elements of Hasidism, but he denies—to the point of running the danger of manifest self-contradiction—that this has anything to do with the creative impulses which avail themselves of myth and transform it. The infinite slipperiness of his formulations permits him to surmount such contradictions.

Buber began his activity as spokesman for Judaism in his "Three Addresses on Judaism." In contrast to the great gesture represented by these speeches stand the speeches published in 1952 at the end of his life, which are permeated by deep resignation and depression. The voice has become soft, the spokesman stands at the brink of despair and is aware of the bitter irony that he, the philosopher of dialogue, never reached the point of engaging in a dialogue with his own people.[81] Few will be able to read these speeches—the legacy of an old man

80. Ibid., p. 953. This polemic against gnosis recurs very frequently in his later writings; see, for example, *Der Jude und sein Judentum*, pp. 194–97.

81. The situation was formulated very precisely in this way by one of his American critics, Chaim Potok, in *Commentary* (March, 1966), p. 49.

who once more summarizes the insight of his life—without being moved. At the high point of his life and influence, in a speech delivered in 1933, "Biblical Humanism," he had still answered with much greater assurance the questions he now poses for himself and leaves unanswered.[82] Previously he had contrasted Western humanism with the Biblical variety, which is to say the summons to become a person "worthy of the Bible," a person "who permits himself to be addressed by the voice speaking to him in the Hebrew Bible and who responds to it with his life."

Buber demands a rebirth of the normative primal powers to which life is subject.

> Even he who, like me, is . . . incapable of letting the Biblical word take the place of the voice, even to him it must be certain that we will never again truly attain to the normative in any other way except by making ourselves accessible to the Biblical word. . . . We are no longer a community which possesses [what was proclaimed by revelation], but if we open ourselves to the Biblical word . . . we may hope that those who are gripped in this way—differently and yet in common—will grow together again into a community in that original sense. . . . Biblical humanism, unlike the Western variety, is unable to lift one above the problems of the moment; it wishes to educate us to steadfastness in, and confirmation of, the moment. This present stormy night, these bolts of lightning hurling down, this threat of corruption: do not flee from them into any world of logos, into any world of perfect form; stand fast, hearken to the word in the thunder, obey, respond! This fearful world is the world of God. It challenges you. Confirm yourself as God's person in it!

These words sum up Buber's understanding of Judaism. Buber's activity is contained in the tension between the summons from the year 1933, marking the onset of the great catastrophe of the Jewish people, and the still, small voice of those speeches called "At the Turning Point." Perhaps the melancholy words of praise with which one of the great Hebrew poems of this century begins hold good for Buber, too:

> Blessed are those who sow but do not reap.

82. *Schriften*, II, pp. 1087–92. ("Biblical Humanism" appears in *On the Bible*, op. cit., pp. 211–16.—Ed.)

Walter Benjamin[*]

I

In 1965 it will be twenty-five years since Walter Benjamin—for as many years a close friend of mine—took his own life when, on his flight from the Germans, he had crossed the Pyrenees into Spain with a group of refugees, and the local official at Port-Bou threatened to turn them back and extradite them to France. He was forty-eight years old at the time. A life lived entirely beyond the footlights of the public scene, though linked with it through his literary activities, passed into complete oblivion, except for the few who had received an unforgettable impression from him. During over twenty years, from the onset of the Nazi era in Germany to the publication of a collection of the majority of his most important writings in 1955, his name was as thoroughly forgotten as any in the intellectual world. At best he was the subject of an esoteric whispering campaign that some of us assiduously promoted. It is due largely to the intense efforts of Theodor Wiesengrund Adorno that this has changed in the German-speaking world. Adorno never tired of pointing out Benjamin's towering stature; moreover, at a time when it was by no means easy to find a publisher for a venture of that kind, he succeeded in winning over the Suhrkamp Verlag for the publication of a two-volume edition of Benjamin's writings (*Schriften*). In the generation of authors as well as readers now coming into

[*] A lecture in German delivered at the Leo Baeck Institute, New York, October 1964. Published in *Neue Rundschau*, LXXVI (Frankfurt, 1965), pp. 1–21. English version published in *Yearbook of the Leo Baeck Institute*, X (London, 1965), 117–36; translated by Lux Furtmüller, and reprinted here, slightly revised.

its own, he is greatly respected as the most eminent literary critic of his time; some of his writings have come out in new editions, the large volume of selected writings, *Illuminations*, was published conspicuously and in a substantial edition, and in the course of the current year we can expect the publication of a fairly comprehensive selection of his letters—some of them very important—edited by Adorno and myself. They will present a picture of his life and work.

I first set eyes on Walter Benjamin late in the autumn of 1913 at a discussion between the Zionist youth and Jewish members both of Wynecken's "Anfang" group and the Free German Student Association, which he attended as the main spokesman of the latter group. I have forgotten what he said but I have the most vivid memory of his bearing as a speaker. This left a lasting impression because of his way of speaking extempore without so much as a glance at his audience, staring with a fixed gaze at a remote corner of the ceiling which he harangued with much intensity, in a style incidentally that was, as far as I remember, ready for print. I noticed the same behavior on some later occasions. At the time he was considered the best mind in that circle in which he was fairly active during the two years before the First World War, for a while as president of the Free Student Association at Berlin University. By the time I made his acquaintance—one day in summer 1915 during my first term, when we were following up a discussion on a lecture by Kurt Hiller who had treated us to a passionate rationalist debunking of history—he had completely withdrawn from his former circle. In the years 1915 to 1923 when, living in almost complete seclusion, he followed his studies and took the first steps to launch out beyond them I was on very close terms with him and spent much of that time, especially 1918 and 1919 in Switzerland, together with him. The problem of Judaism and its discussion occupied a central place in our relationship in those years. Between 1916 and 1930 Benjamin considered again and again, on various occasions and in the most different situations, whether he should not leave Europe and go to Palestine. Actually he never got beyond the initial efforts and preparations, and this, I am convinced, was not by accident. Late in the summer of 1923 I went myself to Jerusalem. In the following years he embarked—

hesitantly at first, afterwards, especially from about 1930, with growing determination—on the attempt to absorb historical materialism into his mental system and make it the basis of his literary production. During that period there were only two occasions, in Paris, when I spent days or even weeks in his company and we had lively, indeed at times tempestuous discussions about the new turn in his thinking, which I was unable to approve and considered a denial of his true philosophic mission. Until his death we conducted a correspondence which was very intense at times, and his letters are among my most precious possessions. Thus my picture of Walter Benjamin, though authentic in its way, has always been determined by personal decisions.

In his youth his character was marked by a profound sadness. I remember a postcard to him from Kurt Hiller who took him to task for his "unserene cast of mind." I would assume that his profound understanding of the nature of sorrow and its literary manifestations which dominates so many of his works is related to this trait. At the same time he had in his earlier years an element of personal radicalism, even personal ruthlessness, strangely contrasting with the almost Chinese courtesy that generally characterized his social intercourse. When I first came to know him, he had with utter harshness and lack of compunction severed nearly all relations with his friends of the youth movement, because they had ceased to mean anything to him. In the process he deeply hurt some of his former friends. In conversation he hardly ever mentioned such matters. That conversation of his—a meeting place of wit and gravity—was of extraordinary intensity. In it his passionate logic was probing depth after depth, and straining after ever greater precision of utterance. What thinking really means I have experienced through his living example. At the same time he had an effortless command of felicitous metaphors and striking images saturated with meaning yet always direct and to the point. Faced with unexpected views, he was utterly free of prejudice and sought to illuminate their sense or their place in a wider context from no less unexpected angles. This undogmatic manner of thinking contrasted with his pronounced firmness in judging people.

His most enduring personal passion was the collecting of

books. In him the author and the collector were combined in rare
perfection, and this passion added an admixture of gaiety to his
somewhat melancholy nature. An essay published in his
Schriften—"Unpacking my Library"—beautifully displays that
gaiety. We read there the sentence inspired by Jean Paul: "Of all
the methods of acquiring books, the one considered most
reputable is to write them," whereas "among the customary
means of acquisition the most genteel for collectors [is] that of
borrowing with subsequent nonreturn." His own library, which I
knew quite well, clearly mirrored his complex character. The
great works which meant much to him were placed in highly
baroque patterns next to the most out-of-the-way writings and
oddities, of which—both as an antiquarian and as a philosopher
—he was no less fond. Two sections of this collection have
remained most vividly in my memory: books by mentally
deranged authors and children's books. The "world systems" of
the mentally deranged, which he had brought together from I do
not know what sources, provided him with material for the most
profound philosophical reflections on the architecture of systems
in general and on the nature of the associations that nourish the
thinking and imagination of the mentally sound and unsound
alike.

But the world of the children's book meant more to him. It is
one of Benjamin's most important characteristics that throughout
his life he was attracted with almost magical force by the child's
world and ways. This world was one of the persistent and
recurring themes of his reflections, and indeed, his writings on
this subject are among his most perfect pieces. (Only some of
them are included in the *Schriften*.) There are the entrancing
pages on the subject in his volume of aphorisms, *One-Way Street*
(*Einbahn-strasse*), which include what must be the most beautiful
passages ever written about postage stamps; there are no less
outstanding essays about exhibitions of children's books and
related topics, works dedicated to the as yet undistorted world of
the child and its creative imagination, which the metaphysician
describes with reverent wonder and at the same time seeks
conceptually to penetrate. Further passages on this subject occur
very frequently in his other writings. To Benjamin the work of
Proust marks the point where the worlds of the adult and the

child are most perfectly interfused, and accordingly one of the cardinal points of his philosophical interest. Lastly, this fascination found an outlet in the records of his own childhood that he wrote down in the early 1930s under the title *A Berlin Childhood around 1900*. Much of this appeared at the time in the *Frankfurter Zeitung* in the form of separate pieces, but it was not published as a complete work, in the form originally conceived, until after World War II. Here poetry and reality have become one. It has often been asserted that Schelling, the philosopher, at the height of his creative powers wrote *Nachtwachen* (*Night Vigils*), one of the most important romantic prose works, under the pseudonym of "Bonaventura." It is not certain whether this is correct. If it were, it would be the most exact parallel to Benjamin's book, written as it is in a prose that combines crystal limpidity with continual pervasive movement and appears relaxed as well as thoroughly tough, a prose that could only have been conceived in the mind of a philosopher turned storyteller. "Narrative philosophy" was Schelling's ideal. In this book by Benjamin it has been achieved in an undreamt-of manner. The philosopher and his outlook is present behind every one of these pieces, but under the gaze of memory his philosophy is transmuted into poetry. Though lacking in all the attributes of a German patriot, Benjamin had a deep love for Berlin. It was as a Jewish child whose forefathers had been settled in the regions of Mark Brandenburg, Rhineland, and West Prussia that he experienced his native city. In his description the city's flagstones and its hidden corners, which open themselves up before the child's eye, are transformed back into a provincial island in the heart of the metropolis. "In my childhood I was a prisoner of the old and the new West, the two city quarters my clan inhabited at the time in an attitude of defiance mingled with self-conceit. This attitude turned the two districts into a ghetto upon which the clan looked as its fief." How a child of that golden ghetto explores its length and breadth, how he shines the light of his imagination into all its corners as if it were the child's universe, was brought vividly to life by Benjamin thirty years later in his recollections.

It was the small things that attracted him most. To create, or discover, perfection on the small and very smallest scale was one of his strongest urges. Authors like Johann Peter Hebel or the Hebrew writer S. Y. Agnon, who achieved perfection in stories of the smallest compass, enchanted him time after time. That the greatest is revealed in the smallest, that—as Aby Warburg used to say—"The Lord God dwells in the detail": these were fundamental truths to him in many ways. This inclination lends a special note to his volume, *One-Way Street*. For what matters here is not the aphoristic form but the underlying intention: to present in the briefest literary utterance something complete in itself. The same trait was manifest in his handwriting which reflected that extreme bent toward smallness, yet without the slightest sacrifice of definition or accuracy in his minutely shaped characters. It was his never-realized ambition to get a hundred lines onto an ordinary sheet of notepaper. In August 1927 he dragged me to the Musée Cluny in Paris, where, in a collection of Jewish ritual objects, he showed me with true rapture two grains of wheat on which a kindred soul had inscribed the complete *Shema Israel.*

II

In the years that have passed since the publication of his *Schriften*, a good deal has been written about Benjamin, much of it silly or petty. He had too strong an element of the enigmatic and unfathomable in his mental makeup not to provoke that sort of thing. And his critics' misunderstandings would surely have been a source of amusement to him who even in his brightest hours never abandoned the esoteric thinker's stance. As Adorno said very aptly about him, "What Benjamin said and wrote sounded as if born of mystery, yet its force derived from cogency." The peculiar aura of authority emanating from his thought, though never explicitly invoked, tended to incite contradiction, while the rejection of any systematic approach in all his work published after 1922—a rejection that he himself proclaimed boldly from the hoardings—screened the center of his personality from the view of many.

That center can be clearly defined: Benjamin was a philosopher. He was one through all the phases and in all the fields of his activity. On the face of it he wrote mostly about subjects of literature and art, sometimes also about topics on the borderline between literature and politics, but only rarely about matters conventionally considered and accepted as themes of pure philosophy. Yet in all these domains he derives his impulse from the philosopher's experience. Philosophical experience of the world and its reality—that is how we can sum up the meaning of the term *metaphysics*, and that is certainly the sense in which it is used by Benjamin. He was a metaphysician; indeed, I would say, a metaphysician pure and simple. But it was borne in on him that in his generation the genius of a pure metaphysician could express itself more readily in other spheres, any other sphere rather than in those traditionally assigned to metaphysics, and this was precisely one of the experiences that helped to mold his distinctive individuality and originality. He was attracted more and more—in a fashion strangely reminiscent of Simmel, with whom otherwise he had little in common—by subjects which would seem to have little or no bearing on metaphysics. It is a special mark of his genius that under his gaze every one of these subjects discloses a dignity, a philosophic aura of its own which he sets out to describe.

His metaphysical genius flowed from the quality of his relevant experience, its abounding richness pregnant with symbolism. It was this latter aspect of his experience, I believe, which invests many of his most luminous statements with the character of the occult. Nor is this surprising. Benjamin was a man to whom occult experiences were not foreign. Rarely though—if ever—do they appear in his work in their immediate unprocessed form. (This is presumably why he was able to recapture the occult character of Proust's decisive experience with unsurpassed precision.) In his personal life, incidentally, this trait found expression in an almost uncanny graphological gift of which I witnessed a good many instances. (Later on he tended to conceal this gift.)

Even where he takes up controversial topics of literary and general history or politics as his starting point, the metaphysician's eye penetrates deep below the surface, and reveals in the objects of his discourse fresh layers bathed in a light of strange radiance. In his earlier works he seems to describe the configuration of such layers as if writing under dictation, while later on this immediacy gives way to an increasingly precise understanding of the tension and the dialectic motion astir in his subjects. He proceeds from the simplest elements, and entirely unexpected vistas open themselves up to him; the hidden inner life of his subjects is manifest to him. His discursive thinking commands great trenchancy, as displayed, for instance, in his first book, on the concept of art criticism among the early German romantics. In most of his work, however, this discursive element of strict conceptual exposition takes second place to a descriptive method by which he seeks to let his experience speak. It is this descriptive method which seems so strangely to open his subjects up to him, and which invests even short papers and essays of his with a character at the same time fragmentary and final.

To say that Benjamin is a difficult author would be an understatement. His major works demand an unusual degree of concentration from the reader. His thought was greatly compressed and inexorable in the often excessive brevity of exposition. Accordingly, his works—if I may say so—need to be meditated upon. At the same time they are written in a masterly prose of rare incandescence. His essay on Goethe's *Elective Affinities* (*Wahlverwandtschaften*), which moved Hofmannsthal to enthusiasm, combines in a manner unique in aesthetics the highest elevation of style with the deepest thought. The same applies to the last section of his book on the *Trauerspiel*. By contrast many of his smaller and smallest pieces—especially the essays in *Die Literarische Welt, Die Gesellschaft,* and *Frankfurter Zeitung*—are written with a gusto and facility of expression that seem to veil the profundity of interpretation. As his masterpiece in this genre I would rate the essay on Gottfried Keller, although others—for instance those on Johann Peter Hebel, Paul Scheerbart, Robert Walser, Nikolai Leskov, and Max Kommerell—come close to it. No wonder that the combination came off, sprang into life spontaneously as it were, where he was able to pay homage. Among the scholars of his own generation in the field of German literary history there was but one whom Benjamin recognized without reservation, "notwithstanding the decisive difference of his own views [as a Marxist?] from the author's." Yet this was not a Marxist like Georg Lukács, or some other "Left" author, but a man from the opposite camp. It was Max Kommerell, younger by several years, who had broken free from Stefan George's school and who, later on, by a stroke of irony, was granted the *venia legendi* in German literature at Frankfurt University that had been denied to Benjamin on his one and only bid for an academic position. He admired in him the very qualities which he himself so conspicuously possessed, although he used them very differently: "The mastery of physiognomic description and the dynamic range of his understanding which assessed not only the characters, but also, and above all, the historical constellations in which they encountered one another."

His metaphysical genius dominates his writings, from the unpublished "Metaphysics of Youth," which he wrote in 1913 at the age of twenty-one, to the "Theses on the Philosophy of History" of 1940, his latest extant piece of writing. It is manifested especially in two spheres that increasingly interpenetrate in his work: the philosophy of language and the philosophy of history. The one bent led to a growing preoccupation with literary critical analysis, the other similarly to social-critical analysis. But throughout it was always the philosopher speaking, unambiguous, an unmistakable voice. For about ten years he upheld the concept of the philosophic system as the form proper to philosophy, after which he himself was groping. Kant exerted a lasting influence on him, even where—as in the recently published "Program of the Coming Philosophy"—he passionately challenges the validity of the experience expressed in that philosophy. He expected that an experience of infinitely greater richness would still have to be fitted into what was basically Kant's frame of reference, however great the necessary modifications. But this ideal of the system, reflecting the traditional canons of philosophy, was corroded and eventually destroyed in his mind by a skepticism that stemmed in equal proportions from his study of neo-Kantian systems and from his own specific experience.

Margarete Susman has referred to an "exodus from philosophy" said to have occurred in Germany after World War I and to have ushered in a completely new mode of thinking. What she meant, to judge from her examples, was the tendency to turn from idealism to existentialism and theology. Few men can have provided more drastic an illustration of this exodus than Walter Benjamin, who forsook systematic philosophy to dedicate himself to the task of commenting on the great works, a task which at that time—with his prime interests still belonging to theology— he considered preliminary to commenting on sacred texts. This goal, though clearly envisaged, he never reached; the provisional, halfway stage remained the ever-changing and yet enduring field for his productivity, and the form of his philosophy was determined by the method of commentary. After the liquidation of the driving force of system, a dialectic unfolds in his commentaries that seeks to record the intrinsic movement of each object of contemplation at its specific historical locus. True, everything is still viewed from one common angle of vision here, but the separate pieces can no longer cohere into a unified system, which in his eyes became increasingly suspect of brutality.

The themes of most of his papers now become those of literary criticism, different though Benjamin's writings in this field are from the customary ingredients of that genre. Only rarely are his analyses and reflections literary in the conventional sense of being concerned with the structure and value of an important work. They are almost invariably philosophical prob- ings of their specific and in particular their historical aura, to use a concept that often recurs in his writings, seen from many different angles. Each of his pieces outlines, as it were, an entire philosophy of its subject. Clearly, having set himself the task of interpreting and plumbing the depths of the great works of literature—in his eyes, incidentally, greatness did not always coincide with public fame—the philosopher did not surrender to the methods of literary history he had come to recognize as more than dubious, but worked all the time with the inheritance of the philosophical inspiration that never deserted him. He was at his most inspired where he felt the appeal of a kindred impulse or an inspiration close to his own—nowhere more so than in the cases of Marcel Proust and Franz Kafka to whose world he devoted years of intense exploration, of impassioned reliving and de- tached rethinking. In such cases there were virtually no limits to the overflowing metaphysical richness at his command in re- capturing the unique historical situation that he saw reflected in these works, its very uniqueness manifesting complete universality. It is nearly always this combination of historical cum philosophical insight with a wide-awake and highly articulate awareness of artistic values that turns his essays—and sometimes the shortest among them in particular—into true masterpieces. What was the anatomy of the imagination of "his" authors— though in fact he was theirs, possessed rather than self-possessed —and how was the mainspring of their imagination connected in each case with the characteristic tension of the historical and social ambience that determined their production? These were the questions that fascinated him.

To Benjamin, mystics and satirists, humanists and lyricists, scholars and monomaniacs are equally worthy of philosophical study in depth. As he proceeds he is liable without warning to switch from the profane to the theological approach, for he has a precise feel for the outline of theological substance even when it seems dissolved altogether in the world of the wholly temporal. And even where he thinks that he can successfully avail himself of the materialist method, he does not close his eyes to what he has perceived with the utmost clarity. For all his renunciation of system, his thought, presented as that of a fragmentarian, yet retains a systematic tendency. He used to say that each great work needed its own epistemology just as it had its own metaphysics. This constructive tendency in his mode of thinking —constructive even where applied to destructive facts or phenomena—also conditions his style. Meticulously pointed, shining with a contemplative luster that refuses the slightest concession to the fashionable expressionist prose of those years, this style is deeply embedded in the processes of a mind striving after order and cohesion. Benjamin's "texts" really are what the word says: "woven tissues." Although in his youth he was in close personal contact with the rising expressionism which celebrated its first triumphs in Berlin at that time, he never surrendered to it. In his best works the German language has achieved a perfection that takes the reader's breath away. It owes this perfection to the rare achievement of blending highest abstraction with sensuous richness and presentation in the round, and thus bears the hallmark of his notion of metaphysical knowledge. In a wonderful fashion his language, without abandoning depth of insight, closely

and snugly fits the subject it covers and at the same time strives
in competition with the subject's own language from which it
keeps its precise distance. I know very few authors of this
century whose writings include a comparable number of pages of
sheer perfection. The tension between the language of Benjamin's analyses or interpretations and the texts on which they are
based is often stupendous. The reader—if I may use a mathemati-
cal simile—finds himself between two transfinite classes recipro-
cally related, though not by a one-to-one correspondence. The
perfection of language in Goethe's *Elective Affinities* or in Karl
Kraus's polemical pages is matched in Benjamin's treatment of
those works by the new beauty of the interpreter's language,
which seems to descend from the language of a recording angel.
Small wonder, then, that Hofmannsthal was overwhelmed by the
long essay on the *Elective Affinities*; small wonder, too, that
Kraus, while acknowledging that the essay devoted to him was
"well meant," did not understand a word of it.

In his finest works, philosophy in a converted form, transfigured as it were and pellucid, recedes into a wonderfully
concentrated language of humanity. In the flow of periods it
becomes visible only as an aura. Benjamin's greatest achievements in this direction are *A Berlin Childhood around 1900* and
his introductions to letters from the century 1783–1883 that he
had collected and published under the pseudonym of Detlev
Holz at the end of 1936 during the Hitler era in the volume
Deutsche Menschen which, in dedications to friends, he described as "an ark I built when the fascist deluge began to rise."
This volume owed its utter anonymity—its shining brilliance
radiating inwards and never penetrating to the public—to the
grotesque circumstances of its publication by a forgotten Swiss
publisher who soon after went bankrupt. For many years
collectors paid high prices for secondhand copies of the allegedly
lost book until—not untypical of the fate of Benjamin's work in
general—the bulk of the original edition was found stored in the
cellar of a Lucerne bookseller, just when the book had been
reprinted in Germany in 1962.

III

For more than two years Benjamin worked to attain habilitation as a *Dozent* (lecturer) in modern German literature at Frankfurt University, encouraged at first by the head of the department, Professor Franz Schultz, who promptly backed out as soon as he received the thesis, covering his retreat with polite maneuvers. He and the head of the Aesthetics Department, Professor Hans Cornelius, complained in private that they did not understand a word of the work. Yielding to strong pressure, Benjamin unfortunately agreed to withdraw the thesis, which was sure to be rejected. He had already lost his rapport with the university and with the university way of organizing the pursuit of learning. Having felt obliged to undertake the attempt, its failure in circumstances bound to arouse bitterness nevertheless moved him to a sigh of relief, expressed in his letters. He was all too well aware of the kind of game that was being played in the academic disciplines of philosophy and literary history. Yet, by withdrawing the paper as a thesis, he lost the opportunity of publishing it with a foreword that would have recorded for posterity the ignominy of the university that turned the thesis down. He had actually written the foreword and it is still in my possession. Indeed, it may be said that this paper—published in 1928 under the title *Der Ursprung des deutschen Trauerspiels* (*The Origin of German Tragic Drama*)—is one of the most eminent and epoch-making habilitation theses ever submitted to a philosophical faculty. Its rejection, which set Benjamin finally on the road of the free-lance writer—or more aptly of the *homme de lettres*—compelled to earn his living by his pen, was a symbol of the state of literary scholarship and the mentality of the scholars during that Weimar period that has lately been the subject of so much praise. Even when it was all over, long after World War II, a highly equipped representative of that branch of learning was capable of dismissing the failure of Benjamin's academic bid with the nefarious and insolent phrase that "one cannot habilitate *Geist*." It was in keeping with that state of affairs that the book, when published, encountered a profound silence, and that in the years before Hitler only one specialized journal deigned to review it.

Admittedly, Benjamin did not make things easy for his readers. He prefaced his book with a chapter on epistemology in which the guiding philosophical ideas underlying his interpretation were flaunted as a warning to the reader rather than explained. The secret motto behind it—he used to say—was the nursery rhyme's injunction: "Hurtle over root and stone, ware the boulder, break no bone." This introduction has always frightened off many readers. It stands forbiddingly in front of the book—an angel with the flaming sword of abstract reason by the gates of a paradise of the written word. Benjamin held in reserve the advice to potential readers to skip the chapter and return to it at the end, but he did not make this generally known. Accordingly the experts' silence, which for years enveloped the book like a heavy veil, is to some extent understandable.

It is impossible to deal in a few words with this immensely rich book, the only one, incidentally, which Benjamin ever completed as such. In his philosophical exploration and dynamic portrayal of German tragic drama in the Baroque period, his main object was to vindicate the philosophical reputation of the category that was crucial not only to tragic drama but to the world of the Baroque altogether: the category of Allegory, whose hidden life nobody has more movingly recaptured than Benjamin in this work. He was perfectly aware that German tragic drama could not stand comparison with the accomplished forms of Baroque drama in the hands of a Calderón or Shakespeare, but the very uncouthness and crudity of construction of the works seemed to him to bring out all the more clearly the structure and interplay of the motive ideas working in them. What ostensibly was intended as a continuation or imitation of classical tragedy, with its roots in the world of mythology, is here recognized as its counterimage, decisively determined by wholly different spiritual patterns. Benjamin undertook to show how aesthetic ideas are most intimately bound up with theological categories. It was his aim to uncover the inner life, the dialectic movement in the fundamental concepts of that world of Baroque allegory, indeed to reconstruct it out of that dialectic. That he did succeed is perhaps the outcome of the special way in which here the philosophy of language and the philosophy of history, though dialectically dissociated, are fused in his metaphysical attitude in

a union fed—through channels at that time still unobstructed—
by the most fertile impulses of his thought.

In his later works the materialist method—however subtly
and (if I may say so) heretically he applies it—to some extent
intrudes between his intuition and its conceptual exposition, and
to the same extent that union becomes again problematic. He
sought to identify his dialectic—the dialectic of a metaphysician
and theologian—with the materialistic dialectic, and for doing so
paid a high price—too high a price, I would say. About those
works which Benjamin conceived under the aegis of historical
materialism a critic has said that at any rate his interpretation of
the doctrine was "so brilliant and self-willed that it escapes the
characteristic boredom usually engendered by the purblind
application of that system to literary history in particular." There
is a good reason for that self-willedness, for the idiosyncratic trait
in his materialism. To Benjamin, the approach of historical
materialism was a heuristic method which, he said, had to be
checked against its results every time to see how far it would take
one in earnest, but which at least held out some promise of a way
out of the manifest bankruptcy of bourgeois literary scholarship.
From his point of view, then, he was embarking on a large-scale
experiment when working with that method which, he hoped,
would prove the best vehicle for the expression of his dialectic
insight.

Now it may be said that in the course of the interminable
discussions that have raged during the past forty years about the
nature of historical materialism and of the Marxist method in
general, interpretations so vastly different were put forward that
they might be thought to cover almost anything. From what
Benjamin called the "unsubtle analysis" of Kautsky and Mehring
in *Die Neue Zeit*, the path leads, somewhat tortuously, to modes
of reasoning where Marxism itself is again so deeply embedded in
the Hegelian world of thought where its origin lies that the
differences become problematical. It could be argued that this is
Benjamin's position; but I do not believe that it is. Indeed, the
peculiar self-willedness of Benjamin's materialism derives from
the discrepancy between his real mode of thought and the
materialist one he has ostensibly adopted. His insights are in all
essentials still those of the metaphysician who, it is true, has

evolved a dialectic of inquiry, yet one that is worlds apart from the materialist dialectic. His insights are those of a theologian marooned in the realm of the profane. But they no longer appear plainly as such. Benjamin translates them into the language of historical materialism. Sometimes it happens in a flash, and then the translation turns out well and serves its purpose. At other times the operation is carried out all too laboriously and self-consciously. Deep insights of the philosopher of history and of the critic of society, which have their source in his own entirely metaphysical mode of thinking, are thus presented in materialistic disguise. I have certainly found no evidence that such insights ever flow from the use of the materialistic method itself, least of all in the most admirable works of his late period. Herein lies both the strength and the weakness of those works. Their strength, because the undiminished fertility of his intuition is still revealed in the subjects of his inquiry, and so seems to invest the materialist approach with tremendous depth and inexhaustible riches. Their weakness, because his genius tends to forsake its very essence in that transplantation, and this brings a shadowy and ambiguous element into some of his works. It is not hard to distinguish between the method and the insights accommodated in it. The critical reader still stands to profit abundantly. Yet it seems to me that there is undeniably something disjointed in those works as a result of that contradiction.

Yet, whenever his intuition was allowed to flow freely without being forced into the materialist mold, Benjamin was able, even in that late period, to produce works of compelling force and inviolate beauty unmarred by the faintest false note. This is demonstrated by some of his later essays, foremost among them "The Storyteller, Reflections on the Works of Nikolai Leskov"—writing of a quality unexcelled in its own genre—and the great essay on Franz Kafka. In contrast there stand two great pieces from the last five years of his life that embody the most valuable results of his attempt to commit his thought with utter intensity to the materialist categories and establish the affinity, or indeed identity, of the two worlds. They are "The Work of Art in the Age of Mechanical Reproduction" and "On Some Motifs in Baudelaire." The former was for a long time only available in a

French translation, which presented formidable hurdles to understanding, until the German text at last became accessible in 1955.
This essay—on which André Malraux drew amply for his
philosophy of art—is one of the most important contributions of
the last generation to the philosophy of art and can be
confidently expected to remain a potent influence. And yet, even
in the magnificent design of what Benjamin considered the first
serious materialist theory of art, the reader is struck by a glaring
discrepancy between the two parts.

The first part offers a metaphysical-philosophical interpretation hinging on the concept of the *aura* of a work of art—defined
by him as "unique revelation of a distance, however close"—and
its loss in the photomechanical process of reproduction. This part
is packed with exciting discoveries and illuminations of problems
in the philosophy of art which he was the first to perceive. It rests
on a purely metaphysical concept taken over from the mystical
tradition. In the contrasting second part, on the other hand,
Benjamin attempted to develop from Marxist categories what I
am inclined to describe as an enchantingly wrongheaded philosophy of the film as the one true revolutionary form of art. Against
the background of Chaplin's art he analyzes the reality and the
Utopian potential of the film, with its promise of infinite
happiness.

Benjamin pinned the highest historical hopes on the cinema
as the art form proper and congenial to the proletariat on the
threshold of its rule. In a long passionate conversation about this
work in 1938, he said in answer to my objections, "The missing
philosophic link between the two parts of my essay, about which
you complain, will be supplied more effectively by the Revolution than by me." I would say his Marxist faith had an element of
naïveté that was utterly alien to his thinking. This thinking once
more emerges in its full stature in his paper on one of his favorite
authors, Baudelaire. In its most superb section, where he uses
philosophical-historical analysis to deduce Baudelaire's situation,
that inherent contradiction which we have discussed here is all
but completely laid bare.

Even as a historical materialist Benjamin, apart from one
exception, is preoccupied only with so-called "reactionary"
authors such as Proust, Julian Green, Jouhandeau, Gide, Baude-

laire, and Stefan George. The exception is Brecht, who for years held Benjamin spellbound and fascinated. Brecht, after all, was the only author in whom he was able to observe the creative processes of a great poet at close quarters. Also, he had much in common with Brecht's at first strongly anarchistically tinged brand of communism. Although Brecht did not provide the first impulse, it was undoubtedly his influence which made Benjamin attempt in earnest to absorb historical materialism into his thinking and his work or even to fit all his thinking and work into the frame of historical materialism. Brecht, the tougher of the two, left a profound imprint on the more sensitive nature of Benjamin, who had nothing of the athlete in him. That it was in any way for Benjamin's good is more than I would dare to claim. Rather, I am inclined to consider Brecht's influence on Benjamin's output in the thirties baleful, and in some respects disastrous.

From 1927 on Benjamin worked on, apart from his published writings, a plan for another book in which he intended to fuse and at the same time test his historical-philosophical and his poetic intuition by tackling a subject of the highest order. The project underwent many transformations. It began as an essay "Paris Arcades"—passages dating from the middle of the nineteenth century, framed with shops and cafés that became a characteristic feature of the city. But the subject kept expanding into an historical-philosophical work for which he eventually chose the title *Paris—Capital of the Nineteenth Century (Paris— Hauptstadt des 19. Jahrhunderts)*. The book was never finished, and this may be put down as much to his precarious material circumstances which did not leave him enough time either for meditation on his theme or for its final execution, as to his mental development which led to a point where the project appeared to him a self-liquidating venture. Here, indeed, the philosophy of history and the philosophy of language were to have merged with such finality and cogency that the philosopher's comments became redundant. Eventually the ideal form of the work—unattained, unfinished, and presumably unfinishable—was conceived as a montage of quotations from the literature of the period that was to epitomize the Marxist metaphysician's analysis which, coming full circle, had now returned to its sources. Thus the work was designed as a lucid counterpart to the profundities of the book on tragic drama. Impracticable as the idea proved to be in the end, we owe to Benjamin's unremitting endeavors in those long years a large number of important drafts and completed manuscripts of varying length on a variety of themes both in his immediate and in his wider field. Some of the most important were published at the time in the *Zeitschrift für Sozialforschung* and some others later from his posthumous papers. Benjamin's sketches and selected excerpts from his source material for the Parisian book were found among these valuable posthumous papers that—unlike their author—safely survived the troubled war years in France, hidden away in the Bibliothèque Nationale, and have yet much to contribute to a better appreciation of his way of thinking.

IV

There is a profound difference between the main body of Jewish authors who have become famous in German literature and one group among them that is very small, though of the highest rank. Those in the former group—including in the last generation such writers as Arthur Schnitzler, Jakob Wassermann, Franz Werfel, Stefan Zweig—unquestioningly look upon themselves as forming part of German culture and tradition, as belonging to the German people. It was a lurid and tragic illusion. Berthold Auerbach, one of the first authors of that type, at the end of his life and at the beginning of Stoecker's anti-Semitic movement, summed it up in words that have become famous, though, alas, they were spoken into the void: "In vain have I lived, in vain have I suffered." Only very few among the first-rate minds of German-speaking Jewry did not succumb to that illusion. Freud, Kafka, and Benjamin belong to those few. Almost throughout their productive lives they shunned German phraseology, even the phrase "we Germans," and they wrote in full awareness of the distance separating them from their German readers. They are the most distinguished among the so-called German-Jewish authors, and it is as much their lives that bear witness to that distance, its pathos and its creative quality or potentiality, as their writings in which things Jewish figure rarely if at all.

They did not fool themselves. They knew that they were German writers—but not Germans. They never cut loose from that experience and the clear awareness of being aliens, even exiles, that most other authors from among the German-Jewish elite labored with so much earnest and ardor and yet with utter lack of success to evade or repudiate. Closely as they knew themselves tied to the German language and its intellectual world, they never succumbed to the illusion of being at home—an illusion, it is true, against which they were forearmed by specific personal experiences (though these availed nothing in other cases). I do not know whether these men would have been at home in the land of Israel. I doubt it very much. They truly came from foreign parts and knew it.

Benjamin undoubtedly had his quirks. I have sometimes been asked whether his attitude toward Judaism was not perhaps one of those quirks to which he clung with all his obstinacy. But this is not the case. On May 25, 1925, shortly after the world of Marxist dialectic had first appeared in his field of vision, he said in a letter that two crucial experiences lay still ahead of him: contact with Marxist politics (he still thought little of the theory of Marxism at the time) and with Hebrew. This statement provides a key to the understanding of Benjamin, for these are precisely the two experiences that never came his way. It is a deeply and authentically revealing statement in a matter where my own personal experience, which in any case is scarcely communicable in a convincing way, might be found inconclusive.

When we inquire after the Jewish element in this man and his production, it is entirely in character with Walter Benjamin's contrariness and complexity that the Jewishness of which he was intensely aware as the root of his being, and often also as the ultimate destination of his thought, should be present only in overtones in the bulk of his work, though admittedly in very conspicuous places, for instance in the prospectus for the projected journal *Angelus Novus*, or in the "Theses on the Philosophy of History," his last work. But there is much more behind it.

In the years of withdrawn study and preparation during

World War I and immediately afterward, the phenomenon of Judaism occupied him a great deal, and he read sporadically but widely about the subject. When I told him in 1916 that *Philosophy of History or Reflections on Tradition (Philosophie der Geschichte, oder über die Tradition)*—a large four-volume work on the *kabbalah* by Franz Joseph Molitor, a pupil of Franz von Baader—published sixty to eighty years earlier, was surprisingly still available at the publishers', this was one of the first works on Judaism which he acquired. For many years it occupied a place of honor in his library. In Franz Rosenzweig's *Star of Redemption*—the most original work of Jewish theology of our generation, of which Benjamin, on the evidence of many of his own writings, was an avid reader—as well as in the kabbalist writings, he experienced that profound attachment of genuine Jewish theological thinking to the medium of language that became so marked a feature of his own work. In letters and conversations, he returned time after time to Jewish issues, and while going out of his way to emphasize his own factual ignorance, he would yet quite often approach them with his relentless intensity and delve into problems of Judaism as a matter that concerned him personally and fundamentally. Many a letter of his stands as a curious testimony to this interest.

In the autumn of 1916, Benjamin was writing to a correspondent to whom he usually gave his views on literary subjects. In connection with some remarks about the writer Rudolf Borchardt—who had tried so hard to blur his Jewish origin—Benjamin felt impelled to write an enthusiastic epistle in praise of Judaism. He had just read Ahad Ha-am and been profoundly impressed by his essay "The Law in the Heart" (*Die Thora im Herzen*). Benjamin even said it was not certain whether he would not himself go to Palestine after the war. His correspondent, also a Jew, wrote in his reply in December 1916 that he had been amazed by Benjamin's profession of faith in Judaism and found it altogether inexplicable unless there was a woman behind it. I can still see Benjamin's sly winks when he read that letter to me. The correspondent did not know that Benjamin was actually about to marry the daughter of one of the well-known pioneer-members of the Zionist movement, Professor Leon Kellner, the editor of Theodor Herzl's Zionist writings and of his diaries. This young woman naturally encouraged his Jewish awareness, but was hardly in a position to influence it to any great extent. It is true, on the other hand, that his approach to the second great subject to which he meant to dedicate his experience, to revolutionary Marxist policy, was palpably made under a woman's influence.

Benjamin's "theological thinking"—a marked tendency of his early years that impressed itself on all who came into close contact with him at the time—took its bearings (instinctively, I almost added) from Jewish concepts. Christian ideas never held any attraction for him. Indeed, he had an undisguised distaste for the type of neo-Catholicism which, at the time, was much in vogue among Jewish intellectuals in Germany and France.

Two categories above all, and especially in their Jewish versions, assume a central place in his writings: on the one hand Revelation, the idea of the Torah and of sacred texts in general, and on the other hand the messianic idea and Redemption. Their significance as regulative ideas governing his thought cannot be overrated.

Over and over again one meets in his writings, often indeed in the most unexpected places, instances of a preoccupation with the problem of sacred texts, for instance in most of his papers on the philosophy of language, in the essay "The Task of the Translator" in the book on German tragic drama (*Trauerspiel*), but also in his remarks about the verbal imagination of children, when he says that "sentences formed in play by a child out of words [given in advance] are more akin to the language of sacred texts than to the colloquial language of the grown-ups." For many years he considered the confrontation with the sacred texts of Hebrew tradition as the crucial literary experience of which he stood in need to come really into his own. I shall never forget the superb manner in which he declared his commitment to his coming task as a commentator of Jewish texts in a great discourse—of which I was a witness—with Dr. Judah Magnes, the chancellor of the nascent Hebrew University of Jerusalem, in Paris in August 1927, when he contemplated the idea of preparing himself for a teaching assignment at the university. Yet, from his pen we have only one example of such a confrontation with the Bible. (Benjamin, incidentally, was no great admirer of Buber's Bible translation but a keen reader of the old translation edited by Leopold Zunz whose austerity deeply impressed him.) This one instance is provided by the comments he wrote in 1916 and 1927 about the statements on the nature of language in the first three chapters of Genesis— pages of rare concentration and beauty.

It must be emphasized that later on when he had turned to historical materialism, out of those two categories of Revelation and Redemption only the latter was preserved *expressis verbis*, but not the former, closely though it was bound up with his basic method of commenting on great and authoritative texts. In the process of transformation of his thought the notion of Revelation vanished—or rather, I am inclined to suspect, remained unsaid, having become truly esoteric knowledge. The proud emphasis which, to the last, characterizes his references to the *utopian* category of religion, to Redemption and the messianic idea, whereas its *existential* (more aptly perhaps: its substantive) category disappears, must be related to the structure of what I would call his materialist theology. (I would characterize his latter-day thinking as a materialist theory of Revelation whose very subject no longer figures in the theory.)

I said that for years Benjamin sought to go all the way to Judaism which, he hoped, would offer scope for the homecoming of his innermost intentions. Around 1930 he abandoned that hope as unrealizable in *his* life; yet echoes of fundamental Jewish concepts continued all the time to reverberate in his writings, now stamped with the seal of the Marxist dialectic. Thus he brings to light the Jewish element in Karl Kraus even at the stage of ultimate estrangement, when he identifies the "Jewish certainty" that "the world was the scene for the sanctification of the name" as the root cause of the contrasting attitudes to language of Karl Kraus and Stefan George; or he will base his analysis of the world of Franz Kafka on the categories of the *halakhah* and *haggadah*.

In addition, an apocalyptic element of destructiveness is preserved in the metamorphosis undergone in his writing by the messianic idea, which continues to play a potent part in his thought. The noble and positive power of destruction—too long (in his view) denied due recognition thanks to the one-sided, undialectic, and dilettantish apotheosis of "creativity"—now becomes an aspect of redemption, related to the immanence of the world, acted out in the history of human labor. A new concept of *subversiveness* now appears in his writings frequently and in the most surprising contexts, and illuminates for him patterns of profound meaning behind the phenomena he studies. There are few important works of his during that period where this concept does not play a central part, avowed or hidden, in inspiring his analyses, as for instance in the most characteristic essay *Der Destruktive Charakter*, or in the great essays on Kraus, Proust, and Kafka. He developed an extremely accurate and sensitive feeling for the subversive elements in the *oeuvre* of great authors. Even in authors whose picture of the world exhibits mostly reactionary traits he heard the subterranean rumblings of revolution, and generally he was keenly aware of what he called "the strange interplay between reactionary theory and revolutionary practice." The secularization of Jewish apocalyptic doctrine is plain for all to see and nowhere denies its origin. The talmudic image of the angels created anew each moment in countless hosts, only to be destroyed and return into naught after having raised their voices before God, unites his earlier with his later writings. It appears at the end of his announcement of the projected journal *Angelus Novus*, which was never to materialize. This was in 1922, at the height of his theological period. It appears again at the end of his seemingly materialist essay of 1931 on Karl Kraus, which ushers in his later production with a Marxist bugle call. Yet, those ever new angels—one of them he found in Paul Klee's painting *Angelus Novus*, which he owned and deeply loved—bear the features of the angels of judgment as well as destruction. Their "quickly fading voice" proclaims the anticipation of the apocalypse in history—and it was this that mattered to him.

Jewish inspiration pure and simple, with no adjustment even to the terminology of the materialist dialectic, dominates Benjamin's tireless striving after an understanding of Kafka, whose writings he studied from the first with passionate involvement. This tendency is manifest above all in the great essay of 1934 to which Bertolt Brecht responded with the charge that "it was aiding and abetting Jewish fascism." It reveals itself also in his formidable letter of 1938, in which he sketched a new portrait of

Kafka that he intended to execute in a book if a publisher could be found. The concepts of justice, of the study of Scripture and of exegesis are here consciously introduced and developed as Jewish concepts. "Study"—we read here—"is the gate of justice. And yet Kafka dared not attach to study those promises that tradition held out for the study of the Torah. His acolytes are beadles, but they have lost the house of prayer; his scholars are disciples, but they have lost the scripture." Equally far removed from Max Brod's optimistic interpretation of Kafka and from the existentialist interpretation which has been the fashion in recent years, Benjamin perceived the negative inversion to which the Jewish categories are subjected in Kafka's world; there the teaching no longer conveys a positive message, but offers only an absolutely Utopian—and therefore as yet undefinable—promise of a postcontemporary world. We are left nothing but the procedures of a "Law" that can no longer be deciphered. These procedures became the central feature of Kafka's vision. Benjamin knew that in Kafka we possess the *theologia negativa* of a Judaism not a whit less intense for having lost the Revelation as a positive message.

Benjamin, who was aware of a close affinity with this author—Proust and Kafka were probably the authors truly familiar to him at the deepest level—saw in the exegetic passages so often presented by Kafka the crystalization of Torah tradition mirrored in itself. The twelve lines on the interpretation of *Don Quixote* he considered to be the most perfect extant piece of Kafka's writing. Benjamin's commentaries on Brecht, among which the one on the "Legend of the Origin of the Book of T'ao teh Ching on Lao-tse's Way into the Emigration" is perhaps most outstanding, represent the ultimate form assumed by the commentary in Benjamin's hands. He fully realized that he was embarking on a problematic venture when he put this form in the service of interpreting revolutionary rather than archaic and authoritative texts. Indeed, these commentaries display a rare and pathetic helplessness—disconcerting in a mind of Benjamin's sovereign power—that is entirely absent from his interpretation of other texts. And yet, it is obvious that he had made up his mind—even if the price was high—not to forgo the explosive force which he more than any Jewish contemporary had rediscovered in the mysterious life of the commentary as a decisive religious category.

Among the Jewish categories which he introduced as such and upheld to the last is the messianic idea; nothing is wider of the mark than the notion that he took it over from Ernst Bloch, though the two met on common Jewish ground. Another is the idea of remembrance. The last paragraph in Benjamin's work that can be chronologically placed, representing a *confessio in extremis* as it were, reads—all the more strikingly for being part of a quasi-Marxist text on historical time—like an apotheosis of Judaism: "The soothsayers who found out from time what it had in store for them certainly did not experience time as either homogeneous or empty. Anyone who keeps this in mind will perhaps get an idea of how past times were experienced in remembrance, namely in just the same way. We know that the Jews were prohibited from investigating the future. The Torah and the prayers instruct them in remembrance, however. This stripped the future of its magic, to which all those succumb who turn to the soothsayers for enlightenment. This does not imply, however, that for the Jews the future turned into homogeneous, empty time. For every second of time was the street gate through which the Messiah might enter."

The Judaism encompassed in this description was the goal which Walter Benjamin approached asymptotically throughout his life, without ever attaining it. Yet it may be stated that his deepest intuition, in the spheres of creation and destruction alike, sprang from the very center of that Judaism; and this statement about Benjamin, the thinker, loses nothing of its dialectic range by the fact that it is also about a life often beset by the dread shadows of loneliness, consumed in longing for fellowship, though it be the apocalyptic fellowship of revolution; by the fact that it illuminates the story of that burning, pining life with a deep radiance.

Walter Benjamin and His Angel*

I

Among the peculiarities of Benjamin's philosophical prose—the critical and metaphysical prose, in which the Marxist element constitutes something like an inversion of the metaphysical-theological—is its enormous suitability for canonization; I might almost say for quotation as a kind of Holy Writ. In this respect it enjoys *one* advantage over the canonical texts of Marx, Engels, or Lenin, so beloved by Marxists: its deep connection with theology, the inspiration of which remained enduringly vital to Benjamin until the end, determining its special form, which cloaked so many important sayings of Benjamin's (and, Heaven knows, unimportant ones as well) in the aura of the *ex cathedra*. At a very early stage, his enemies spoke of the authoritarian ontology [*Konstatierontologie*] in his writings. Indeed, I am not the only one who has noticed that young Marxists "quote Benjamin like Holy Writ." [1] His sentences often enough have the authoritarian stance of words of revelation, as which they were in fact considered by him to no slight extent during his youthful metaphysical period. "It is a metaphysical truth that . . ." was a favorite sentence of Walter Benjamin's in the years in which I came to know him, and it was followed by an assertion deeply enmeshed in the theological, and frequently surpassingly odd. In

* "*Walter Benjamin und sein Engel,*" in Siegfried Unseld, editor, *Zur Aktualität Walter Benjamins* (Frankfurt-am-Main: Suhrkamp Taschenbuch No. 150, 1972). Translated by Werner J. Dannhauser.

1. C. Z. von Manteuffel in the *Neue Zürcher Zeitung*, December 13, 1970, in the supplement *Literatur und Kunst*, p. 53.

regard to this manner, there is hardly a difference between the "Metaphysics of Youth" of 1913 and the "Theses on the Philosophy of History" of 1940, notwithstanding all contrasts in substance. Basically he would have accepted his appointment as Church father, or as some now like to put it, Marxist rabbi, quite graciously, though with dialectical reservations. The gesture of the esoteric writer perceived in him by Adorno and me was that of the producer of authoritative sentences, and that, to be sure, also means, from the very outset and because of their essence, sentences lending themselves to quotation and interpretation. What is illuminating in them is meshed with the thoroughly enigmatic, as in none of the other authors who now, with varying degrees of plausibility, are quoted together with him (from Bloch or even Lukács to Brecht and Adorno). They are sentences from the Holy Writ of an initiate, scarcely and scantily disguised, at once rational and mystical, as is becoming to sentences of this kind.

In stretches of Benjamin one finds original impressions, insights, or experiences transposed into or communicated by direct language and focused into Marxist reflection, or at least dressed up as such. A judicious reader like Marianne Kesting has said of Benjamin's tendency to "cast a bridge between Marxist conceptualization and aesthetic procedures" that he associatively kept up this tendency, especially in the late writings centering around the work about the *Pariser Passagen* ("The Arcades"), and that much that was fruitful had come out of this. To be sure: "His associations are those of genius and lead further, but they are no longer Marxist." [2] It is this fact with which the Marxist readers of Benjamin find it so hard to come to terms, or of which they take no cognizance.

Everyone knows how Benjamin's Marxist writings point in a definite direction, even though no end can be seen to the discussions about the definition of the direction. One can hardly doubt Benjamin's resolution in his attempt to use the matter and terminology of the class struggle as the content not only of world history but of philosophy as well. And yet doubts force themselves on the careful reader of this "mountain" of thoughts,

2. *Deutsche Zeitung—Christ und Welt*, September 10, 1971, p. 11.

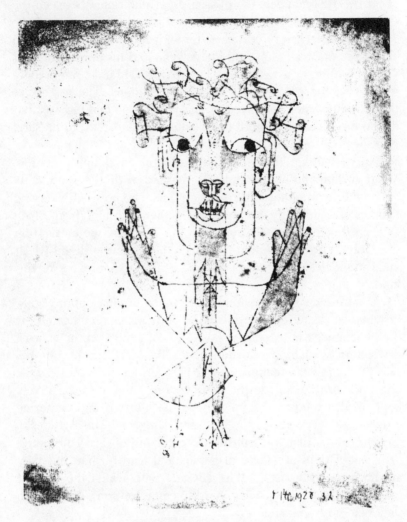

Paul Klee, Angelus Novus

which, as he himself expressed it in a letter of May 1935 to Werner Kraft,[3] was to have been transformed in such a direction.

3. Walter Benjamin, *Briefe*, II (1966), 659. Noteworthy is the parallel formulation in an (unprinted) letter to Alfred Cohn of May, 1935, where the talk is of the "beneficial process of recasting, in which the whole, originally directly metaphysically organized mass of thought [of "The Arcades"] has been transferred into an aggregate condition [*sic*] more suitable to present existence."

Untransfigured, in fact offering stiff-necked resistance to this well-advertised transfiguration—and sometimes overpowered or executed only by purely verbal-rhetorical means, sometimes not even that—many of the pieces and notes connected with "The Arcades" offer open and unfeigned refuge to the mystical tradition and confess their continuity with it. That such pieces as those about Leskov and Kafka and others destroy the legend of the unequivocal line of development in Benjamin's productivity has, as suggested above, often led to their suppression in the minds of his Marxist commentators among the New Left. That is understandable enough, though not to the advantage of a real understanding of Benjamin's work. Embedded in a Marxist (and vociferous) vicinity, they represent true *pièces de résistance* for the reception of Benjamin that has now become fashionable.

It is, therefore, appropriate to point to aspects of Benjamin's person and thought that are neglected by his current interpreters, or cast aside embarrassedly. To these belong, and perhaps above all else, his ties to the mystical tradition and to a mystical experience which nevertheless was a far cry from the experience of God, proclaimed by so many oversimplifying minds as the only experience deserving to be called mystical. Benjamin knew that mystical experience is many-layered, and it was precisely this many-layeredness that played so great a role in his thinking and in his productivity. If I may speak from my own experience, Benjamin's most amazing trait was the connection between pronounced clairvoyance and the gift for dialectical subtlety on the one hand, but also the inclination to connect this clairvoyance with fantastic theories, which in earlier times he readily surrendered if contradicted and then by burrowing sought to penetrate deeper into the matter itself; while in his later period he often stuck to them stiff-neckedly under the pretext of a purely heuristic procedure. The intimate interweaving of mystical-cosmic and Marxist insights, which penetrate each other or appear one alongside the other, is first visible in his little book *One-Way Street*, about the last piece of which, "To the Planetarium," a critic has said with very good reason, "Here enthusiasm divulges a mystical fixation before some artifice withdraws the former to a rational and morally aloof dialectic." [4]

4. Dietrich Böhler in *Neue Rundschau*, LXXVIII (1967), 666.

In my essay about Walter Benjamin[5] I have emphatically pointed
to this two-track aspect of Benjamin's thinking, in which mystical
intuition and rational insight are frequently only seemingly
connected by dialectic, and in what follows I am going to present
a striking example of that aspect.

Behind many of Benjamin's writings stand personal, indeed
most personal, experiences which by projection into the objects
of his works disappeared or were put into code, so that the
outsider could not recognize them or at least could do no more
than suspect their presence. Such is the case, for example, in *The
Origin of German Tragic Drama (Trauerspiel)* with the theory of
melancholy, by which he described his own constitution. So, too,
fifty years after the composition of his famous treatise on
Goethe's *Elective Affinities*, which represents a high point of the
literature of aesthetics, one may be allowed to divulge the simple
but hidden truth that this work—"altogether incomparable" as
Hofmannsthal called it—and its insights were possible only
because they were written by Benjamin in a human situation that
corresponded uncannily to that of the novel. It was, after all, the
"plantlike muteness" and beauty of that "Ottilie" who at the
time entered his life so consequentially, which stood at the source
of his intuitions about the meaning of the beautiful, and about
the Luciferian depth of the "appearance" in which the beautiful
conceals and reveals itself. Along the same line is the small piece
of an autobiographical nature, about himself and his angel, to
which I wish to direct attention here. It represents a depiction of
Benjamin's self—disquieting, to be sure—so important to him
that on two consecutive days he wrote it down in two versions.
As such it seems to me illuminating and precious, even though it
is admittedly very much in need of a commentary.

II

This piece, with a title that seems truly enigmatic, of
"Agesilaus Santander," is in a notebook of Walter Benjamin's
that is to be found among his literary remains in Frankfurt, which

5. See above, pp. 172–97.

after Theodor Adorno's death are under the control of a panel constituted to assume such responsibility. This notebook contains writings from the years 1931 and 1933, in which his most diverse observations, Marxist and wholly incompatible with Marxism, are intermingled. Thus it contains (pp. 15–16) "Reflections on Broadcasting" and (pp. 25–27) under the caption "Art for the People—Art for the Connoisseur" the summary of a discussion held in the autumn of 1931 with Willy Haas, the editor of the *Literarische Welt*, in which Benjamin, in Marxist terms, squarely defends the thesis that art is meant for connoisseurs of art. On pp. 31–35 there follows a sketch, "Doctrine of Similarity," [6] written during the spring of 1933 on the island of Ibiza after his flightlike departure from Berlin in March, and which contains a theory of occult phenomena of which he sent me an abridged version (omitting essential material); only the latter has previously appeared in his collected works (Vol. 1, pp. 507–10). Afterwards follows, on pp. 37–39, the "Agesilaus Santander" in a shorter form (p. 39) dated Ibiza, August 12, 1933, and in a somewhat longer and final version (pp. 37–38) dated the following day. From April to October of 1933 Benjamin lived on Ibiza (in San Antonio), where he had first taken up residence from May to the middle of July 1932, a period from which the first pages of the notebook "Notes on the *Jugendstil*" possibly stemmed.

The circumstances under which the piece originated are not known. One may, however, raise the question posed to me by Peter Szondi during a discussion I had with him about the piece, whether "Agesilaus Santander" might not be the product of a fever delirium. According to Jean Selz (*Über Walter Benjamin*, [Frankfurt, 1968], p. 49) Benjamin had malaria in the summer of 1933. He indicates no exact dates, only that Benjamin left Ibiza in October. Opposed to this, to be sure, is the indication of Benjamin himself, who in a later application to a French administrative office—obviously in connection with his planned naturalization or extended residence permit in France—gave the dates and duration of his stays. We possess a copy of this application, according to which he left Ibiza on September 25,

6. Now available in *Zur Aktualität Walter Benjamins* (Frankfurt-am-Main: Suhrkamp Taschenbuch No. 150, 1972), pp. 23–30.

1933. From there he jumps over to October 6 and indicates a Paris address for this date. According to a letter to me of October 16, 1933, from Paris, we know that he arrived in Paris seriously ill and that toward the end in Ibiza he had been "generally no longer healthy," and that the day of his departure from there "coincided with the first of a series of highest fever attacks." After his arrival in Paris, malaria had been diagnosed. Could he perhaps have already suffered from this malaria on August 12 and 13, six weeks before his departure? In his letter to me of July 31, 1933, in which he reports about the composition of the important piece, "Loggien" in *A Berlin Childhood*, he tells me that he had been ill for about two weeks. On the other hand, one finds there the passage, "The great heat has begun here. The Spaniards, who know its effects, speak of 'August madness' as a completely common thing. It gives me much pleasure to follow its onset among the foreigners." Obviously, then, he himself had not yet at this time felt its appearance. Nevertheless, one cannot exclude a possible connection between the origin of the piece and a first, still relatively slight, attack of malaria, however hypothetical this must remain. In any case, Selz in his recollections drew the indication from his later knowledge of the diagnosis of Benjamin's malaria, about which he learned only in Paris after Benjamin's return and thus provides no certain proof that the latter really had malaria as early as August. The whole problem carries little weight, I am convinced, for the understanding of the text, for the latter's construction and world of images have an immanent logic that does not differ from his usage in many other writings.

In what follows I reproduce the text of both versions:

[First Version]

Agesilaus Santander

When I was born the thought came to my parents that I might perhaps become a writer. Then it would be good if not everybody noticed at once that I was a Jew: that is why they added to the name I was called two very unusual ones. I do not

wish to divulge them. Suffice it to say that forty years ago parents
could with difficulty see farther ahead. What they held to be a
remote possibility has come true. But their precautions, meant to
counter fate, were rendered without force by the one most
concerned. Instead of making public the two provident names by
his writings he locked them within himself. He watched over
them as once the Jews did over the secret name they gave to each
of their children. The latter did not come to know it before the
day of their attainment of maturity. Since, however, that can
occur more than once in life, and perhaps, too, not every secret
name remains always the same and untransfigured, its transfiguration might reveal itself on the occasion of a new maturity. It
does not, therefore, remain any the less the name that contains in
itself all the life forces, and by which the latter can be summoned
forth and guarded against the unauthorized.

Yet this name is in no way an enrichment of him who bears it.
It takes away much from him, but above all the gift of appearing
wholly as he was of old. In the room I last occupied, the latter,
before he stepped out of the old name, armored and encased,
into the light, put up his picture at my place: New Angel. The
kabbalah relates that in every instant God creates an immense
number of new angels whose only purpose is, before they dissolve
into naught, to sing His praise before His throne for a moment.
Mine was interrupted in doing so; his features had nothing about
them resembling the human. As for the rest, he made me pay for
having disturbed him at his work. For in taking advantage of the
circumstance that I came into the world under the sign of
Saturn—the planet of slow rotation, the star of hesitation and
delay—he sent his feminine form, after the masculine reproduced
in the picture, by way of the longest, most fatal detour, even
though both were so very much adjacent to each other.

He did not, perhaps, know that thereby he brought to the
fore the strength of him whom he accosted. For nothing can
overcome my patience. Its wings resemble those of the angel in
that very few pushes are enough for them to preserve themselves
immovably in the face of her whom my patience is resolved to
await. But it, which has claws like the angel and knife-sharp
wings, does not look as though it threatens to pounce on her
whom it has sighted. It learns from the angel how he encom-

passes his partner in his view, but then yields by fits and starts, and incessantly. He pulls him along on that flight° into a future from which he has advanced. He hopes for nothing new from the latter except the view of the person he keeps facing.

So I journeyed with you, no sooner than I had seen you for the first time, back from whence I came.

Ibiza, August 12, 1933

[Second, final version]

Agesilaus Santander

When I was born the thought came to my parents that I might perhaps become a writer. Then it would be good if not everybody noticed at once that I was a Jew. That is why besides the name I was called they added two further, exceptional ones, from which one could see neither that a Jew bore them nor that they belonged to him as first names. Forty years ago no parental couple could prove itself more far-seeing. What it held to be only a remote possibility has come true. It is only that the precautions by which they meant to counter fate were set aside by the one most concerned. That is to say that instead of making it public by the writings he produced, he proceeded with regard to it as did the Jews with the additional name of their children, which remains secret. Indeed, they only communicate it to them when they reach maturity. Since, however, this maturity can occur more than once in life, and the secret name may remain the same and untransfigured only to the pious one, its change might reveal itself all at once with a new maturity. Thus with me. It therefore remains no less the name which joins the life forces in strictest union and which is to be guarded against the unauthorized.

Yet in no way is this name an enrichment of the one it names. On the contrary, much of his image falls away when that name becomes audible. He loses above all the gift of appearing anthropomorphous. In the room I occupied in Berlin the latter,

---

° Benjamin had first written *journey* (*Fahrt*), then changed it to *flight* (*Flucht*) and written the word *flight* under it once more.

before he stepped out of my name, armored and encased, into the light, put up his picture on the wall: New Angel. The *kabbalah* relates that in every instant God creates an immense number of new angels, all of whom only have the purpose, before they dissolve into naught, of singing the praise of God before His throne for a moment. The new angel passed himself off as one of these before he was prepared to name himself. I only fear that I took him away from his hymn unduly long. As for the rest, he made me pay for that. For in taking advantage of the circumstance that I came into the world under the sign of Saturn—the star of the slowest revolution, the planet of detours and delays—he sent his feminine form after the masculine one reproduced in the picture by way of the longest, most fatal detour, even though both happened to be—only they did not know each other—most intimately adjacent to each other.

He did not, perhaps, know that the strength of him whom he thus wanted to accost could show itself best in this way: namely by waiting. Where this man chanced upon a woman who captivated him, he was at once resolved to lurk on her path of life and to wait until sick, aged, in tattered clothes, she fell into his hands. In short, nothing could enfeeble the patience of the man. And its wings resembled the wings of the angel° in that very few pushes were enough to preserve themselves long, immovably in the face of that which he was resolved no longer to leave alone.

The angel, however, resembles all from which I have had to part: persons and above all things. In the things I no longer have, he resides. He makes them transparent, and behind all of them there appears to me the one for whom they are intended. That is why nobody can surpass me in giving gifts. Indeed, perhaps the angel was attracted by a gift giver who goes away empty-handed. For he himself, too, who has claws and pointed, indeed knife-sharp wings[,] does not look as though he would pounce on the one who has sighted. He fixes his eyes on him firmly—a long time, then yields by fits and starts but incessantly. Why? In order to pull him along with himself on that way into the future on which he came and which he knows so well that he traverses it

---

° First Benjamin wrote *those of the angel*, and crossed it out.

without turning around and letting the one he has chosen out of view. He wants happiness: the conflict in which lies the ecstasy of the unique,° ["once only"] new, as yet unlived with that°° bliss of the "once more," the having again, the lived. That is why he can hope for the new on no way except on the way of the return home, when he takes a new human being along with him. Just as I, no sooner than I had seen you, journeyed back with you, from whence I came.°°°

Ibiza, August 13, 1933

III

Before I undertake to explain this thoroughly hermetic text, something must be said about the picture central to it, *Angelus Novus* by Paul Klee. That picture was painted by Klee in 1920 in Munich and carries the signature "1920/32." From 1919 to the end of his life, the work of Klee is interspersed with pictures and drawings of angels on some fifty sheets, in large part from the last years of his life. As his son Felix Klee wrote in a letter of March 1972, "it enticed Paul Klee to render the messenger of the gods—often even in human tragicomedy." Thus there happens to exist a picture *Angel Brings What Was Wished* with the signature 1920/91 in which the angel seems rather like a waiter or waitress serving the order wished for by Klee. In the works and portfolios about Klee a whole number of such angels is to be found, above all from his later years, as, for example, in the two books by Will Grohmann, *Paul Klee* (1954) and *Paul Klee— Handzeichnungen (Sketches)* (1959). Since, as far as is known, no remarks by Klee himself are to be found about these angels, no reason exists in connection with what is to be considered here for going more closely into the sentences which Grohmann in 1954 (pp. 348–50) dedicated to this theme in Klee. There he attempts to place the angels closer to those of Rilke's "Duino Elegies"

° First only: *in that the "once only," new, as yet unlived with it;* then improved as in the text.

°° *"That" (jener)*—instead of the crossed out, preceding *"that" (dem)*.

°°° First: *journeyed back from whence;* then crossed out and newly written *journeyed back with you from whence*.

which, according to Grohmann, "like Klee's angels, live in the great unity embracing life and death and see in the invisible a higher order of reality" (p. 348). For an analysis of the significance and position possessed by Klee's picture *Angelus Novus* in Benjamin's life and thought, these (rather doubtful) pronouncements are not relevant, since Benjamin's contemplation of the picture was nourished by completely different motives, as will presently be shown.

Klee's picture was exhibited in May and June of 1920 in the great Klee Exhibition of the Hans Goltz gallery in Munich; in the latter's catalog, which appeared as a "special Paul Klee issue" of the periodical *Der Ararat*, it is listed on page 24 as number 245 but not reproduced. It is a relatively small watercolor, which was first reproduced at page length opposite page 128 in Wilhelm Hausenstein's book, *Kairuan oder eine Geschichte vom Maler Klee* (Munich, 1921). Hausenstein, who lived in Munich, could have seen the picture while it was still in Klee's studio or at the Goltz gallery. It was later reproduced again—obviously from Hausenstein's book—in the monograph "Paul Klee" by Carola Giedion-Welcker (Stuttgart, 1954), on page 184. At the time Benjamin was not in Munich, but he might have seen it at a small Klee Exhibition which took place in April 1921 in Berlin somewhere on the Kurfürstendamm, and which he mentioned as a special attraction in a letter to me of April 11, 1921 (*Letters*, Vol. I, p. 262). I do not, however, even know whether the picture was actually exhibited there.

In any case it was returned to Goltz, for Benjamin obtained it in Munich, when he visited me there in the end of May and the beginning of June 1921. He brought me the picture with the request to keep it for him until he once more would have a permanent lodging in Berlin, where great personal difficulties had arisen in his life. Until the middle of November 1921 the *Angelus Novus* hung in the residence—first Türkenstrasse 98, later Gabelsbergerstrasse 51—I shared with my subsequent first wife, Elsa Burchardt, in whose room it was hanging, a fact to which Benjamin referred in several letters. On November 27, 1921, he had already received the picture in Berlin, where I had sent it to him according to his wish (*Letters*, Vol. I, p. 282). Until his divorce it hung in the study of his residence at Delbrückstrasse

23, over the sofa, and later in his last residence at Prinzregenten-strasse 66. In the Hitler era, a female acquaintance brought him the picture to Paris around 1935. At the time of my visit in February 1938 it was again hanging in his large room at 10 Rue Dombasle. When, in June 1940, he fled from Paris and stored his papers in two suitcases—which George Bataille, connected with Benjamin through the Collège de Sociologie, founded by Bataille, temporarily kept hidden in the Bibliothèque Nationale—Benjamin cut the picture out of the frame and stuffed it into one of the suitcases. And so after the war it made its way to Adorno in America and later in Frankfurt. Benjamin always considered the picture his most important possession, even though he obtained another picture by Klee in the preceding year, namely *Performance of the Miracle*, but one I have never seen. When at the end of July 1932 he wanted to take his own life and wrote a testament, he designated it as the special personal gift he bequeathed me.

Klee's picture fascinated him most highly from the very first moment on and for twenty years played a significant role in his considerations, as Friedrich Podszus said in his biographical sketch about Benjamin, using a formulation expressed by me in the course of a conversation (Benjamin, *Illuminationen*, p. 441): as a picture for meditation and as a memento of a spiritual vocation. To be sure, the *Angelus Novus* also represented something else for him: an allegory in the sense of the dialectical tension uncovered in allegories by Benjamin in his book about tragic drama. In his conversations as well as in his writings, he frequently had occasion to speak of the picture. When he obtained it we had talks about Jewish angelology, especially of the talmudic and kabbalistic kind, since at that time I was just writing a piece about the lyric of the *kabbalah*, in which I gave a detailed account of the hymns of the angels in the representations of the Jewish mystics.[7] From my own long contemplation of the picture also stems the poem "Gruss vom Angelus," which I dedicated to Benjamin on his birthday on July 15, 1921, and which I published in the notes to the collection of his letters (Vol. I, p. 269).

7. This essay, a critique of a book by M. Wiener, *Lyrik der Kabbala*, appeared in the autumn of 1921, in the monthly periodical edited by Buber, *Der Jude*, VI, 55–68; concerning the hymns, see especially pp. 60–61.

In Benjamin's letters, the picture is first mentioned in a postcard of June 16, 1921, which he and his wife Dora jointly wrote me from Breitenstein on the Semmering, when the picture was already on my wall. There the *Angelus Novus* is designated by his wife as the "newly created protector of the *kabbalah*," and Benjamin himself indulged in humorous intimations in the form of quotations from nonexistent periodicals. In the *Journal of Angelology* he pretended to have read: "Under the influence of the Turkish climate the heavenly *Klee*-leaf has added three new leaves. It is henceforth reckoned among the species of the four-leaved (*lucerna fortunata*). We will keep our subscribers informed about the further development of the magic plant." In contradiction to this, he simultaneously quotes "a private report of the central organ for little books": "The dear little demonology does not agree with the Angelus. He requests the removal of the same to Berlin. Signed: Dr. Delbrück." The heavenly Klee-leaf was, naturally, the picture by Klee hanging in the Türkenstrasse, and the three new leaves referred to me, Elsa Burchardt, and his friend Ernst Schoen, who was then visiting with us in the Türkenstrasse. That at the time Benjamin did not yet connect any Satanic-Luciferian thoughts with the picture follows from his remark about the "little demonology" the angel could hardly bear. This little demonology was a booklet without title and text, consisting only of the reproductions and symbols ("characters") of demons, in reality the *Tafelband* to *Dr. Faust's Book of Black Magic*, which had been published about 1840 in Stuttgart by lithography. The little book was originally in the possession of Benjamin,[8] who gave it to me as a gift in the latter half of April 1921, in gratitude for my intervention in a matter touching his life deeply; at that time he also suggested we adopt the familiar form of address "Du" instead of "Sie." I still have the book.

Benjamin frequently made use of the signature "Dr. Delbrück" in humorous or satiric communications; in doing so he alluded to the house of his parents at 23 Delbrückstrasse in

8. Hugo Ball described this copy in his journal (*Flucht aus der Zeit*, 1927, p. 243) after his visit with Benjamin on March 3, 1919: "A kabbalistic book on magic with demonological illustrations. Devils who bring to view an intentional banality in order to conceal that they are devils. Plump chubby-faced wenches who trail off into a lizard's body. Offspring of the fiery sphere, of a fat obtusiveness. . . . Banality corpulent and strapping, accentuated in order to mislead."

Berlin-Grünewald. In the letters to me from the year 1921, he made several further references to the *Angelus Novus*, in whose name he held forth or thanked me about various matters. On August 4, 1921, when he accepted the offer of the Heidelberg publisher Richard Weissbach to edit a periodical for him and notified me of it (*Letters*, Vol. I, p. 271) he had already decided to call it *Angelus Novus*. For the periodical, as he expressed himself in its prospectus (all that was to reach the printing stage), was from the beginning to have in common with the angel the ephemeral character of the latter. This ephemeral quality seemed to Benjamin the just price it had to exact for its striving after what Benjamin understood as true actuality: "Why according to a talmudic legend even the angels—new ones each moment in innumerable bands—are created so that, after they have sung their hymn before God, they cease and dissolve into the naught. Let the name of the periodical signify that such actuality as is alone true should devolve upon it." [9] Klee's picture itself is not mentioned here.

In the course of the years, Benjamin associated very diverse conceptions with the angel, whom he apostrophized in the text reproduced above. In an (unprinted) letter of November 18, 1927, shortly after my return from Europe to Jerusalem, he referred to my poem to the *Angelus* in a rather cheerful connection—in relation to the "University of Muri," invented by us, from whose *Transactions* at that time I had had my brothers in Berlin, who were printers, print, with his active intercession, a "Philosophical Alphabet" which was dedicated to Benjamin and presented itself as the "official didactic poem of the Central and State University of Muri." Here he called my poem "the poem to the guardian angel of the university." The guardian angel of the *kabbalah* from the year 1921 has become the guardian angel of the University of Muri, in whose *Transactions* a "philosopher" and a "kabbalist"—who in a traditional sense were neither a philosopher nor a kabbalist—made the traditional university and its scholars the object of their derision. The angel, not yet sunk in melancholy as he was later to be, still speaks to both of us, joined

9. *Schriften*, Vol. II (1955), p. 279. (Vol. II of the final edition *Gesammelte Schriften* has not yet appeared.)

in a common cause. One "lays him down on twigs of roses [*Rosenzweigen*]," which is to say he still finds in Franz Rosenzweig's Jewish-philosophical work an abode where he can tarry.

The angel whom Paul Klee evoked in his picture was certainly enigmatic—though enigmatic in a completely different way than, say, the angel of the "Duino Elegies" and other poems, in whom, after all, the Jewish element of the messenger who transmits a message is altogether lost. In Hebrew, after all, the word for "angel" is identical with that for "messenger" (*malakh*). Everlasting angels like, say, the archangels or Satan, seen as the fallen angel of the Jewish and Christian tradition, were evidently less important for Benjamin than the talmudic theme of the formation and disappearance of angels before God, of whom it is said in a kabbalistic book that they "pass away as the spark on the coals." To this, however, was added for Benjamin the further conception of Jewish tradition of the personal angel of each human being who represents the latter's secret self and whose name nevertheless remains hidden from him. In angelic shape, but in part also in the form of his secret name, the heavenly self of a human being (like everything else created) is woven into a curtain hanging before the throne of God. This angel, to be sure, can also enter into opposition to, and a relation of strong tension with, the earthly creature to whom he is attached, as is reflected in Benjamin's assertions in the "Agesilaus Santander." In August 1927, when Benjamin and I spent an extended period of time together in Paris, I had just published a Hebrew work of research containing, among other things, detailed texts on the angelology and demonology of the kabbalists of the thirteenth century, and I told him about these.

The Luciferian element, however, entered Benjamin's meditations on Klee's picture not directly from the Jewish tradition, but rather from the occupation with Baudelaire that fascinated him for so many years. The Luciferian element of the beauty of the Satanic, stemming from this side of Benjamin's interests, comes out often enough in his writings and notes. His recently published notes "On Hashish" referred, in a record of a hashish-impression of January 15, 1928, to a "Satanic phase" he went through during this intoxication: "My smile assumed Satanic features: though more the expression of Satanic knowing,

Satanic contentment, Satanic serenity than that of Satanic destructive activity." [10] However, while the "indescribably beautiful face" of a human being can appear as "Satanic features— with a half-suppressed smile" about 1932 in Benjamin's partly unpublished "Self-portraits of the Dreamer," the anthropomorphous nature of Klee's angel, now changing into the Luciferian, is no longer present when one (perhaps two) years later he wrote the piece concerning us here. But the theme of the message transmitted by the angel has not disappeared. Its content, to be sure, changes along with Benjamin's conceptions. Does he bring news from Above? News about the Self of him who views him and about his fate? Or perhaps news about what is occurring in the world of history, as it finally appeared to Benjamin, when he recognized the angel of history in the *Angelus Novus*? The following considerations will provide more exact information about this.

IV

When Benjamin wrote this piece on Ibiza, his situation was that of the refugee who in every sense leads an existence on the brink of desperation. Three weeks earlier, he had written me on July 24, 1933, that he had lowered his necessities of life to a "minimum that could hardly be lowered any further." His capacity of concentration on spiritual matters was of an almost miraculous intensity precisely in such situations. A relative of his quoted to me from a lost letter from him during such a condition an unforgettable sentence she had retained verbatim: "I pluck flowers on the brink of subsistence." The review of his life occupied him most deeply during these months. Out of it also arose the new meditation about the angel that is set down here—when the picture itself was no longer with him but present only in his imagination. The latter allied itself with the review of his life as writer, as Jew, and as unrequited lover. That in so desperate a situation he nevertheless decided on writing an

10. Walter Benjamin, *Über Haschisch. Novellistisches. Berichte. Materialien.* Edited by Tillman Rexroth. Introduction by Hermann Schweppenhäuser (Frankfurt-am-Main: Suhrkamp Taschenbuch No. 21, 1972), Sentence 69.

observation which for all its melancholy is harmonious and does
not totally slip into the hopeless, an observation establishing a
certain equilibrium of the impulses moving his life—this permits
a glance at the forces which then and for so long after prevented
his self-destruction and which he summarized by the image of
patience, for which he here praises himself with such overwhelming justification.

The following explanation is based on the text of the second,
final version, but the important variations of the first one are
taken into consideration.

Benjamin proceeds from the fiction that at his birth his
parents gave him, besides the name Walter, two additional and
thoroughly peculiar names, so that he might if necessary use
them as a literary pseudonym without directly being recognized
as a Jew, as was inevitable in case of the employment of the name
Walter Benjamin. (In Germany, "Benjamin" would invariably be
a Jewish name.) To be sure, by, as it were, anticipating his
relation to his angel—even if only in Benjamin's imagination—his
parents expressed more than they could have guessed. For what
conceals itself behind the enigmatic name of the Spartan king
Agesilaus and the city of northern Spain, Santander? [11] Nothing
other than a significant anagram. Benjamin's taste for anagrams
accompanied him through his whole life. It was one of his main
pleasures to make up anagrams. In several of his essays he used
the anagram Anni M. Bie instead of the name Benjamin. A whole
page on which he had written anagrams in his own hand is to be
found among his posthumous papers in Frankfurt. In his book on
tragic drama he wrote that in anagrams "the word, the syllable,
and the sound, strut around, emancipated from every handed-

11. A young scholar who became familiar with Benjamin's sketch in connection with a
lecture by me pointed out the possibility to me that Benjamin was stimulated to the use of
this name by a passage in Karl Marx's *The Eighteenth Brumaire of Louis Napoleon*, where
a famous ancient anecdote about King Agesilaus is quoted; cf. the edition in Volume 8 of
the *Werke* of Karl Marx and Friedrich Engels (Berlin, 1960), pp. 175 and 623. This
conjecture is, however, unacceptable, for while Benjamin had read just this writing by
Marx (of whom he otherwise read very little), he did so only in June 1938, during his last
visit with Brecht in Skovsbostrand. This follows from Benjamin's carefully kept list of
books read by him, the main part of which has been preserved, and on which the book by
Marx is listed as number 1649. Before 1933, Benjamin had completely read only one
writing by Marx at all, namely in 1928 the book *Klassenkämpfe in Frankreich*, number
1074 of his list.

down association with meaning, as a thing that may be exploited allegorically," [12] whereby he defined as much the inclination of Baroque writers for anagrams as his own inclination.

Jean Selz also most clearly observed this same feature about him. "Sometimes he also investigated and considered a word from all sides and in so doing often discovered in its individual syllables an unexpected meaning" (*Über Walter Benjamin*, p. 40). And Selz observed this feature precisely on Ibiza, where the present piece was written. And what he says here about the syllables of a word holds as much for the combination of individual letters in the words that make up the anagrams.

Agesilaus Santander is, sealed as it were with a superfluous "i," an anagram of The Angel Satan (*Der Angelus Satanas*). Such an Angel-Satan is spoken of not only in Hebrew texts as, for example, the Midrash Rabba for Exodus, Section 20, paragraph 10, but also in New Testament texts, where, in Paul's Second Letter to the Corinthians, Chapter 12:7, there is talk of the *Angelos Satanas*, who is identical with the fallen, rebellious Lucifer.

Benjamin, who published his own writings under his civil name, made no use, as he says, of this name; he "proceeded . . . as did the Jews with the additional name of their children, which remains secret" and which they reveal to them only when they reach maturity. This is an allusion to the Hebrew name which every male Jewish child receives at circumcision and which is used instead of the usual civil first name in religious documents and synagogue services. In fact this name is "secret" only insofar as no use is made of it by assimilated Jews, even though their children after the completion of the thirteenth year of life—when, according to Jewish law, they reach maturity—are called up by this name for the first time in order to read from the Torah in the synagogue (*bar mitzvah*). Among Jews this "reaching of maturity" means only that they are now obligated under their own responsibility to keep the commandments of the Torah, and that for purposes of public prayer, requiring at least ten "mature" participants, they are among those counted. Indeed, on this solemn occasion, the father pronounces a—to say the least—peculiarly sober blessing: "Praised be [He] who has removed my responsibility for this one here [*sic!*]."

Benjamin transposes this conception further into the mystical. Maturity, which for the Jewish tradition has a sexual character only marginally, is now related to the awakening of love, which can occur more than once in life, namely with each real new love. For the pious man, which is to say the man true to the Law, his "secret name" remains "perhaps" unchanged throughout his life, because apart from the marriage sanctified by the Law he knows no renewed sexuality in reference to other women. For him, by contrast, who like Walter Benjamin does not count himself among the pious, the change of his name can reveal itself all at once with a new reaching of maturity, which is to say with a new love. "Thus with me"—with a new, passionate love there was revealed to him, in place of the name Agesilaus, allegedly given to him by his parents, the new name which is hidden in the old one as an anagram. To the formula employed here, "Thus with me" [*So mir*], there corresponds, at the end of this sketch in the final version, the phrase "Just as I" obviously referring to the same event in his life.

But even in the new transformation of the old name it retains its magic character. It is the name Angelus Satanas, which joins together the angelic and demonic forces of life in the most intimate union, indeed one by which (in the first version) those forces are even summoned forth. Like every truly secret magic name, it may not be trusted or disclosed to unauthorized ones. No wonder that in this sketch, too, Benjamin does not make it public undisguised. To be sure, here a part is also played by the association with the words Benjamin wrote at the end of *One-Way Street* (1927) in a no less mystically inspired sentence about the teaching of antiquity, one closely connected with his notes "Concerning the Mimetic Faculty," which were written in the spring of 1933. In his book *One-Way Street* (in the piece "To the Planetarium") he does not, it is true, speak of the bond of the life forces in the magic name, but of the future which will belong alone to those who "live from the forces of the cosmos," in other words just those in whom the cosmic forces of life are tied together most intimately—even though not as in the case of Agesilaus Santander in a name, but in the intoxication of cosmic

experience that the human being of antiquity possessed and that
Benjamin still sought to rescue for the expected seizure of power
by the proletariat—more in the spirit of Blanqui than of Marx.

From this point Benjamin's piece turns to the angel and the
latter's association with his own, obviously secret, name. For this
name is for Benjamin no enrichment of him who bears it, as is
clearly stated in the first version. Unexpectedly the human person
of Benjamin now changes into the angelic-Luciferian nature of
the angel in the picture by Paul Klee, a nature connected so
unfathomably deeply and indeed magically with his own. The
first version still states, unambiguously referring to the name
Agesilaus Santander as Benjamin's name, that the new name,
which he discovered in it due to a new situation of life, takes
away much from him, above all the gift of perseverance by virtue
of which he was able "to appear wholly as he was of old."
Somehow he is no longer identical with himself. In the final
version, however, the talk turns to the *picture of this new name*,
which was revealed to him. Everything said here about this
picture must, in connection with what follows, be referred to the
picture by Klee.

Now if this picture is called *Angelus Novus*, whereby its
proper name—which is to say the one it should have according to
Benjamin—"becomes audible," then at the same time it loses
much. While in the first version Benjamin's secret name took
from him the gift of being himself, of seeming wholly as of old;
the picture of this name, the Luciferian angel, loses the gift of
appearing anthropomorphic, as is said in the final version. Here
Benjamin transcends the old angelogical tradition according to
which the angel of a person preserves the latter's pure, arche-
typal form [*Gestalt*] and thereby becomes anthropomorphic. The
next sentence deals with the transformation of the name
Agesilaus Santander, the "old name" as it is called in the first
version, into the name Angelus Satanas, which comes to light out
of it, "armored and encased," through a permutation of the
letters. For Benjamin the name projects itself on a picture,
instead of the customary view, according to which a picture is
approximately circumscribed by a name. This picture, however,
does not call itself *Angelus Satanas*, though it is that, but rather:
new angel. The second version makes precisely clear that this was

not the true name in Benjamin's sense. For the angel passed himself off as a new one belonging to those whose only function consists of a hymn before the throne of God, "before he was prepared to name himself." On the picture in Benjamin's room he did not name himself, but Benjamin knew with whom he was dealing. The description "armored and encased" refers to the way of the depiction of the angel in the picture. Benjamin interrupted the angel from the singing of his hymn, or else, in that in Klee's picture he confined him for years in his room, he took him away "unduly long" from the chanting of his hymn, as the second version says.

The following is intelligible only if one takes into consideration the situation in which, as Benjamin sees it here, the new name, upon the reaching of a new maturity, stepped out of the old name and at the same time settled down in the picture by Paul Klee in his room. Benjamin's marriage from 1917 to April 1921 proceeded unimpaired, unaffected by other experiences of love, in spite of many other difficulties. It came to a destructive crisis in the spring of 1921, one full of consequences for his life, when on seeing Jula Cohn again in Berlin he developed a passionate inclination for her. She was a young artist and sister of a friend of his youth, a woman to whom he was tied only by a casual friendship between 1912 and 1917 and whom he had not seen again since then. This love remained unrequited, but for years it constituted the discreet center of his life. When he obtained the Klee picture he was in the throes of his love, through which also, as he sees it in these pieces, his new secret name was revealed to him, transmitted by Klee's picture.

Benjamin was born under the sign of Saturn, as he expressly testifies only here in all the writings of his known to me. Thus the angel, to whom astrological characterology was no less familiar than to the author of *The Origin of German Tragic Drama* and to his melancholy nature, could make him pay for the disturbance of his heavenly and hymnal performance.[13] For after he had

13. One may perhaps point to an almost obtrusive parallel between Benjamin's relation to the angel and a Jewish tradition about Jacob's battle with the angel in Genesis 32:27. Here, too, the tradition of the Talmud and the Midrash fluctuates about whether the angel with whom Jacob wrestled at the break of day was an angel of light or perhaps Samael, the name of Satan or Lucifer in the Jewish tradition. The "man" who, according to the text of the Bible, wrestled with Jacob and at the break of day said to him, "Let me

appeared to Benjamin in masculine form in the picture by Paul
Klee, he sent him, as if to square his account with Benjamin, his
feminine form in the earthly appearance of the beloved woman;
not, to be sure, in the direct fulfillment of a great love, but rather
"by way of the longest, most fatal detour," which is probably an
allusion to the difficult, and for Benjamin fatal, situation into
which this relationship, remaining essentially unconsummated,
had brought him. One could perhaps also interpret the sentence
to mean that the detour refers to the time from 1914—when he
met the girl, indeed extraordinarily beautiful—to 1921 during
which his life made long, and for him fatal, detours, as for
example his first engagement in 1914 and his marriage, which in
retrospect, at least during certain periods, he experienced as fatal
to himself. This interpretation corresponds with the sentence
about Saturn as "the planet of detours and delays": he became
conscious of his love only after great delay.

What does not seem transparent is the concluding remark of
this sentence to the effect that the angel and his feminine form in
the figure of the beloved did not know each other though they
had once been most intimately adjacent to each other. In the
same year in which the Angelus appeared in his life, there also
appeared almost at the same time this woman in the center of his
life, although they did not see each other in spite of this
"adjacency": when she was in Berlin, the Angelus was not yet
there—if, that is, he was not to be seen in the above mentioned
Klee exhibition which Benjamin visited at the time. And later,
when he had obtained the picture, she was in Heidelberg, her

go, for the dawn is coming," supposedly said to him, according to one version of the
Jewish legend: "I am an angel and since I have been created the time has until now not
come for me to say my hymn [before God], but just now the hour for the singing has
come." And just as Benjamin's angel makes him suffer for having prevented him from the
singing of his hymn, by detaining him in his room, so also does the angel of the Biblical
narrative, and the legend spun out of it, exact suffering for the delay of his hymn by
dislocating Jacob's hip joint. In the Midrash (Genesis Rabba 78, §1) an opinion is expressly
brought up that Jacob's angel is among those "new angels" ever and again created anew,
whose task is limited to the singing of hymns. Just as Benjamin in his encounter with the
angel transfigured his own name Agesilaus Santander to a new secret name, so too does
Jacob, according to the Biblical narrative, change his own name in his battle with the
angel and is from then on called Israel. And in the Jewish legend, too, the angel refuses,
upon Jacob's question, to give his own name: "I do not know into what name I will
transfigure myself"—completely like Angelus Novus's not wishing to give his real name to
Benjamin.

residence at the time. When in the late summer of 1921 she was in Berlin, where I made her acquaintance, the picture was still hanging in my place in Munich. However, the sentence about adjacency could also refer to the fact that before Klee's picture itself had been painted in Munich, Jula Cohn, who was a sculptress, had her studio in Munich at the time Benjamin studied there from autumn 1915 to 1916.

Benjamin's virtue of patient awaiting, which is exhibited by the Saturnian features of hesitation, the slowest revolutions and decisions, is, as he now says, his strength. The angel, in this a genuine Satanas, wanted to destroy Benjamin through his "feminine form" and the love for her—in the first version the text says "accosted" him; the second version speaks of the fact that he "wanted to accost" him in this manner—but in the history of this love the angel first really demonstrated Benjamin's strength. For when he ran into a woman who cast her spell on him, he was resolved (the first version is silent about this) to assert the fulfillment of this love by "lying in wait" on the life path of this woman, until at last, "sick, aged, in tattered clothes" she would fall to his lot. The general formulation of the sentence (in the second version) possibly includes a number of women who cast this spell over him, and could refer to both of the women who played a role in Benjamin's life after the crisis of his marriage: to the "feminine form" of the angel in the person of Jula Cohn and to Asja Lacis, who had great influence on his life from 1924 to 1930, especially on his political turning to revolutionary thinking, but over whom he could cast his spell as little as he could over his earlier (and partly concurrent) great love. He lay in wait on the life path of both women, but above all, when he wrote the piece under consideration, still on that of Jula Cohn, from whom he did not wish to leave off, although in 1929–1930 he divorced his wife for Asja Lacis, without this divorce then leading to marriage or closer ties with her. When he wrote this piece in 1933, she had already been back in Russia for three years, and he never saw her again, while during these years Jula Cohn, married and the mother of a child, lived in Berlin and at the time also made a wooden bust of him—lost in the chaos of war—of which I possess two photographs. The expectation to which he gives expression in the sketch was not fulfilled. But Benjamin had the right to say of

himself, "Nothing could enfeeble the patience of the man."
Benjamin was the most patient human being I ever came to
know, and the decisiveness and radicalism of his thinking stood in
vehement contrast to his infinitely patient and only very slowly
opening nature. And to deal with Benjamin one had to have the
greatest patience oneself. Only very patient people could gain
deeper contact with him.[14]

Thus in the following sentences he praises the wings of his
patience, which resemble the wings of the angel that are open in
Klee's picture, in that they maintain themselves with a minimum
of exertion in the presence of the beloved one for whom he waits.
The reason Benjamin passed from the unequivocal formulation of
the first version, referring to the person of the beloved, to the
more equivocal formulation of the second version is probably
connected with the clearer specification of the figure of the angel
in the latter. For the final formulation contains not only the
possible reference to the presence or countenance of the beloved
one—whom he was resolved never to leave even though he did
not possess her—but also an assertion about the angel himself,
who maintains himself in the presence of Benjamin, onto whom
he casts his wide-open eyes, whose glance never seems to become
empty, and whom as the person chosen by him, he was resolved
never to leave. From a statement about the wings of patience, the
second version goes on to a statement that refers more precisely
to the wings of the angel, who, after he has once descended from
heaven, holds him, as his Angelus Satanas, under his sway for
years, indeed in some way until the end. This passing from the
patience of Benjamin to the angel himself is also carried through
in the further sentences of both versions. In both versions the
Satanic character of the angel is emphasized by the metaphor of
his claws and knife-sharp wings, which could find support in the
depiction of Klee's picture. No angel, but only Satan, possesses
claws and talons, as is, for example, expressed in the widespread

14. Even during his internment in the stadium near Paris and in Nevers in the autumn
of 1939, Benjamin made an indelible impression on people who came into closer contact
with him at the time, by his infinite and stoic patience, which he demonstrated without
any ostentation whatever and under the most difficult conditions. This has been made
grippingly clear to me only recently by the oral descriptions I owe to Moshe Max Aron
(from Frankfurt, now in Jerusalem) who lived closely together with Benjamin during
Benjamin's whole stay in the camp from September 1 to the middle of November 1939.

notion that on the Sabbath witches kiss the "clawed hands" of Satan.[15]

In the first version, Benjamin speaks further of his patience, which, though it conceals a secret sharpness in itself, nevertheless makes no arrangements actively to pounce "on her whom it has sighted," which is to say the beloved. Instead, it learns from the angel, who likewise encompasses his partner in his view, though he does not accost him, but rather yields and thereby pulls him along, as Benjamin here interprets Klee's picture. From here on the first version at once goes on to the conclusion. The second version is, by way of contrast, decisively different and more detailed. In a wholly new turn of Benjamin's view, the angel no longer resembles that which Benjamin has or is, but rather all that from which in his current state he has had to part, what he no longer has. He mentions not only the people from whom he has had to part, but also the things that meant something to him, especially emphasizing the latter. As a refugee at the beginning of a new turn of his life he is removed from those who were close to him. At a distance they take on something of the angel, who, after all, is also no longer with him.

But more: it was precisely in the things he possessed in his room in Berlin and toward which he had attuned a deep contemplative relation that the angel had settled. By entering into these objects he made them transparent, and behind the surface of these things, which he remembers with a lively imagination, Benjamin sees the person for whom they were destined. This sentence finds its explanation in Benjamin's testament of July 27, 1932, written by him only one year earlier, in which he enumerated those objects which meant much to him and bequeathed one to each of his male and female friends. Thus he sees himself as a gift giver into whose gifts the angel has wandered. This pleasure in giving often occupied Benjamin as a predominant feature of his character, and whoever knew him, knows how right he was. In the *Berlin Chronicle*, which was also written on Ibiza, but a year earlier, he speaks of it as one of two features he has inherited from his maternal grandmother (Hed-

15. As, for example, it is mentioned in Hölty's *Hexenlied*. See *Gedichte* by Ludwig Heinrich Hölty (Hamburg, 1783), p. 143. The claws of Satan are a common metaphor in the Christian tradition.

wig Schoenflies): "my pleasure in giving and my pleasure in traveling." [16] The angel himself—so he sees it now—was perhaps allured by a "gift giver who goes away empty-handed," who had to part from everything that was near to him.

The turn of the phrase about the gift giver who goes away empty-handed reminds one of the conclusion of the book on tragic drama (p. 233) that quotes the famous verse from Psalm 126:6 in a paraphrase by one of the Baroque writers: "With weeping we strewed the seed into the fallow land/and went away in grief." Whereupon Benjamin then notes "Empty-handed does allegory go away." Just like the melancholy view that discovers in things the infinite depth of allegories, without however being able to complete the step over the transitory into the religious sphere and therefore at long last goes away empty-handed, because here salvation can fall to one's lot only by way of a miracle; so does it also happen to the gift giver, who goes away empty-handed, who never attains to the beloved whom he has given great portions of his creative power as a gift, even though in his imagination he had realized the deepest community with her, of which the conclusion of the piece is to speak.

Before this, however, Benjamin's consideration becomes engrossed once again in the form and nature of the angel, who, before he took up residence in the vanished things, used to confront him daily. Reference has already been made to the difference between the two versions, in which an assertion about Benjamin's patience is transformed into one about the angel himself. For now it is the angel who, though he possesses claws and knife-sharp wings for attack, does not look as if he is about to "pounce on the one who has sighted." It is difficult to decide whether in this dependent clause the word "him" [*ihn*] has been omitted due to Benjamin's neglect or whether it remains meaningful even without this supplement. I incline toward the first conception. While in the first version it is the beloved whom Benjamin's patience keeps in his field of vision, it is now Benjamin himself who has sighted the angel who was allured by

16. Cf. *Berliner Chronik* (Frankfurt-am-Main: Bibliothek Suhrkamp, No. 251, 1970), 80.

him. Even though the angel would have reason enough to pounce on Benjamin who, after all, interrupted his hymn, he proceeds completely differently. He grasps him who has attained a vision of him, who lets himself be tied eye to eye, firmly in his own eye. Then, however, after he has tarried long with Benjamin, he withdraws inexorably. He does so because it corresponds to his being, only now really disclosed to Benjamin. He takes with him the human being who encounters him or whom he encounters, for whom he perhaps has a message—not wholly in vain is the head of the angel in Klee's picture there, where curls are to be expected, encircled by scrolls of writing on which his message may have been inscribed.

The following sentences now disclose the nature of the angel. In the first version it still says that he pulls along his partner in the flight into a future "from which he has advanced." He knew the latter for it was his origin, and so he can hope for nothing new from it except the view of the person he keeps facing. He has been pushed forward from the future and goes back into it. This is wholly in the sense of the verse Karl Kraus put into the mouth of God in his poem, "The Dying Man" (*Der Sterbende Mensch*).

"You remained at the origin. Origin is the goal."

(*Du bliebst am Ursprung. Ursprung ist das Ziel.*) [17]

This verse was well known to Benjamin and he quoted it in an important passage, to be discussed below, in his last piece, which is intimately connected with the one we are considering.

In the final version there is, to be sure, more cautious talk of "that way into the future on which he came." Did he also come from the future? It is not directly said here but seems implied by the continuation. For how else should he know this way so well "that he traverses it without turning around and letting the one he has chosen"—that is to say Walter Benjamin himself—"out of view." Also pointing to this is the talk of the way of the return home, which is precisely the way into the future. Holding him in his sway, he pulls his human partner along with him and

17. Karl Kraus, *Worte in Versen*, I (1916), 67. Cf. also Werner Kraft, *Die Idee des Ursprungs bei Karl Kraus* in *Süddeutsche Zeitung*, July 25, 1971.

therewith makes him a participant in what the angel really
wants: happiness, even though in this regard he perhaps has as
little success as Benjamin himself, to whose life happiness was
denied, unless it is meant in the one sense here defined and
whose dialectical character corresponded to Benjamin's deepest
intention.

The association of the angel with happiness was first derived
from my poem about the picture by Klee in which the angel says
resignedly:

> My wing is ready for a flight,
> I'm all for turning back;
> For, even staying timeless time,
> I'd have but little luck.

> *(Mein Flügel ist zum Schwung bereit*
> *Ich kehrte gern zurück*
> *Denn blieb' ich auch lebendige Zeit*
> *Ich hätte wenig Glück.)*

The happiness of which my poem spoke referred, to be sure, to
the success of his mission, of which he expected little. For
Benjamin, however, this happiness, as the angel wishes it, has a
wholly new meaning. It refers, amazingly enough, to "the conflict
in which lies the ecstasy of the unique ('once only'), new, as yet
unlived, with that bliss of the 'once more,' the having again, the
lived."

The paradox of this formulation is evident. In contrast to the
familiar formula, "once and never again," happiness is based on
the conflict between the "once only" and the "yet again." For in
this sentence the unique, the "once only," is precisely *not* that
which one has lived through, the now of "lived time," as the
French expression *"le temps vécu"* expresses it, but rather the
wholly new and as yet unlived. In contrast to it stands the "once
more," directed to that which is capable of repetition, to
repetition of that which one has already lived through.[18] In

18. Here, then, already five years before Benjamin's paper on Baudelaire, in the
picture of *Angelus Novus*, the opposition, the "dialectic between the new and the
ever-same" is addressed or sighted, the opposition with which the third part of his
planned book on Baudelaire was to find its conclusion and crown, as he wrote to Adorno,
Briefe, Vol. II, p. 793. A basic theme of Benjamin's thinking is here still enclosed in
mystical form. To be sure, already in 1929, in a polemically skilled opposition to

leaping out of the familiar formula, Benjamin describes the melancholy happiness of the dialectician. Thus, too, there probably corresponds to the angel's way into the future of the as yet unlived and the new, an expectation of happiness that can only be fulfilled on the way of the return home, that once again traverses what one has already lived through. And the new, which he can only hope for on the way of the return home, consists only in taking along a new person to his origin. In the first version this newness was formulated even more reticently. There the new was not the taking along of a new person on the way of the return home, but only the *view* of the person to whom the angel turns his eyes, and which is the only one he can hope for from the future from which he came. In the final version, the way of the return home is no longer the flight into the Utopian future, which, rather, has disappeared here.

Standing over against these delimitations of happiness— which certainly say much about the angel but also something about the nature of Walter Benjamin's expectations of happiness —is the enigmatically ambiguous formulation of the concluding sentence, which poses the question: is the addressee of this sentence the angel or the beloved? Did Benjamin, when he first saw the angel, and Klee's picture affected him like a revelation of his own angel, journey back with the latter into the future that was his origin? Or does he address the beloved, whom he puts in a position parallel to the angel? As if he wanted, as it were, to say: When I for the first time really, that is to say lovingly, perceived you, I took you along to the place from which I came. I consider this second interpretation of the sentence to be the correct one. The "Just as I, no sooner than I had seen you" by which the concluding sentence is introduced, seems to me clearly to refer to the same situation discussed in this version after being introduced by the sentence "Thus with me."

I would paraphrase as follows: Just as with me, Walter Benjamin, the transformation of my secret name was revealed all at once in the moment of the "new maturity," the awakening of love, so I also journeyed, after scarcely having truly seen you for

"experience" [*Erlebnis*] he had formulated: "Experience [*Erlebnis*] wants the unique, and sensation, practical experience [*Erfahrung*], that which is ever the same." (*Gesammelte Schriften*, Vol. III [1972], p. 198.)

the first time "back with you from whence I came," which is to say: I took you, the beloved, along on the way from the origin into the future, or, however, on the way into this origin itself, in which I felt at one with you. Just as the angel takes along a new person on the way of the return home, so also did I take you along, when you appeared to me anew, on my way to the origin. Of what, precisely, this origin from whence he came consisted— this remains unsaid. Is it the future of happiness, which in the sense of the happiness desired by the angel, he hoped to enjoy with her, even though he did not achieve it, or is it an origin in another area, lying beyond the erotic sphere? I do not dare to decide between these possibilities. In any case the turn of the phrase "saw you for the first time" cannot at all refer to Benjamin's first encounter with Jula Cohn, whom after all he had in no way seen for the first time in 1921, when the angel appeared to him and he himself was transformed in love along with him. It seems to me that the context also precludes referring the sentence to Asja Lacis, whom he did not see at all until 1924.

In his encounter with the angel, Benjamin, in accordance with this piece, undergoes an illumination about himself. Benjamin expressed himself about the character of such an illumination in an essay on surrealism written in 1928 (published in the *Literarische Welt* in the beginning of 1929), employing a formulation the equivocality of which may have escaped some of his more recent readers. He speaks there about occult experiences and phantasmagoria:

> All serious research into occult, surrealistic phantasmagoric gifts, and phenomena has as its presupposition a dialectical interweaving which a romantic mind will never appropriate. . . . Rather we penetrate the mystery only to the extent that we rediscover it in daily life. . . . The most passionate investigation of telepathic phenomena, for example, will not teach one half as much about reading (which is an eminently telepathic procedure) as the profane illumination of reading will about telepathic phenomena. Or: the most passionate investigation of a hashish intoxication will not teach one half as much about thinking (which is an eminent narcotic) as the profane illumination of thinking will about hashish intoxication. The reader, the thinking one, the waiting one, the *flâneur* are as much types of the illuminated as

are the opium-eater, the dreamer, the drunken one. Not to speak of that most fearful drug—ourselves—which we take in solitude.[19]

According to Benjamin's sentence about the profane illumination of the reader and other types, out of the experience of daily life—if one would only get to the bottom of it—there leaps the mystical experience, the occult event still hidden in it. Reading is for him an occult event, although the philosophers do not like to admit this. For "profane illumination" is nevertheless still illumination and nothing else. The experience of the reader, the thinker, or the *flâneur* already contains everything that the so-called mystical experience contains, and does not first have to be forced into the latter. But in contradistinction to the materialistic conception of such experience, which causes mystical or occult experience to disappear, the latter is still present precisely there (in everyday experience).[20] In the phantasmagoria of his imagination, the picture of the *Angelus Novus* becomes for Benjamin a picture of his angel as the occult reality of his self.

V

It has been shown how in 1933 Benjamin understood the picture *Angelus Novus* in a deeply personal manner. But already in 1931 a perspective of Klee's picture had opened up to him, in which, in addition to the personal-mystical conception of the angel depicted above, a historical one first asks to be heard. Here, too, the angel appears in a prominent place, at the end of the great essay on Karl Kraus, in which almost for the first time in Benjamin's writings a Marxist way of thinking seeks to make its way alongside one based on the philosophy of language and metaphysics. Just at the end of his considerations—guided by such inspiration—of the social function of Karl Kraus, he comes to speak again of the *Angelus Novus*, in whom he once more recognizes the mission of Karl Kraus:

One must rather have followed the architect Adolf Loos in his

19. W. Benjamin, *Angelus Novus*, 1966, pp. 213–14.
20. This interpretation of the sentence contradicts the one by K. H. Bohrer, *Die gefährdete Phantasie oder Surrealismus und Terror* (Frankfurt, 1970), p. 44.

battle with the dragon "ornamentation," [21] one must have absorbed the Esperanto of the stellar creatures abounding in Scheerbart's stories, or have sighted Klee's *New Angel*, who would rather free human beings by taking from them than make them happy by giving to them, in order to grasp a humanity which confirms itself by destruction.

Seen that way, the emancipation that is perhaps hidden in the mission of the angel stands in opposition to happiness—an emancipation somewhat remote from the Revolution's auguries of happiness. Because of this, too, the humanity of justice, which is Karl Kraus's strictest feature, is destructive. The demon contained in Karl Kraus has been conquered by the angel:

> Not purity and not sacrifice have become the master of the demon; where, however, origin and destruction find each other, it is all over with his dominion. His conqueror stands before him as a creature made out of child and cannibal, not a new man; an inhuman creature, a new angel. Perhaps one of those who, according to the Talmud, are created anew each moment in innumerable hosts, in order—after they have lifted up their voice before God—to cease and to vanish into nought. Lamenting, accusing, or jubilating? No matter—the ephemeral work of Kraus is an imitation of this quickly vanishing voice. Angelus—that is the messenger of the old etchings.[22]

Before Benjamin dared to put his own confrontation with the angel down on paper, when he himself, almost hopeless like the angel, sat on Ibiza and had had to separate himself from everything that was part of him, he had already recognized the "perfect nature" of Karl Kraus—if I may use the expression of the old masters of hermetics—in the form of the angel (an inhuman angel as also in "Agesilaus Santander"). He, who undertook language's revenge on its destroyers, the press, is still one of the angels of the talmudic legend. It is no longer certain whether this angel recites a hymn, a song of jubilation, before God, for he would rather recite lamentations or accuse the destroyers of language, true to his hidden Satanic nature; indeed, in Hebrew the word *Satan* has the meaning of "accuser." But as

21. An allusion to the essay by Loos, *Ornament und Verbrechen*, 1907.
22. *Schriften*, Vol. II, pp. 194–95.

in the announcement of the periodical *Angelus Novus*, the truly actual is the ephemeral, and therefore the work of Karl Kraus imitates that quickly vanishing voice of the angel which has remained from the Jewish conception.

The final form which the angel assumed for Benjamin emerged from a new connection between these two views in the essay of 1931 and the sketch about himself of 1933. In the beginning of 1940, after his release from the camp in which, like almost all of the refugees from Hitler's Germany, he had been interned after the outbreak of the war, Benjamin wrote those "Theses on the Philosophy of History" in which he accomplished his awakening from the shock of the Hitler-Stalin pact. As a reply to this pact, he read them at this time to the writer Soma Morgenstern, an old acquaintance and companion in misfortune. They are as much a discussion of social democracy, as they constitute a metaphysical justification of a "historical material-ism," which owes more to theology—to which it so emphatically refers—than could be stomached by its current "Marxist" readers. These, after all, as their writings prove abundantly, feel themselves completely capable, like Marx himself, of managing even today without theology and therefore in their interpreta-tions they must emasculate the relevant passages in Benjamin. With good reason did an open-minded reader like Jürgen Habermas describe these theses, and precisely the one that will concern us here as "one of the most moving testimonies of the Jewish spirit." [23] For Benjamin, at the end of his life, historical materialism is no longer anything but a "puppet" that can win the historical game only by taking into its service the hidden mastery of theology, "which today, as we know, is wizened and has to keep out of sight." It did not, to be sure, remain all that invisible in these theses, in which frequently nothing remains of historical materialism except the term itself.[24]

Following the above cited verse from my poem of 1921, which serves as a motto, one reads in the ninth of these theses:

There is a painting by Klee called *Angelus Novus*. It shows an angel looking as though he is about to move away from something

23. J. Habermas, *Philosophisch-politische Profile* (Frankfurt-am-Main: Suhrkamp Taschenbuch No. 265, 1971), p. 55.

24. In 1940, his conception of the significance of theology had not deviated essentially from the one advocated in 1928, in which, in a sketch in memory of a hashish "trip," he still found the "deepest truths" in the sphere of the theological (*Haschisch*, p. 75).

he is fixedly contemplating. His eyes are staring, his mouth is open, his wings are spread. This is how the angel of history must look. His face is turned toward the past. Where we perceive a chain of events, he sees one single catastrophe that keeps piling wreckage on wreckage and hurls it in front of his feet. The angel would like to stay, awaken the dead, and make whole what has been smashed. But a storm is blowing from Paradise; it has got caught in his wings with such violence that the angel can no longer close them. This storm irresistibly propels him into the future to which his back is turned, while the pile of debris before him grows skyward. This storm is what we call progress.[25]

Here, then, Benjamin's personal angel, who stands between past and future and causes him to journey back "from whence I came," has turned into the angel of history, in a new interpretation of Klee's picture. He stares into the past, from which he is removing himself or just about to remove himself, but he turns his back to the future into which a storm from Paradise is driving him. This storm from Paradise blows into his wings and prevents him from closing them and tarrying. So he proceeds along like a herald before this storm, which in profane language is called progress. He announces the future from which he came, but his countenance is turned toward the past. The new turn of phrase in the conception of the angel's mission quotes almost verbatim the old text he had in front of him in his notebooks, at the time of writing. Whereas in Agesilaus Santander there stood the concrete human being Walter Benjamin, whom the angel drew along with him, or after him, into the future out of which he had been thrust, there now stands man as a general essence, as bearer of the historical process. But if before it was the *patience* of the lover who waits, it is now the *storm* from Paradise that drives him into the future, though he does not so much as turn around his countenance.

The antithesis in the transformation of the sentences from patience to storm, which all the more casts light on Benjamin's changed conception, is a striking one. But what is more, Paradise is at once the origin and the primal past of man as well as the utopian image of the future of his redemption—a conception of the historical process that is really cyclical rather than dialectical.

25. *Gesammelte Schriften*, Vol. I, pp. 697–98.

"Origin is the goal"—even at this time, and not for nothing, does this sentence by Kraus stand as motto over the fourteenth thesis. Even in the earlier sketch the angel yields and withdraws back into the future "incessantly" or "inexorably." Why incessantly? The reasons are given only in the theses, in which the storm prevents him from tarrying and drives him on. What is really deeply moving and melancholy in this new image of the angel is that he walks into a future into which he does not look at all and will never look, so long as he, as the angel of history, fulfills his sole and singular mission.

This angel no longer sings any hymns. Indeed, it is more than doubtful whether he will fulfill his angelic mission at all. That is connected with Benjamin's conception of the past in this thesis. That which appears as history and past to the human observer—I should say to the undialectical philosopher of history—the angel sees as one great catastrophe, which in a pernicious eruption incessantly "keeps piling wreckage on wreckage" and hurls it at the feet of the angel. He knows of his task: he would really like to "awaken the dead and make whole what has been smashed." In this sentence two themes come together that were well known to Benjamin, a theme from the Christian Baroque and another one from Jewish mysticism. It is already said in "The Origin of German Tragic Drama" that for the Baroque writers of allegory history was not a process in which eternal life takes shape, but rather a "process of incessant decay." The Baroque dismemberment, of which there is so much talk in the book on tragic drama and which the angel of this thesis takes up again when he wishes "to make whole what has been smashed," is connected with the melancholy gaze at the past of history. The process of decay has turned into the one great catastrophe which brings the past before the angel's eyes only as a pile of debris. At the same time, however, Benjamin's meaning includes the kabbalistic concept of *tikkun*, the messianic restoration and repair which mends and restores the original being of things, and of history as well, after they have been smashed and corrupted by the "breaking of the vessels." [26] To be sure, for the Lurianic *kabbalah* the awaking of

26. On this concept, with which Benjamin was familiar from conversations with me as well as from F. J. Molitor's work, *Philosophie der Geschichte*, cf. my exposition in *Major*

the dead and the joining together and restoring of what has been smashed and broken is the task not of an angel but of the Messiah. Everything historical, unredeemed, has according to its nature a fragmentary character.

The angel of history, however, as Benjamin sees him here, fails in this task, which can be fulfilled, in the last thesis of this sequence, only by the Messiah, who might enter through the "strait gate" of every fulfilled second of historical time, as Benjamin says in an exposition concerning the relationship of the Jews to time and the future. What prevents the angel from such a completion of his mission? Precisely that storm from Paradise, which does not permit him to tarry, but also the unredeemed past itself, which as a pile of debris grows skyward before him.[27] That he can overcome this pile of debris or go so far as to join it together in a Utopian or redeemed unity, of this nothing is said. It is precisely "progress" which causes the real *tikkun* of redemption to turn into an ever more threatening and insoluble problem. The solution of that problem, then, in the language of theology, lies with the Messiah; in the language of historical materialism, however, for the sake of which Benjamin annexes theology, it consists of the dialectical leap "in the open air of history," of the revolution which for Benjamin is "a tiger's leap into the past," as is said in the fourteenth of these theses.

The angel of history is, then, basically a melancholy figure, wrecked by the immanence of history, because the latter can only be overcome by a leap that does not save the past of history in an "eternal image," but rather in a leap leading out of the

Trends in Jewish Mysticism (1961), pp. 268–74. Benjamin also knew my presentation of these thoughts appearing in 1932 in the article *Kabbala* of the (German) *Encyclopaedia Judaica*, Vol. IX, columns 693–98.

27. Hannah Arendt says of the situation of the angel: "The angel of history observes the field of debris of the wholly unparadisical past, but the storm of progress blows him backwards into the future" (see her Introduction to Walter Benjamin, *Illuminations* [New York, 1969], pp. 12–13. That book contains a translation of "Theses on the Philosophy of History" by Harry Zohn, pp. 253–64, from which the passages quoted in this essay have been adapted). But precisely in the "Agesilaus Santander," which was unknown to Hannah Arendt, the angel in fact retreats into the future, as there is no mention yet made of progress. She further remarks on the above-quoted sentence: "that a dialectically sensible, rationally interpretable process could present itself to such eyes—that is out of the question." But is that right? Certainly not an unequivocal process, but why not a dialectically sensible one? The immanent logic of Benjamin's conception, as I have attempted to present it here, seems to me sensible in spite of the paradox inherent in it.

historical continuum into the "time of now," whether the latter is revolutionary or messianic. It is a matter of dispute whether one can speak here—as I am rather inclined to do—of a melancholy, indeed desperate, view of history for which the hope that the latter might be burst asunder, by an act like redemption or revolution, continues to have about it something of that leap into transcendence which these theses seem to deny but which is even then implied in their materialistic formulations as their secret core. To be sure, with what one is accustomed to call historical materialism, this angel of the last datable writing by Benjamin has left in common only the ironic relation of the *termini technici*, which, however, signify the opposite of what a more robust, less mystical materialist than Walter Benjamin would like to understand by them.

Benjamin divided up the function of the Messiah as crystalized by the view of history of Judaism: into that of the angel who must fail in his task, and that of the Messiah who can accomplish it. In this division, if one keeps in mind the writings of ten years discussed here, the angel itself has become, *sit venia verbo*, "transfunctioned." But his image has remained a "dialectical image" in the sense of Benjamin's usage of this concept. This concept first appears in his work in a connection not yet estranged by Marxism.[28] Later he says of it what certainly holds good of his interpretation of Klee's angel: "The dialectical image is a flashing one . . . an image flashing in the Now of Knowability." In it the "salvation of what has been is accomplished"—and only in it.[29]

The reality of the messenger from the world of Paradise who is incapable of accomplishing his mission is dialectically burst asunder by the storm wind blowing from Paradise. I would interpret it this way: by a history and its dynamic determined by Utopia and not, say, the means of production. As angel of history he really has nothing to hope for from his efforts in its behalf, nothing other than what became of the angel in "Agesilaus Santander," who "can hope for the new on no way" except on the way of the return home on which, because of an encounter

28. Cf. the piece "Nach der Vollendung," *Gesammelte Schriften*, Vol. IV (1972), p. 438.

29. In the piece "Zentral-Park," *Gesammelte Schriften*, Vol. I, (1974), p. 682.

with a new human being, the human being Walter Benjamin, he takes the latter along with him.

If one may speak of Walter Benjamin's genius, then it was concentrated in this angel. In the latter's saturnine light Benjamin's life itself ran its course, also consisting only of "small victories," and "great defeats," as he described it from a deeply melancholy point of view in a letter which he addressed to me on July 26, 1932, one day before his intended, but at the time not executed, suicide.[30]

30. *Briefe*, Vol. II, p. 556.

Two Letters to
Walter Benjamin*

I

Jerusalem, February 20, 1930

. . . It may be good, after your recent letters—especially the first one, which aroused a most peculiar feeling of uneasiness in me—in which you have broached the matter of our acute mutual concern in a manner altogether unmistakable to me, that we go on to make it clear to ourselves where we stand. Three years ago you were of the opinion, which I shared with you, that you had arrived at a point where a fruitful coming to terms with Judaism appeared as the one and only way to a positive progress in your work. On the basis of this insight, about which both of us seemed to be certain, I did what I did, for the purpose of securing you the possibility of realizing your intentions.°° Now the question—and after three years have elapsed, it seems to answer itself on the basis of your position and preoccupations—is as follows: has not that idea, at one time even described and advocated by you to Magnes, become a thing of the past? After all, you prove *in actu* that, on the one hand, the cluster of problems into which you have delved, and, on the other hand, the position of the most outstanding literary critic you have achieved—or in any case, I am sure, can achieve—prove to be continuously fruitful and positively self-fulfilling for you, and all this, contrary to your own expectations, altogether beyond that Jewish world of which we

° From Walter Benjamin, *Briefe* (Frankfurt-am-Main: Bibliothek Suhrkamp, 1966), edited by Gershom Scholem and Theodor W. Adorno, Vol. II, pp. 510–12; 525–29. Translated by Werner J. Dannhauser.

°° Scholem had secured him a stipend that was to make it possible for him to devote himself exclusively to the study of Hebrew for one year.—Ed.

thought at that time. I deem it advisable that we get this clear, if only so that I am not put into a false position here in Jerusalem, since, after all I can't very well maintain year after year that you are about to come to a decision at which, it seems to me ever more probable, you will never really arrive.

Since, however, both of us know all too well from long experience that with you more than with most people, it is only your inner inhibitions that bring about your outer ones, we must face the following question. Isn't it obvious that the inhibitions that have now been asserting themselves for twelve years as regards your position on these Jewish matters, though in a different spiritual or physical form in each epoch of your life, are so fundamental, that instead of indulging in false illusions about a coming to terms with Judaism that can never come to be, though for fifteen years we considered such a coming to terms as our common cause, it would be better and preferable squarely to face the reality (still distressing to me, but at least unequivocal) of your existence beyond that world? It is, after all, evident that from your present absorption in problems you are posing for yourself you will turn to new and different ones; that the opinion you expressed three years ago to the effect that without the way to Hebrew the only way of unobjectionable activity would lead from literature into the labors of pure party politics—that this opinion has turned out to be exaggerated and false and that especially from the loftiness of your presumptive position as the one genuine critic of German literature one can see no *necessity* of a way to Hebrew.

With these considerations I would like to induce you not only to come to terms with yourself about this matter—I have the impression that you will, after all, hardly contradict, that in this case you do not like to do that, and especially not with due passion—but to explain it to me with the same frankness I offer you and believe I have a right to expect from you concerning this question above all others; so that, come what may, we do not mutually deceive ourselves by means of a private apocalypse about the divergences of our courses of life. I am, after all, certainly the man who will endure things with composure and perhaps even a tolerable degree of understanding, if it should turn out to be a fact that in this life you can and do no longer count on a real encounter with Judaism beyond the medium of our friendship.

Sometimes I believe that in speaking about these things you show more consideration for me than consideration for yourself. As paradoxical as that may sound, I really think it is a correct rendering of your position in many a moment and I would have to feel differently about you than I do feel if I were not to suffer from this situation. Now and then I say to myself: out of friendship to me Walter does not dare to furnish a clear account of his condition, he avoids "transferring himself into the center of that condition in a knowing way" *—but I assure you that neither morally nor symbolically can or should this be a valid reason for you. For me it is far more important to know where you really are than where you perhaps hope to betake yourself one day, since, after all, the constitution of your life makes it certain that you—more than anyone else—will always arrive at a place different from the one you desired. If, however, I should prove to be completely wrong in these thoughts—of course, I don't believe I am—well; it is all the better to have expressed them for once. In any case, your biography for the last ten years provides ample occasions for such errors, even among your friends. All the more must we wish that the crisis of your external life**—which I must infer from the intimations of your letters, without, however, having the power to intercede—will at least also result in securing you clarity about where you belong as well as where you stand.

Thought in friendship and written with all my heart.

Yours,
GERHARD

II

Jericho, March 31, 1931

Dear Walter:

I am staying in Jericho for a week, occupied by doing nothing

* Quotation from a piece by Benjamin.—Ed.
** His divorce.—Ed.

and the like, in preparation for a visit from my mother and my brother occurring in Jerusalem next week; tomorrow morning I am going to take a little journey on the Dead Sea, on which I have never been in all these years. My idleness was interrupted by the copies of your letters, those to [Bertolt] Brecht and [Max] Rychner,° which will have to substitute for an "original letter." The letter to Brecht confirms my expectation, which I have had all the while, that nothing could come of the journal of which you write me, though in my ignorance I can't say much about the matter. On the other hand, I would like to tell you a few things about the other letter, which to a certain extent strikes me as being addressed to me as well. I very much regret not knowing Rychner's essay, which may well contain real insights. However, what can be said about your letter is presumably independent of that—the question *dic cur hic?* °° is in any case well formulated. I beg of you to receive my remarks as an abbreviation and in the same spirit of benevolence, which you were entitled to expect from the reader of the letter.

Since I have become familiar with more or less comprehensive specimens from your pen of the consideration of literary matters in the spirit of dialectical materialism, the insight has taken hold of me in a clear and distinct manner that in this production you perpetrate a self-deception in a peculiarly intensive way; for me this is especially and most significantly documented by your admirable essay on Karl Kraus, which I unfortunately do not have here with me.

The expectation you express that so obviously understanding a reader as Mr. Rychner will know how to find in this essay, in any sense whatever, a justification of your sympathies for dialectical materialism "between the lines" strikes me as completely misleading: the exact opposite is much more likely to be the case, by which I mean the following. It seems to me that it is clear to every open-minded reader of your writings that while in recent years you have exerted yourself frantically—pardon me for saying so—to expound your insights, which are in part very

---

° A Swiss literary historian and journalist (1897–1965) and friend of Hugo von Hofmannsthal and Paul Valéry, who labored to bring classical world literature to the attention of German readers.—Ed.

°° "Say why you are here"—a medieval proverb—Ed.

far-reaching, in a phraseology approaching the Communist one as far as possible, but that—and this is what seems to me to matter—a stupendous incompatibility and lack of relation exists between your *real* and *alleged* process of thinking. You reach your insights not, say, by a strict application of a materialist method, but completely independent of it (in the best case), or (in the worst case, as in some of your pieces of the last two years) by playing with the ambiguities and dissonances (*Interferenzerscheinungen*) of that method. As you yourself put it with perfect correctness to Mr. Rychner, your own and solid insights grow out of—to put it briefly—the metaphysics of language, which is quite properly the field in which, having attained undisguised clarity, you could be a highly significant figure, the legitimate heir of the most fruitful and authentic traditions of a Hamann and Humboldt.

By contrast, the ostensible effort now to fit these results into a framework, in which they suddenly present themselves as the seeming results of materialist reflections, introduces into your thought a wholly alien form-element, one easily detached by every intelligent reader, and one which imprints on your productions of the time the stamp of the adventurous, ambiguous, and prestidigitatious. You will understand that I do not use such a demonstrative mode of expression without the greatest reluctance; but when I picture to myself the altogether fantastic discrepancy gaping between the true method and the one alleged by the terminology in so excellent and crucial an essay as the one on Karl Kraus; when I think of the way everything suddenly limps there *because the insight of the metaphysician about the language of the bourgeois,* or let us even say that of capitalism, is in an artificial and all-too-transparent manner *identified with those of the materialist about the economic dialectic of society* to such an extent that it might almost seem as if one entailed the other!—then I am dismayed to have to tell myself that this self-deception is possible only because you will it, and more: that it can last only as long as it is not put to the materialist test.

The complete certainty I maintain to having about what would happen to the body of your writing, if it were to chance to appear *within* the Communist Party is quite woeful. I almost believe that you will this state of suspension, when you ought really to welcome every means of ending it. That your dialectic is not that of the materialist to which you try to approximate it would turn out to be unequivocally and explosively clear the moment your fellow dialecticians, as could not fail to take place, would unmask you as a typical counterrevolutionary and bourgeois. As long as you write for bourgeois citizens about bourgeois citizens, the *genuine* materialist can afford not to care, I might say not to give a damn, whether you wish to harbor the illusion of being at one with them. On the contrary, he ought really to have every interest, from a dialectical perspective, to strengthen you in your illusion, for presumably even he could realize that on *that* terrain your dynamite might be stronger than his. (Comparable, let us say—pardon the parallel—to the way he encouraged certain psychoanalytic Bolshevists in Germany à la Erich Fromm, whom in Moscow he would immediately send to Siberia.) You are of no use to him in his own camp, for there the first steps to the heart of the matter would lead to a blowup revealing the purely abstract identification of your spheres of interest. Since it happens that you yourself, in the other corner, are to a certain extent interested in a certain *in suspense* state, you get along quite well with each other. The only question is, to say this in a seemly way as well, how long, given so ambiguous a relationship, the morality of your insights, one of your most precious possessions, can remain healthy.

Yet it is *not* the case, as you may perhaps see it, that you ask yourself how far one can get, say, by way of experiment with the attitude of the materialist, since in your creative procedure it is evident that you have never yet and in no case assumed that position; what is more, as an old theologian, I believe I am permitted to say that you are totally incapable of doing so successfully. It is, of course, conceivable, given a certain robustness of your resolution which I believe I can presuppose in this case, that you can pretty well project your insights—reached as you so truly say by theological procedures—onto the terminology of materialism, along with a few inescapable dislocations to which nothing corresponds in that which is to be duplicated—*dialectica dialecticam amat.* Therefore the two of you may after all keep up your illegitimate association for a long time, namely exactly as long as circumstances will permit you to persist in your ambiguity; and that, with the historical conditions now obtaining, can be a very long time. Thus as much as I dispute that there was something, as you maintain to Rychner, that led you to the application of the materialistic view, to which your work, after all, adds no significant contribution whatever, as much do I understand that you have succumbed to the self-deception that the introduction into metaphysics of a certain slant and terminology in which there is reference to classes and capitalism, though hardly to their opposites, turns your reflections into materialist ones.

The sure means of proving the full truth of my view, namely your entry into the ranks of the Communist Party, is, to be sure, one I can recommend to you only ironically. After all, to test how far a strict observation of the economic-materialist methods of research leads away from the ideal attitude of the metaphysical-dialectical activity and procedure of science (in order to vary your formulation)—to undertake such a test, which can only end in a *capitis diminutio* of your existence, is something that as a friend I am incapable of advising you without any further ado. I am rather inclined to assume that one fine day this connection will end as inadvertently as it began. If I am mistaken about that, then the high expenses of that mistake will, as I fear, have to be borne by you, which, to be sure, will be paradoxical, but only fitting to the situation that will then have arisen: you would, to be sure, not be the last, but perhaps the most *incomprehensible* victim of that very confusion between religion and politics, the articulation of which in their proper relation could be expected more definitely from none other than you yourself. But, as the ancient Jews of Spain used to say, What time can do, reason can also do.

About other matters, another time. I am always waiting for letters from you; perhaps this one will set your fountain pen into polemical motion!

With the most heartfelt greetings,
YOUR GERHARD

Israel and the Diaspora[*]

I

If I am to speak about Israel and the Diaspora and, more precisely, about their mutual interdependence, I can scarcely cherish the illusion of saying anything really new on this subject. In recent years, indeed since the establishment of the State of Israel, no subject has been treated with greater intensity and passion than this one. Whatever could have been said, from every possible point of view and in every possible way, has long ago been said. I almost believe that I am just about the only Jew with any power of articulation who has still not spoken about this topic.

There is, to be sure, a good reason for my reticence about expressing myself on this subject: I have no firm, certain, unequivocal answer to offer. My own thoughts—and which one of us could be without thoughts on this topic?—were of a contradictory nature, and I could not get anywhere with myself. Throughout my life I was tossed hither and yon by expectations and disappointments; expectations from the Jewish people in general and, in particular, from us who were at work in the land of Israel. I have come to know many phases of this process, from highest expectation to deepest disappointment, indeed despair; and I have gone through them myself. That has left me without any inclination to speak with any semblance of authority, which

* "Israel und die Diaspora," a lecture delivered at the annual convention of the League of Swiss Jewish Communities, Geneva, May 14, 1969. Published in Gershom Scholem, *Judaica* 2 (Frankfurt-am-Main: Bibliothek Suhrkamp, 1970), pp. 55–76. Translated by Werner J. Dannhauser.

in this case could have been nothing but presumption and pretense. I would nevertheless like to present and offer for reflection some considerations that seem to me to be of special relevance to the discussion of this complex problem. It is certainly true that throughout my life I have believed in the rebirth of the Jewish people through the Zionist movement, but within the framework of that belief—which, nonetheless, in oh so many an hour, threatened to dissolve because it struck me as deceptive—I belonged much more to the group of those who posed questions than to those who knew how to give answers. Given the multiplicity of aspects disclosed by a consideration of the relationship between Israel and the Diaspora, aspects I wish to consider here, an answer can, after all, be only an affirmation of a faith and a hope—and one might say that even that would amount to a good deal.

There is an old saying that is the basis for many a Jewish legend: on the day of the destruction of the Temple, the Messiah was born. This bold sentence, which, coming from the old Rabbis, certainly is food for thought, probably expresses in a paradoxical form the feeling—not to say the knowledge—that the great historical catastrophe of the Jewish people and redemption are inseparably connected, dialectically intermeshed. With the falling into ruin of the Temple, the main focus of a people that had understood itself as God's chosen people, the possibility of redemption is disclosed from another level and from a focal point that cannot as yet be determined. Of what did this "redemption" consist? Concerning this question, one finds the most various and contradictory views in the history of Judaism and its theology. This is not the place to speak of that. But in whatever way "redemption" was understood, even in the formulations of the faithful and the mystics, it always terminates in a restitution of the destroyed central focal point; a restitution drawing its strength not only from the intercession of a supernatural, divine power, but also from the depth of the catastrophe itself, from the experience of exile, which was the experience of Israel's homelessness in the world of history.

The religious categories in which the experience is described have undergone a change in recent generations, certainly not for everyone, but for very many of us. But even the most secular forms in which this experience defines itself in the large circles of those who do not deny their Jewish identity—who, indeed, affirm it passionately—still vibrate in resonance with a secret tone of the religious. After all, the old saying of Dostoevsky's, certainly no great admirer of the Jews, that he could not conceive of a Jew who had no God, has been confirmed by the religious passion with which the Jewish socialists and fighters for the social revolution took up their cause.

This falling apart of, and indeed conflict between, conceptions that are on the one hand religious and tradition-oriented, and on the other hand secularized and directed to a metamorphosis of Judaism into rejuvenated forms—it is this point which here, too, in the discussion occupying us, plays a highly significant role. The relationship between Israel and the Diaspora, Jewishness in *galut,* cannot be illuminated unless we give an account of the processes and differentiations connected with the emergence of Zionism and especially persistently with the founding of the State of Israel. What I mean by this can be rendered clearly.

At the time of the appearance of the Zionist movement, the Jewish communities of the Diaspora represented institutions in which a Judaism, on which the struggle for Emancipation had left its imprint, defined itself in purely religious categories, originating in trains of thought that were religiously orthodox but which might also have been liberally reinterpreted. Measured against the totality of Jewish life in the period before Emancipation, it was a most watered-down version of Judaism; in fact, many people were effectively involved who were completely indifferent to religion but who devoted much energy to the social tasks of the communities. The moving force in all this was much less the religious tradition affirming such activity than it was a thoroughly irrational tie, often enough in contradiction to its own ideology, and a readiness to assume responsibility for the Jewish community. As yet such activity was not backed by a conscious affirmation of what may be called profane tasks by people who anxiously set great store on emphasizing that only religious convictions (which often they no longer even had) separated them from their fellow citizens.

Zionism broke with all this and sought to replace fictions and games of hide-and-seek in Jewish life with honest and open relationships. It was—if I may for once avail myself of a fashionable term—an avant-garde movement, borne by a small minority that was bound to provoke the opposition of the Jewish communities precisely because of its contempt for the fictitious element in the latter's conventions. Nor is it any wonder that a breakthrough to a freer stance, and one felt to be revolutionary by the spokesmen of the time, appealed precisely to not a few of the most active elements among the youth.

If Zionism triumphed—at least on the level of historical decisions in the history of the Jews—it owes its victory preeminently to three factors that left their imprint on its character: it was, all in all, a movement of the young, in which strong romantic elements inevitably played a considerable role; it was a movement of social protest, which drew its inspiration as much from the primordial and still vital call of the prophets of Israel as from the slogans of European socialism; and it was prepared to identify itself with the fate of the Jews in all—and I mean all—aspects of that fate, the religious and worldly ones in equal measure.

These were the characteristics that called forth the courage of a departure and a new start, of the construction of a life that was no longer a fiction, in one's own land, and then, when the time came, the courage to liberate and help organize those forces leading to the foundation of Israel. It is true that no one can say it would have come to that without that monstrous catastrophe, which in an equal manner concerned all Jews, whether they happened to think of themselves as a people, religious community, or whatever—even when it did not physically affect the individual. It is idle to speculate about this question. But that in this period there was on hand a concentration of force which could crystalize the will to life of the Jews and their exertions on their own behalf, no longer secretly but on the open and exposed plane of history, and if absolutely necessary even the history of war—that is the great and unique achievement of Zionism.

Ever since its above-mentioned origins, however, this great achievement has contained built-in contradictions which are eminently significant precisely for the questions we are now posing and pondering, and which it would be completely impossible to pass over in silence. The different tendencies,

whose often extreme confrontation dominates the life of Israel in
so many respects, are an expression of these contradictions. The
focal point of these contradictions, however, is a question that
has never been clearly resolved in the Zionist movement, and for
the good reason that no unequivocal answer to it was possible. I
am thinking of this question: was Zionism a revolution in the life
of the Jewish people, a rebellion against the latter's existence in
galut, which it negated radically in order to inscribe on its banner
an equally radical new beginning in the land of Israel; or was it
rather to be understood from the perspective of an awareness of
historical continuity, as a continuation and evolution of those
forces that have determined the existence and endurance of the
Jewish people even during the long years of dispersion? Did it
merely represent a metamorphosis of those forces, which had to
prove themselves in different historical conditions and in new
social relationships and, therefore, would the physiognomy of this
community or society not deviate very much from the one that
had characterized Judaism in the times of exile? Or was it not
rather a question of a break with just this past, of a summoning
up of wholly new forces, which would seek their roots not so
much in our historical heritage as in the resolution to a
wholehearted effort on behalf of a new humanity? Could the two
tendencies—the conservative, indeed reactionary one, and the
revolutionary, indeed Utopia-oriented one—reach an understanding or at least a common ground on which they could meet
without mutually annulling and negating each other?

The Zionist movement was the arena of lively discussions of
these questions. They took place essentially beyond the properly
political setting of goals and the partisan political maneuvers
which outwardly determined the history of the movement. For
even within the framework of common political ideas, opinions
about this highest and deepest question diverged widely and were
to a great extent a matter of temperament and personal decision.
Added to this should be the fact that the most clearly visible
exponents of these conceptions hardly played a role on the level
of politics, even completely rejecting the latter or at least
maintaining the greatest reserve toward it. That is as true of
Ahad Ha-am, the most influential spokesman of a rather conser-

vative conception of the rebirth and renewal of the Jewish people, as of Micha Josef Berdyczewski and Josef Haim Brenner, who were the most important mentors of those who advocated and affirmed the break of the new Jew with his past. It was precisely they who exercised a considerable influence on the socialist *halutz* movement. That movement, concerned with the concrete formation of new styles of life and community—to grow out of the socialist communes of those who worked the land— was marked by a particularly strong awareness of a break with the past. It will always remain notable how in this case such incompatible elements as the critique of society from a socialist, Tolstoyan, and, paradoxically, Nietzschean point of view were often strongly at work alongside each other. At this point the conscious passing over of the history of Israel in exile, in *galut*, the reaching back to primal Biblical times, which was later to become significant, played hardly any role yet, except perhaps in romantic fantasies. Since, however, the historical situation did not demand a decision, the different tendencies, each in its sphere, could coexist with a minimum of friction. After all, the provisional nature of all that happened within the framework of the avant-garde, which before World War II constituted the heart of the new *yishuv*—the Jewish settlement—was clear to all the participants. Since they felt themselves to be the avant-garde *halutzim*, they awaited the great reinforcement, the masses, who were to procure a real embodiment for their versions of the future.

It was also characteristic of this situation that the ideas of Ahad Ha-am, for whom the relations between the new Center and the Diaspora were from the start a focal point for his thought—that is to say, the setting up of a spiritual center for the whole Diaspora, one that was to rise on a new social foundation —that these ideas could maintain themselves almost without any conflict alongside of the properly political conceptions. Only a handful of radical adherents of Ahad Ha-am's thought, to which I myself belonged for a great many years, anticipated an inescapable conflict between these conceptions. But of whatever kind the conceptions were that I have briefly identified here, their adherents without exception drew their strength from the great reservoir of the yet-unawakened Diaspora, and it did not matter at all in this respect whether in their theories they "affirmed" or "negated" that Diaspora.

II

To be sure, when the historical hour was at hand and in the wake of World War II—of the destruction of the Jews precisely in those countries from which Zionism had drawn its strongest impetus, and the establishment of Israel as a state—the great immigration set in of which we had all dreamed for so long; then everything turned out differently. Millions of those Jews on whom we had counted most, who were to us more than all the others the very embodiment of the Jewish people and its capacities, were dead; they had died in a way, moreover, that burdened the collective consciousness of the Jews with a shock, a trauma in its deepest strata that no analysis will ever resolve. Everything that from now on came to pass among the survivors stood—and stands—in the shadow of this trauma. That is as true of Israel, where all those tendencies of which I have spoken were deeply affected and transformed by the attempts to master this trauma, as it is of the Jews in the Diaspora. All were confronted by a fact with which they had not reckoned, a fact that boggled the mind, and the reaction to which involved a task for one's awareness that was as urgent as it was insoluble. It is this community of a deeply felt experience concerning and agitating all of us so directly, that—far above and beyond all theories or even theologies—represents the strongest emotional bond between Israel and the Diaspora. I do not want to go so far as to say that the questions about our relation to tradition and to the history of Judaism as a society molded by religious inspiration have become insignificant or even meaningless. But let us not delude ourselves: compared to the inconceivable, incomprehensible concrete fact that has intervened so destructively in our life as Jews, these things recede into the background. The "existential situation" of the Jews, as perhaps one can say in this case, has changed in our generation.

The establishment of the State of Israel ensued under

completely unique conditions that can never occur again. The unsolved questions that went along with that establishment, and with which we will have to come to terms in these decades, were no less serious and urgent than the necessity of this positive act of founding, which represented our response to the situation in which we found ourselves. Though this establishment of Israel is inseparable from the history of the Jews that preceded it, it was surely accompanied by an idea—and one playing a decisive role—connected with the inability of the Diaspora to secure the life of the Jews and their existence *as* Jews, no matter how these Jews understood themselves and their connection with Judaism. That trauma of which I have just spoken assumed in Israel the form of the slogan: Never again! We would never again live under conditions in which our existence, its affirmation or negation, is determined by others and we are the passive recipients of our fate. We wanted ourselves to bear the responsibility for the vital decisions we could not evade. That led to reactions such as had previously almost never been experienced in our community, and certainly never as central phenomena of this community.

The passion for taking care that the tragedy of the Jews, accompanied by the ambiguous and uncanny silence of those who had power, would never again be repeated, determined much that happened in Israel. The problem of force and violence, which previously had played only a marginal role in our lives, and as such had indeed been rejected by many of us or not reached the level of awareness, now posed itself emphatically and inescapably. In fact, this was the case even before we were forced to defend ourselves in battle with the Arabs. The discussion about the conditions and limits of force and violence, about the meaning of the army, of armed intervention, for the constitution and progress of our lives is to a great extent based on the determination expressed by the slogan never again to be exposed, defenseless, and passive to our fate. The deep aversion of the Jews to the glorification of anything military, which can be felt in Israel as well, was forced to confront the experiences of our most recent history. The past twenty-five years have not been without certain tendencies to overemphasize the elements of force and violence, but it is evident that to a most extraordinary degree Israel relates to its army not as to a military caste capable of having a life of its own, but as to a people's militia.

But it would be deceitful to delude oneself about the fact that the affirmation of force and violence in situations in which our existence is at stake has appeared in our generation in a completely different light than it did previously, and not only in Israel but very widely in the Diaspora as well. It is most remarkable that it was precisely a question so remote from the traditional spheres of Jewish life, and which nevertheless forced a decisive change in our attitude, that led to no conflict between Israel and the Diaspora; but that precisely on this point—I would almost say the most unexpected one—an overwhelming unanimity came about quite spontaneously. In view of the strong quietistic element in the attitude of the Jews—and particularly of the spokesmen of Jewish communities—toward their environment, as we know it from the past, this is no small matter.

When we look back on the most recent generations of Jews and their relationship to things Jewish, we find, I believe, two ideals or model examples which have played a formative role and which were bound to come into conflict, but one more likely to be fruitful than destructive. I mean the ideal of the *talmid hakham* and the *halutz*. For two thousand years the goal of Jewish upbringing was the *talmid hakham*, the authority on Scripture, the master and keeper of tradition, who was able to pass it on in living form. At his side and in competition with him, there appeared—fifty years ago, with the end of World War I—the ideal of the *halutz*, the pioneer who undertook the founding and establishment of a new life on the old earth in a new spirit, and who understood himself as a vanguard of the great masses who were to follow. Alongside a contemplative, spiritual ideal, there appeared an active one aimed at a transformation of our lives, one which profoundly influenced and moved even many of those who did not themselves join that vanguard. The concept of *vanguard* itself includes two factors, a forward striving aimed at the new as well as a conscious relation directed backward as it were to the totality for whose sake it acts. It was never the intention of the *halutzim*, the pioneers, to run away from their people and form a new one. They knew of their bonds to their people by a common history and a common hope. In spite of all their bitter and radical criticism of the form of existence of Jews in the *galut*, they would never have thought of denying their people—as did a large part of the *arriviste* Jews of the nineteenth century. The education they provided did not consist of a doctrine, but rather, however problematic that may be, was accomplished by furnishing a living example.

What is the significance of these two ideals for the Diaspora and for Israel? In itself the ideal of the *talmid hakham* was independent of any connection with Israel and could be completely realized even in the Diaspora, within the continuity of the Jewish community. But it is precisely in the Diaspora of today that its effect—to say nothing of its reality—has altogether faded. There, people of this type and institutions for their training (called *yeshivot*) can be found in only a very few places. But it is precisely in Israel where the ideal of the *halutz* found its natural home and its fulfillment that, paradoxically, the revitalization of this ideal as well succeeded in no small measure. The seedbeds of the Torah are enjoying a considerable blossoming and exert a strong attraction in Israel itself and in circles of the Diaspora vitally important to us. They constitute an effective connecting link between Israel and the Diaspora. In many of them, to be sure—by no means in all—a tendency is becoming evident toward seclusion, toward separatism, toward the formation of a *caste* that turns its back on life in Israel and on affecting that life—a tendency that is in sharp contrast to the former function of these institutions. After all, the *yeshivah* was always open to Jewish life and the Jewish community and never denied its demands. It not only gathered people in, it also sent them back out. I believe it will be important for future developments whether this tendency toward isolation, alarming to many of us, can be overcome, an overcoming that will be possible only from within.

There is also a life of tradition that does not merely consist of the conservative preservation, the constant continuation of the spiritual and cultural possessions of a community. That, too, certainly is tradition, and education in large part depends on it. But tradition is something else as well. There are domains of it that are hidden under the debris of centuries and lie there waiting to be discovered and turned to good use. There is such a thing as renewed contact with what has been forgotten or has not yet come to the fore. There is such a thing as a treasure hunt within tradition, which creates a living relationship to which much of what is best in current Jewish self-awareness is indebted, even where it was—and is—accomplished outside the framework of orthodoxy.

Even within the ideal of the *halutz*, however, changes have taken place. With the onset of the great immigration and the disappointment that this immigration was nevertheless not great enough to correspond to the expectations we had tied to it, many transformations took place here as well. The *halutzim* are no longer among themselves; the new life takes effect in areas that previously had been far beyond the ken of the original intention to bring about a radical rearrangement of Jewish society. With the building up of the machinery of the state, the absorption of great masses of people who came directly from almost medieval and quasi-feudal environments, reality itself posed wholly new tasks, for which the aristocratic and puritanical models of the *halutz* elite were no longer adequate.

The estrangement between Israel and the Diaspora after 1950 spread out from two points of contention: the Israelis were not "Jewish" enough for the Diaspora, which wanted to see model Jews in them who corresponded to traditional conceptions and who would undialectically continue the latter; and the Jews of the Diaspora disappointed the Israelis no less by not coming *en masse* when gates—and hearts—were open to them. Both points furthered tendencies toward the polarization of contrasts and engendered no little bitterness. Both were based on an oversimplification of events in the Jewish world which could not be handled that way. Both parties were unwilling or unable to grasp the events taking place on the other side, which were in themselves contradictory enough. The absence of a great immigration from the countries of the free world played a large part in the tendencies, which were advocated here and there, to let Israel be on its own and to dismantle the bridges to a Diaspora that had missed its chance. Both of these phenomena which soon became visible contained much despair and defiance of those who had been disappointed.

At the same time, however, the old question of the relation

between Israel and the Diaspora thereby entered a new phase. Tendencies, both negative and positive, which previously were discernible only vaguely and dimly, could now be defined with much greater clarity. That goes as much for the change in the attitude of the Jews of the Diaspora—as individuals and even more as groups—toward the great undertaking that is Israel, as it does for the attitude of Israel to the Diaspora. Not only the experiences since the withdrawal of the English, but above all those of the last two years, since the Six-Day War, have promoted a clarification and resolution of this relationship. It is only natural that on both sides lively developments could be discerned in which centripetal and centrifugal tendencies were bound to be brought into relief and to enter into conflict with each other. That is true, albeit in different ways, of all of us.

Let me speak first of the Diaspora. There was certainly no dearth of signs of dissolution here. It was precisely in a state of separation from others that many individual Jews in the postwar era preferred and found it easier to give up their ties to all that was Jewish and to seek their salvation in a resolute severing of their connections with the Jewish world. They may have been aware of their past, but they no longer wanted to have anything to do with the future of the Jews. During our whole lifetime we have heard this song of the great tasks of humanity, compared to which the parochial interests of Judaism are infinitesimal and of negligible weight. In the first half of this century we frequently engaged in passionate discussion with those holding this view, and we were always clear about the impulses leading to this flight into self-abnegation. Today it is easier to look these tendencies in the face. We know that even the deepest estrangement can again and again issue in a turning to Judaism—spontaneous and transforming those affected that way—whether we qualify it as a return or in some other way. For example, whoever has come in contact with French Jews will know how thin the allegedly firm ground is that favors a turning away, the centrifugal tendency. In the most unexpected places this ground and the atmosphere of declarations which often enough hover in a vacuum are pierced by a deeper feeling of identity. These things do not permit of organization, though it is certainly not only occurrences in the environment that shape them, but indirectly also our intentions and achievements. At the same time, this tendency toward dissolution is countered by an extraordinarily strong centripetal impetus which has gripped the Jews of the Diaspora. The wish not to evade the tasks posed for us as Jews by the present, and even more by our future, the awareness of the indissolubility of the bond between Israel and the Diaspora forges the physiognomy of this generation and determines their decisions. The Jewish community of today looks different from the one with which we had to deal in our youth. It has lost the merely anxious regard for alien frowns and has recognized itself as part of a whole that has to accomplish far more than merely religious and philanthropic tasks. It has absorbed the reciprocality between itself and Israel into its life as a determining force. It is inevitable that this will produce tensions between the two poles around which the community's activity is centered. After all, the securing of duration and the fulfillment of the tasks posed by the Diaspora require actions different from the opening toward Israel now seen as necessary.

This tension, however, is not to be found only among the Jews in the Diaspora. It is even more evident in what is now taking place in Israel. Here, too, it is a matter of centrifugal and centripetal tendencies. I would like to clarify what is at stake here by two metaphors. Can Israel and its function be compared with a rocket—say that Apollo XI of which we have read so much recently, from which parts detach themselves and shoot out into the unknown toward the promised landscape of the moon or toward new stars? The astronauts are, to be sure, directed from the earth but they must themselves see to it that they advance; they struggle for air, have to come to terms with their gravity and weightlessness, and are at first able to use only such knowledge as they have learned on earth. But must not a gradual independence in the progress of their mission be reached? Will not a part of the rocket detach itself completely and lead its own life? Is Israel, created by the forces of the Jewish people and out of the native soil of the Diaspora, not destined to detach itself once and for all from that native soil and to lead a new life as a new nation with a new rootedness in the events of recent years? Or are we rather dealing—to counter the technological metaphor with a biological and historical one—with a whole whose parts are all mutually dependent on each other, where the isolation of one part, no matter how crucial a link or constituent, must lead to the destruction of the whole?

We all know the question so often put to us, and which we put to ourselves: are we first and foremost Jews or Israelis? The posing of this question entails a parting of minds in Israel as well. The past twenty years have seen a crystalization into unmistakable clarity of the centrifugal tendencies which strive to dismantle Israel's connection with the Diaspora. Their spokesmen have liquidated for themselves the history of the Jews and their rootedness in it, or at least they claim to have done so. In place of the reliance on the Jewish people and its tradition, they recommend to us that we give up Zionism, which is to say any orientation by "Zion," which is to say any scale of values that understands itself as Jewish. They recommend to us a merging into an allegedly "Semitic world," a term whose sham luster scarcely conceals its total lack of content. The romantic souls among them—and there is no lack of them—have extolled the cult of Baal and Astarte to us, in case we are unable to make do with pure secularization. These cults are to serve the purpose of overcoming the slogans of monotheism that are "hostile to life." The far-reaching propaganda that has been made for the new slogans stands in crying contradiction to their complete lack of seriousness. It is, however, true that behind the extravaganzas of the so-called "Canaanites" who demand to be heard among us, one finds the genuine problem of which I have previously spoken. The question to which that problem can be reduced, and which we encounter everywhere, is, as I have said: what are we first and foremost, Jews or Israelis? It is evident that this question is of decisive significance for the relationship between Israel and the Diaspora. It leads to a parting of minds.

I am convinced that the existence of Israel no less than that of the Diaspora depends on our placing the primacy of our connection with the Jewish people—its history and present state—at the center of our decisions. Indeed, to that pointed question I have mentioned, I reply without hesitation: we are first and foremost Jews, and we are Israelis as a manifestation of our Judaism. The State of Israel and its construction is an enterprise meant to serve the Jewish people, and if one deprives it of this goal, it loses its meaning and will not prevail long in the stormy course of these times. The ideology of an Israel dissociating itself from its historical roots and connections, which is supposed to purchase us political peace, terminates with an inner and horrible logic in the liquidation of the whole, as is most clearly to be seen, admittedly much against the will of the author, in the case of Uri Avneri's *Israel without Zionists*, launched not long ago in Europe amidst great clamor.

Beyond physical survival in extreme situations, the importance of which we have all come to recognize, and in the very actualization of which great human and socially dynamic forces manifest themselves, the question will be always put precisely— and with good reason *to us:* whether we will have more to offer to our people than this survival. The linking up with a preexilic Israel, through a conscious passing over or elimination of two thousand years of Jewish history that have shaped us all, can be accomplished only by way of proclamations and *in abstracto,* but not in historical reality. The return to Zion—which is not identical with dissolving into the Levant—will have incalculable consequences for the formation of our future if it does not try to avoid the fruitful tension between the forces that find expression in that return by coming to a one-sided and all-too-easy decision in favor of one of these forces. That is as true of an orientation directed to an untransformed preservation of tradition as it is of one seeking to cut us off from the roots of that tradition. Zionism was and is the Utopian retreat of the Jews into their own history and thereby, to be sure, a fruitful paradox open in equal measure to the past and the future. This retreat has not ended with the establishment of Israel. Rather, it entered a new phase, one which has most glaringly illuminated its central significance for the fate of the Jews. Without the impulses coming from the new life in Israel, the Judaism of the Diaspora will fall into decay. But Israel, too, is in need of the conscious connection and relation to the whole, the service and transformation of which, in the final analysis, constitutes the justification of its existence, its *ratio essendi.*

It is beyond doubt that the contact with the old and new land, the confrontation of a new historical and social situation, and the necessity of taking an active and positive part in it, have awakened extraordinary energies. No less true, however, remains the old saying that all Jews have to stand up for each other: we are all in the same boat, and the most palpable experience of even the most recent times teaches us that again and again. To be sure, it is possible to jump out of the boat and to disclaim the common responsibility. That is the meaning of those centrifugal tendencies, in Israel as well as in the Diaspora, which I have discussed. As dangerous as they are, they are without significance for our continuity and for the judgment of history upon us.

How profoundly the awareness of the unity of our fate has gripped precisely that younger generation in Israel of which, or in whose name one has so often liked to maintain the contrary—to this a collection of conversations with soldiers from kibbutzim, published shortly after the Six-Day War, bears moving and humanly gripping witness. Notwithstanding all the awkwardness of spontaneous formulations, it is by far the most illuminating document of our spiritual existence hitherto produced by Israel. Never have reflection about ourselves, doubts about ourselves, and astonishment about the experience of our unity been presented in a more honest unpretentious, discriminate manner than in these conversations of young people, scarcely one of whom has ever seen or experienced the Diaspora. Measured against this testimonial, the numerous symposia of Jewish intellectuals which have taken place in Jerusalem, Paris, and New York frequently have—with all their excess of articulation—an air of ghostly unreality about them.

To us, the "old-timers," it was always quite clear that Israel stands or falls with our identification with the Jewish people. Here we sought our true identity, the source of our renewal, above and beyond all formulas and forms. That the "young," however, for whom all this was bound to be much more problematic, had the same experience in a formative hour of our history—that is ground for our hope that the bridges between us, between galut and Israel, will not break down. Israel and the Diaspora are both faced by a crisis threatening their existence. Almost everywhere, the weather forecasts warn of an approaching storm. In order to master the tasks posed by this crisis, we cannot do without each other. The most important of those tasks probably lies in the area of education, which must create a synthesis between tradition and the new values growing out of our coming to terms with the reality of our lives, with the reality of the Jewish people in Israel. It is a task not to be accomplished today or tomorrow, and will for years remain our common cause. The building of a bridge between us and the Diaspora, the wish not to permit an abyss between the two partners, and to overcome any situation threatening to create one, is vital to the common cause of the Jews.

However, as I conclude these observations, I should like to say one thing: it is the personal factor in this mutual concern that will be decisive when all is said and done. Let us not deceive ourselves! No matter how useful and stimulating may be the pilgrimages, visits, educational activities for the preservation and development of what we have in common, and whatever else will come to our minds—they will not be decisive for our relationship. Decisive will be the personal and most intimate factor. What matters is whether we are involved personally, whether we discover a direct connection transcending everything institutional, which is to say whether we discover the unity in our difference, even where this unity of feeling and hope cannot yet be formulated in adequate concepts.

Reflections on
Jewish Theology*

If I undertake here to reflect on the position and possibilities of
Jewish theology today, it should be clear that, as things stand, a
systematic disquisition could only be given by someone possess-
ing a fixed standpoint, an Archimedean point as it were, from
which these questions could be put into systematic order. I am
not among these fortunate ones. What I can do, basically, is to
raise fundamental questions; for I have no positive theology of an
inflexible Judaism. In what follows I hope to make clear why this
is the case.

There are four questions which today are central to me in
discussions of this kind:

(1) The question of the authoritative sources on which such a
theology can draw; in other words, the question of the legitimacy
of Revelation and Tradition as religious categories which can
constitute the foundation of a Jewish theology.

(2) The question of the central values, or of the ideas
underlying such values, that can be established from such sources
and from the conviction that God exists.

(3) The question of the position of Judaism and its tradition in
a secularized and technologized world.

(4) Finally, the question of the meaning, in this context, for
our life and thought as Jews, of the decisive and subverting
events of Jewish history in our time, that is, of the catastrophe of

* Originally published in *The Center Magazine*, Vol. VII, No. 2 (March-April 1974),
pp. 57–71, translated by Gabriela Shalit, and based on a lecture given at the Center for
the Study of Democratic Institutions. The present version is revised according to the
original German manuscript.

the Holocaust and everything connected with it, as well as of the establishment of a Jewish commonwealth in Israel, the *Judenstaat*.

I

It goes without saying that the question of our relation to the tradition of Judaism and to its history as that of a people that even under very different social relations was always formed and developed in a decisive way by religious inspiration has not become meaningless or moot even in an age of secularization.

The fact that so many people from opposing camps, such as that of the pious and that of the consciously and emphatically irreligious, nevertheless confess their identity as Jews with such intensity suffices to make the topicality of the question clear. Yet we should not succumb to the illusion that in the face of the concrete experience of the Hitler years—which affected our lives as Jews in such an overwhelming, unfathomable manner, and in one which basically is probably unthinkable as well—this question was not given a new *Gestalt* or is not represented in a new configuration and against a new background. If I may use a fashionable expression in this context, the "existential situation" of the Jews has changed in our generation. What is more, it is even questionable whether we ourselves are at all capable of formulating the implications of this change adequately, not to speak of doing so exhaustively.

Insofar as we consider ourselves members of a community which is undergoing a historical process of transformation visible to all, which in part is also in a state of beginning the like of which we have hardly known since the destruction of the Temple, one may doubt that we are able to anticipate the multiple facets of this seminal process, which will unfold only in the course of its concrete development. We are necessarily barring our own way, being unable to jump over our own shadow. It is impossible objectively to reflect the experience of a community while the process is still going on. That is why what I am going to say here must necessarily be presented with all due modesty.

How much easier, in this connection, is it for the Orthodox, above all in respect to the first and second questions! They possess a fixed framework, a system of coordinates, that cannot be questioned. They are the fortunate possessors of an Archimedean point which renders senseless such questions as we have posed; that is because their conviction of the divine character of the Torah—which puts it beyond historical questioning—provides them with a standard which, at least in principle, enables them to formulate answers to all the questions arising in the life of the Jew. Beyond this, to be sure, we need not conceal that the meaning of what is called "orthodoxy," i.e., what is meant by the Hebrew expression שלומי אמני ישראל , is altogether controversial. Otherwise, of course, there would not have been those bitter quarrels over this question that took place in the tenth, thirteenth, and from the sixteenth to the eighteenth centuries. Even today one can obtain from Jews who declare themselves Orthodox very different answers to the question of what they mean by that. Perhaps one or another of the participants in this symposium who professes allegiance to this camp will be able to take a more legitimate stand on this question than I can. He will also, perhaps, be able to answer the question as to whether the scale of values which are being proclaimed and propagated as Jewish in theology—moral theology, in particular—is really fixed and unalterable and can stand up even to the tempests of these times in which a secularized world boasts of its possession of entirely different, indeed sometimes diametrically opposed, values.

The first three questions I posed at the beginning are of particular—I would even say bitter—urgency for anyone who no longer possesses the Orthodox system of coordinates. The first question, really the most comprehensive one, also by implication includes the question as to the validity or applicability of important and codified teachings of Jewish theology; I will have occasion to speak of them.

Before one can speak about theology, one must necessarily speak about the sources on which such theology can draw. The observer confronts at least three different stages in which the religious world of Judaism has unfolded, even though each of these stages was itself full of inner flux and rich, indeed overrich, in contradictions. I mean the Bible, the rabbinical tradition, and the *kabbalah;* the last must be regarded as a definitely original fresh beginning on the basis of the two previous sources.

In this context the Bible is not understood as the historical record of Israel's national literature as far as it has been preserved; as such it could contain the most disparate elements without raising any need to harmonize them—a thoroughly legitimate perspective, for which the theological validity of Biblical statements is irrelevant. Here I am thinking of the Bible as a canon of authoritative religious statements, of which at least a part presents itself as the word of God, and to the whole of which religious authority was ascribed by Judaism in the course of its historical crystalization. Both in view of its character as a religious authority and because of the numerous and in part blatant contradictions appearing in it, this whole required interpretation, hermeneutic, and harmonization. This process went on in an impressive manner in rabbinical tradition, in *halakhah* and *aggadah;* the latter was of particular theological relevance because the immediate expression of the religious thinking of wide circles was concentrated in it with particular originality, i.e., by way of the interpretation of Holy Writ.

All three stages here have left an especially impressive stamp on the liturgy of the synagogue, which thus became a precious and true mirror of the religious world of Judaism; the most recent authors, to be sure (as can be seen above all in the case of Franz Rosenzweig), have made only very selective use of its testimony. What these three stages have in common is their unapologetic character, as is particularly evident in *aggadah* and *kabbalah.* The thought processes of the latter tend to be communicated unreflectively, and they forge their own justification as against other categories. In this they differ essentially from the theological literature proper to medieval philosophy of religion from Sa'adia by way of Maimonides to Crescas and Albo, as well as from the more modern reflections on Judaism from Mendelssohn to this day. There religious thought is apologetically oriented toward the respective categories of the dominant philosophies, from the Arabic Kalam and Aristotle to Kant, Hegel, Dewey, and even Heidegger. The outstanding characteristic of these theologies, regardless of their basic differences, is their strictly selective attitude toward tradition. They disregard anything traditional they find undigestible and by its nature unsuitable for apologetic purposes. That, for example, is the reason why the religious world of *kabbalah* is completely excluded from the Jewish theology of the nineteenth century up to the time of Hermann Cohen and others; it falls victim to the censorship of contemporary prejudices. Everybody cuts the slice suiting him from the big cake.

Thus a great variety of choices presents itself. The reader of the relevant literature who expects to find a uniform picture of what is put forth to him as Judaism must be astonished at the multitude of contradictions dominating such depictions. The most important of these contradictions, and precisely for the contemporary observer, surely does not concern the conviction of the existence of God, about which there was no doubt in any of the stages of the religious development of Judaism, and without which I could hardly imagine even a discussion like the present one. It concerns the interpretation to which the concept of Revelation has been subjected. In what sense could a Jew speak of Revelation in the historical context of his tradition? And in what sense can we, here and now, still see in Revelation a category that has meaning for us? Revelation is not a word that has an equivalent in the ancient sources that comprise all occurrences of Revelation. There is a word for the Sinaitic Revelation as well as for the character of Revelation of the Torah as a whole. The occurrence is called *mattan Torah*, "giving of the Torah"; the quality of Revelation is called *Torah min hasha-mayim*, "the Torah from heaven" (i.e., from God). As against this, the theophanies in which God appears to, and communicates with, the patriarchs or distinguished individuals, and above all the prophets, are not included in this concept.

The Rabbinic tradition does, to be sure, recognize a manifestation of the divine presence, but, contrary to the pronouncements about the Torah, this constitutes no authority. It is not experiences of the senses of sight, touch, or taste that constitute authority, but exclusively those within the sphere of hearing. For Judaism, Revelation was the *word* of God, and tradition conceived of the whole of Torah as such a word. The question as to the sense in which one can speak of the word still remains pertinent, even beyond the Orthodox conception. After all, the matter under discussion is the word of God, which was originally thought to be sensibly perceptible. That is no less of an anthropomorphism than those other assertions which ascribe sensible activities to God or speak of His appearance, and which later on, therefore, were subjected to radical reinterpretations with a view to eliminating just this anthropomorphic element.

In these discussions about the significance of Revelation as the word of God, two opposing conceptions came to the fore; both of them, to be sure, were still capable of remaining within the framework of a religious fundamentalism. Here it must be emphasized that fundamentalism was kept alive much longer and with much greater intensity in Jewish-Orthodox circles than among non-Jews.[1] Historical criticism which attacked the immediately divine character of "revealed" texts, that is, the acceptance of the verbal inspiration of Holy Writ and above all of the Torah, was of no importance here—the discussion moved on an entirely different level. With the verbal inspiration of the Torah, a different sphere was introduced into history: a sphere which could nevertheless find its expression within the human and historical mediums and through its means. Of course, such an assumption represents a fundamental paradox. Can the human word contain the word of God in its pure form, or can the word of God, if it exists, express itself within the confines of the human language? This is the paradox leading to the speculations of Jewish theologians on the possible meaning of such Revelations. I would like here to offer some remarks on the subject.

It was hard to evade the above questions by dismissing them as irrelevant, but this was nevertheless done in a particularly drastic manner by S. L. Steinheim, who in 1835 published a great work with the impressive title of *The Revelation According to the Teaching Concept of the Synagogue* (*Die Offenbarung nach dem Lehrbegriffe der Synagoge*), a passionate defense of supernaturalism—influenced by Heinrich Friedrich Jacobi—that is of the thesis that if it is not to be a metaphor devoid of content Revelation must necessarily have as its subject a communication which human reason, even in its most perfect and legitimate

1. This, incidentally, was already noticed by Franz Rosenzweig; see *Kleinere Schriften* (1937), p. 522.

immanent application, could never conceive. Thus human reason must fight against Revelation and the latter must be a paradox. The content of this communication consists of—is both based and concentrated on—the doctrine of creation out of nothing. When in the course of a famous discussion Abraham Geiger asked him where in the writings he accepted as "revealed" the content of this Revelation was to be found, he replied that these convictions were alive in the synagogue and that if he had invented them himself they would henceforth be characteristic of the synagogue. (One can say that such frankness is to be found only rarely in Jewish theology!) To Geiger's further question as to how Revelation reached its first organ, he replied that this he *really did not have to know*—"but probably through the ear." [2]

Yet if there is validity to the supposition that revelation stems from the sphere of hearing—and this is indeed supposed by all the authorities of the rabbinical tradition from Rabbi Akiva to the fundamentalists of our time—we must ask ourselves how the talk of the voice of God could be anything more than an anthropomorphic metaphor. That, however, is a question which, as the history of theology has shown, soon led to the dissolution of the thesis of verbal inspiration, unless it was given a mystical reinterpretation.

It is, after all, noteworthy that the conception of Revelation generally accepted in Jewish kabbalistic circles, no matter how remote it became from its original and naïve meaning, according to its premises not only permitted lively thinking with much inner logic about the concept of Revelation; beyond this it also opened up an astonishing measure of freedom for Jewish thought precisely within the fundamentalist thesis of verbal inspiration and of the divine character of each word—indeed, each letter.

2. Geiger, in his letter to Dérenbourg in the year 1936, cf. *Allgemeine Zeitung des Judentums* (1896), p. 130. In Steinheim's own work (Vol. I, p. 88):

Insofar as Revelation is divine teaching, a new announcement of God by Him and about Himself (not only by Him as mere author, but also about Him as the subject of His announcement), it promises to teach man about a God who to our minds is an *entirely new God*; about a supreme spirit whom the human soul cannot discover and cannot conceive without this outside information and without this message. Neither through reflection nor through experience, nor through any possible means by which the human mind develops other truths within itself or from itself, shall this doctrine of Revelation be explicable, but it shall be of such a character that it can have reached man only through the ear *by an audible word from the outside.*

According to *kabbalah*, God's creative power is concentrated in the name of God, which is the essential word emanating from God. The aspect of God representing this creative power of His—there may be many other aspects still hidden from us—is imbued with His infinity. He is much greater than any human word, any articulate expression, could comprehend. Only through the medium of infinite refraction can the infinite turn into the finite human word, and even then it lends to such a word a depth which goes far beyond anything representing a specific meaning, a communication with other beings. The word of God—if there is such a thing—is an absolute, of which one can as well say that it rests in itself as that it moves in itself. Its emanations are present in everything in all the world that strives for expression and form. In this context the Torah appears as a texture woven from the name of God. It represents a mysterious unity the purpose of which is not primarily to convey a specific sense, to "mean" something, but rather to give expression to that creative power itself which is concentrated in the name of God and which is present in all creation as its secret signature in one or another variation. Not only is the Torah built upon this name and unfolded out of it, like a tree growing forth from its root, but it ultimately represents this name of God. But this also implies that anything which appears to us as the perceptible "Word of God," and in addition contains an intelligible communication about us and our world, is actually something that has already gone through many, many mediations. The word of God must contain an infinite richness, which is communicated by it. This communication, however—and here lies the core of the kabbalistic conception of Revelation—is unintelligible. Its purpose is not a communication that is easily intelligible. Only after it has passed through numerous media can such a message, originally but an expression of the Being itself, become communication as well.

Thus the difference between that which is called the word of God and the human word also contains the key to Revelation. No single definable connection of meaning appears in it but a multitude of such connections into which this word is subdivided *for us*. In other words, the sign of true Revelation is no longer the weight of the statements that attain communication in it, but the infinite number of interpretations to which it is open. The character of the absolute is recognizable by its infinite number of possible interpretations. Revelation does not yield a specific meaning; rather it is that which lies behind the meaning of every word and which thereby lends infinitely rich meaning to every revealed word. To employ the language of the kabbalists: infinitely many lights burn in each word. Or each word of the Torah has seventy—according to some, 600,000—faces or facets. Without giving up the fundamentalist thesis of the divine character of the Scriptures, such mystical theses nevertheless achieve an astounding loosening of the concept of Revelation. Here the authority of Revelation also constitutes the basis of the freedom in its application and interpretation.

Without doubt, this thesis was as far-reaching as it was dangerous. I would venture to say that only a very vital feeling for the significance of theological doctrines and religious values, as many generations developed or derived them from the Torah, and for the continuity of its tradition has prevented a breakup into heretical positions—and even this was not always the case. Small wonder, then, that this also provided the kabbalists with a legitimation for extraordinarily audacious thoughts which appeared defensible before Orthodoxy within the framework of mystical exegesis and a mystical tradition, whereas in the consciousness of those Jewish thinkers who did not share this conception of Revelation they had long ago deviated into heresy or even paganism. To a large extent this also explains those wild protests and bitter complaints about the theology of the kabbalists which abound in the relevant literature, particularly in the nineteenth century.

The fascination which a number of kabbalistic ideas undoubtedly have for a good many Jews of our time, for whom Judaism is a living whole, could only arouse the distaste of those whose aim was an apologia based on the possible rationality of Judaism in a context which seemed to admit only unequivocal dogmatic formulations. They regarded *kabbalah* as a blasphemous (Steinheim) or pagan (Formstecher, Cohen) monstrosity and absurdity. During the nineteenth century and up to Cohen, a dominant feature of this apology was the conviction that Revelation—and everything based on it—represented, or at least initiated, a polemic against, and an overcoming of, myth and (as they saw it) its speculative transformations in pantheism. To be sure, this view was placed in doubt by *kabbalah*, which burst forth in the center of rabbinical Judaism, and in which the primordial mythical element reappears often enough with great force. But in this context I need not deal with that issue.

II

The concept of Revelation, as expounded here, thus had two fundamental aspects whose coincidence constitutes its particular significance for the religious phenomenology of Judaism. On the one hand, the affirmation of the fundamentalist thesis of the divine character of the Torah as the absolute word yielded an absolute system of reference, a common authoritative basis to which all further Jewish thinking could refer. On the other hand, legitimacy was also accorded to progressive insight and speculation, which could combine a subjective element with what was objectively given. If each word of the Torah was pregnant with meaning without being unequivocally bound to any single meaning, it was only a short way to the radical thesis that the sixty myriads of Israel who received the Torah corresponded to the 600,000 facets hidden in every word, each of which gave light only to him for whom it was intended. In principle, then, every one of the community of Israel has his own access to Revelation, which is open only to him, and which he himself must discover.

The extraordinary audacity of such a thesis, in which authority was combined with freedom, was, however, modified in Judaism by the concept of Tradition, which in Judaism stands at the side of the concept of Revelation and is coordinated to it. For if Revelation was an absolute, its application to the lives of its recipients was impossible without mediation. The call implied in it transcends the limits of the single concrete action. Only in the infinite facets, the contingencies of realization in which the absolute word is mirrored, does it become applicable and thus can also be concretely grasped by human action. In other words, the infinite meaning of Revelation, which cannot be grasped in the one-time immediacy of its reception, will unfold only in continued relation to time, in the tradition which is a tradition about the word of God and which lies at the root of every religious deed. Tradition renders the word of God applicable in time. That seems to me to be the basic complementary thesis, through which Judaism was able to realize its concept of Revelation and make it fruitful. From here, the so-called oral Torah obtained its metaphysical legitimation. It comes as no surprise that the "voice from Sinai," which continues to resound every day, and of which the talmudic sources tell us, became for the kabbalists the medium from which Tradition originated. The voice which calls forth incessantly from Sinai receives its human articulation and translation in Tradition, which passes on the inexhaustible word of Revelation at any time and through every "scholar" who subjects himself to its continuity.

What I have said here is a summary of the thoughts which for many centuries were of decisive influence upon the ideas of Revelation and Tradition in Judaism, and which were summed up around the year 1625 in Isaiah Horowitz's *Two Tables of the Law*, one of the most popular books of Jewish literature.[3] It is undeniable, whether one admits it or not, that the book represents a mystical theory, albeit a mystical theory of great scope. It did not circumvent the problem of *how* God could reveal Himself to us in human words by propounding the facile thesis that this just happened to be a miracle; namely an act of freedom and of God's mercy in which God unveils Himself to us in our own language.[4] Obviously, such a mystical conception of Revelation, which at the same time made possible an affirmation of Orthodox fundamentalism, was not something the nineteenth century could absorb or appreciate.

However, with the almost complete, or in any case unlimitedly effective, undermining of the fundamentalist thesis by historical criticism and by the philosophies which supported it just as they were supported by it, the question in Judaism as to

3. See Scholem, *The Messianic Idea in Judaism* (New York: Schocken Books, 1971), pp. 262–303: "Revelation and Tradition as Religious Categories in Judaism," especially pp. 300–303.
4. This is a theory propounded in many Catholic writings, which professed to have found an answer to these questions in their conception of God's word as an "analogous expression." Cf., for instance, Luis Alonso Schöckel, *The Inspired Word* (New York: Herder and Herder, 1965).

whether and in what sense it was still possible to speak of Revelation became inescapable. In practically all the theologians of Judaism whose writings I know, the place which thus became vacant was filled by an attenuating and subjectivist talk of Revelation which was bound to destroy Revelation's authoritative character. Revelation in the sense of a divine communication establishing an authority was now also frequently confounded by the theophanies the Bible mentions in many places, particularly in connection with visions. Above all, however, concepts were introduced which in a disguised form—and denying their origin—adopted mystical concepts.

That is true of authors as different as Kaufmann Kohler, Hermann Cohen, Franz Rosenzweig, and Martin Buber. They all polemicized against mysticism while borrowing its metaphors in case of need. Kohler, the classical theologian of Reform Judaism, defined Revelation as "the appearance of God in the depth of the mirror of the soul," to which, to be sure, he adds an ethical element as being specific to Judaism: "The self-revelation of God as an ethical power is the historic act in which Judaism is grounded." [5] Even Cohen, who finds the progressive development of the religious and ethical sense and consciousness in the records of Revelation, in his later works regards not so much the isolated "fact" of the Revelation on Mount Sinai, but rather the "relocation of Sinai into the human heart" allegedly undertaken by the author of Deuteronomy (30:14)—a mystical formula which has its parallels in the kabbalists, and which appears to be rather peculiar as the culmination of the rationalist yet deeply pious thesis according to which Revelation, by which God enters into a relation to man, is that act "in which the rational human being is born." [6]

Rosenzweig's and Buber's disquisitions on this point, though executed within the framework of a philosophy of the dialogue between man and God, fundamentally acknowledge only one kind of Revelation—the mystical one, even though they refuse to

5. Kaufmann Kohler, *Grundriss einer Systematischen Theologie des Judentums auf Geschichtlicher Grundlage* (Leipzig: Gustav Fock, 1910), pp. 28–29.

6. H. Cohen, *Religion der Vernunft aus den Quellen des Judentums. (Religion of Reason Out of the Sources of Judaism)* (Frankfurt: J. Kauffmann, 1929), pp. 82, 83, 98. (English translation by Simon Kaplan, 1972.)

call it by that name. Thus for Buber, Revelation is a *"gegenwärt-iges Urphänomenon"* (present primordial phenomenon) in the here and now, that is to say potentially in every here and now, namely that of the creative encounter between the I and the eternal Thou in summons and response. In Revelation man receives not a "content" but a "presence as strength." He receives no fullness of meaning but the warranty that there is any meaning at all, "the inexpressible confirmation of meaning." This meaning is not that of another life—not, say of the life of God—but of this our own life, this our own world. Revelation, therefore, is the pure encounter, in which nothing can be expressed, nothing formulated, nothing defined. The meaning founded on it can only attain expression in the action of man. This meaning is not transferable, and not to be forged into knowledge of general validity. It cannot even be rendered as an injunction claiming validity.

> It is not inscribed on any table that should be erected above all our heads. Each of us can only preserve the meaning he received through the uniqueness of his being and through the uniqueness of his life. Just as no prescription can lead us *to* the encounter [with God], so none can lead *from* it. . . . That is the Revelation which is eternally present in the here and now. I know of none which would not be the same in its primordial phenomenon. I believe in none. I do not believe in a self-identification of God or in a self-determination of God vis-à-vis man. . . . What exists *is*, and nothing more. The eternal source of power is flowing, the eternal contact is waiting, the eternal voice is resounding, and nothing more.[7]

In the age of Schleiermacher, the protesting anticipations of Steinheim, a genuine antimystic, were coined against sentences like this. According to Steinheim, "The word Revelation is so great and venerable that even he who, by his deeds, desecrates or destroys it, still believes that he must preserve and honor it in its empty shell, like the corpse of a slain hero or king." [8]

Originally the notion of a one-time Revelation as a historical

7. Martin Buber, *Gesammelte Schriften*, Vol. I (Munich: Kosel-Verlag, 1962), pp. 152–54. See also pp. 158–59 above.
8. S. L. Steinheim, *Die Offenbarung nach dem Lehrbegriffe der Synagoge* (Frankfurt-am-Main: 1835), p. 85.

fact was hardly compatible with that of a continual Revelation which always repeated or renewed itself, as is ultimately presupposed by the category of Tradition even in the rabbinical and kabbalistic sources. Yet when the former notion fell victim to historical criticism—one of its most important victims, if not *the* most important one—there remained only the latter, a doctrine conducive to vagueness and ambiguity about the inspiration of sacred texts or holy men, inspiration which does not manifest itself by a miracle but by a natural process, which in certain circumstances is even repeatable. This, then, corresponded to a large extent—even if it was not so clearly expressed—to the mystics' talk of an "inner light" or "inner word" as the actual basis of all Revelation. Instead of speaking about *ma-amad har sinai* (the event on Sinai) as the formative historical experience of the Jewish people, one now spoke of *ruah hakodesh* (the Holy Spirit) as the instrument of a Revelation that potentially was always possible. Not even the existentialist theologians have been successful in obscuring or obliterating from memory this destructive state of affairs, although one must admit that they—above all, Martin Buber and Abraham Joshua Heschel—employed their considerable eloquence for the purpose of evading the issue.

III

This is the situation in which the large majority of those whose conviction of God's existence cannot be affected by historical criticism find themselves today. The binding character of Revelation for a collective has disappeared. The word of God no longer serves as a source for the definition of possible contents of a religious Tradition and thus of a possible theology. Even where a mystical conception of Revelation is positively admitted, it necessarily lacks authoritative character. The statements of a religious nature which came into being in this manner have no binding force and remain subjective, even when they present themselves as existentially grounded (notwithstanding the protests of their protagonists). I would venture to say that it is no great distance from such a subjective conception, which transplants Revelation into the human heart, to a secular-humanist conception, as is perhaps most readily apparent in Ahad Ha-am. Here some profane, more or less romantic or pragmatic categories such as the *Volksgeist* (genius of the people), assume the place of ethical-religious authority. As a former follower of Ahad Ha-am, I have no illusions regarding the weakness of humanistic foundations for religious statements, in which God can show up at best as a fiction, though perhaps as a necessary one.

Quite recently Alex Derczansky spoke rather felicitously of the "Siamese Twins of Jewish impotence (*impuissance*), humanism and fundamentalism, where the mirage of the former (*le mirage humaniste*) would be the answer to the sclerosis of fundamentalism.[9] When the collective to which Revelation addresses its pronouncements is itself the source from which they emanate, as in Ahad Ha-am, then it is indeed possible to understand the changes undergone by the manifestations of the "genius of the people" during evolution, but surely not their legitimation. The revolutionaries, who negate such ephemeral pretension, subsequently emerge as pioneers of a new metamorphosis by advocating the historical view. The yardstick for what should be considered "Jewish" becomes questionable and credentials uncertain. From such a perspective it even becomes possible to regard Judaism as no longer based upon positive authority, but as an eternal protest, an incitement to revolution which should be evaluated positively, as "The Biblical Call to Revolt," the subtitle of Eric Gutkind's *Choose Life,* one of the most significant attempts at a discussion of the relationship between Biblical Revelation and the modern world of 1950. Nor is it surprising that such an attempt tended to point in the direction of an antitheology whose theological initiatives were doomed to failure.[10]

In the foregoing exploration I started out from the quest for the authoritative sources to which a Jewish theology would be indebted. I did not start out from the faith in God. The reason is obvious. The conviction of the existence of God, insofar as it is

9. *Les Nouveaux-Cahiers,* No. 32 (1973), p. 74.
10. E. Gutkind, *Choose Life: The Biblical Call to Revolt* (New York: Henry Schuman, 1952). As far as I know the book has left no traces in the relevant literature; the same is true of his two other works on Judaism: *The Absolute Collective* (London: C. W. Daniel, 1937) and *The Body of God: First Steps Toward an Anti-Theology* (New York: Horizon Press, 1969).

not itself evoked by Revelation (and that is the only case in which it is in any way connected with the contents of such a Revelation) can be regarded as entirely independent of Revelation. No theology flows from it. It can express itself in as many different forms as correspond to the multifacetness of the human spirit. A theology such as we have recently experienced which denies the existence of its "subject matter," would, of course, be self-contradictory, whereas the affirmation of God is feasible even if no definite theological consequences could be drawn from it. Those consequences which are drawn in the different religions originally emanated from the awareness that there is such a thing as Revelation, and only much later were they translated into philosophical theses. What is left of that in our world, what has remained alive or is capable of maintaining itself in this world with renewed force—this may well be the question to occupy us most. The relevance of religious tradition, of the Holy Scriptures and the traditions and assertions connected with them, can only lay claim to a heuristic value, the value of provocations which may perhaps prove themselves indissoluble in the melting pot of modern nihilism and full of future possibilities.

Even someone who regards Judaism not as something static, but as a vital, varying, and unexhausted whole which has developed under the influence of the basic idea of the oneness of God, confronts the question of how the consequences drawn from Judaism in their basic conception retain their meaning in our time. Here, as so often, the Orthodox have an easier time of it; they find the manifold doctrines, connected in the course of the millennia with the divine monotheistic proclamation, firmly and dogmatically anchored in the Torah, be it the written or the oral one (Tradition). For them the aim, as formulated by Samson Raphael Hirsch, consisted of the "elevation of the age to the level of the Torah, not the degradation of the Torah to that of the age." [11] But for those who do not share Hirsch's premises, probably the majority of those for whom the existence of God presents no problem, questions as to the contents of monotheistic Knowledge or Revelation, and their confrontation with the age,

11. S. R. Hirsch, *Neunzehn Briefe über Judentum* (Frankfurt: I. Kauffmann, 1911), p. 92.

remain pertinent. The concepts in which these contents were formulated, and thus also the values whose recognition was mandatory, are, in their most general version, probably common to all theologians of Judaism. Their detailed comprehension, to be sure, was subject to the most far-reaching differences. This also applies to the three themes in which God's relation to the world and to man was traditionally represented, the themes of Creation, Revelation, and Redemption.

I have already discussed the problem of Revelation, albeit from a rather methodological perspective. Insofar as it contained a message concerning God Himself and His works, no matter how it came into being, it referred, in the original stages of Judaism, precisely to the oneness of God and to his status as creator. A large measure of adaptation to new circumstances was already necessary in order to discover the idea of Redemption as an essential part of Revelation.[12] But once accepted as one of the ingredients of Revelation, the prospect of Redemption proved no less potent in its effect than the idea of the creation of the world by God "out of nothing." It is one of the peculiarities of the present age that the idea of Redemption, either in its pure form or in its secularized metamorphoses, has been maintained much more vigorously in the minds of wide circles than, for instance, the idea of Creation. The very people who talk most loudly about Redemption and its implication are often enough those who want to hear least about the world as Creation. Yet no Jewish theology whatever can renounce the doctrine that the world is a creation—as a one-time event or as a continual always self-renewing process.

Any living Judaism, no matter what its concept of God, will have to oppose pure naturalism with a definite no. It will have to insist that the currently so widespread notion of a world that develops out of itself and even is capable of independently producing the phenomenon of meaning—altogether the least comprehensible of all phenomena—can, to be sure, be main-

12. The process of the interaction of these three links in the chain: Creation—Revelation—Redemption, reached its zenith in the second part of Rosenzweig's *Star of Redemption*. It must be said, though, that in them the architectonic enthusiasm in theology overreached itself considerably. A reaction of disillusionment, as evinced in the writings of Jewish theologians of the last generation in the United States, was unavoidable.

tained, but not seriously held. The alternative of the meaningless-
ness of the world is unquestionably possible if only one also is
prepared to accept its consequences. The philosophical frivolity
with which a number of biologists try to reduce moral categories
to biological ones—one of the most frightening characteristics of
the intellectual climate of our age—cannot deceive us about the
hopelessness of this undertaking. One has only to study one of
these works carefully in order to perceive the equivocations, the
petitiones principii, the latent theologies, and the cracks and
fissures in such intellectual edifices. It will never be possible to
prove the assumption that the world has a meaning by extrapolat-
ing from limited contexts of meaning, yet it is the basic
conviction underlying faith in Creation. Thus it also stands
beyond the ever-changing physical theories which, according to
their very nature, have nothing to say about the origin of the
elements back to which they finally wish to trace all processes.

The Jewish faith in God as Creator will maintain its place,
beyond all images and myths, when it is a matter of choosing an
alternative: the world as Creation and the world as something
that creates itself by chance. The Creation is admittedly not
conceivable in terms of the first chapter of the Book of Genesis,
nor Revelation in terms of Exodus 20, or Redemption in terms of
Isaiah's imagery—and yet all these contain a core which would
be capable of a new articulation even in our time. There is no
doubt that these concepts have undergone changes in the course
of the historical development of Judaism. Their history might be
written. The fact that the Orthodox surprisingly enough and
without opposition have swallowed even the boldest speculations
as they appear, say, in the second volume of Rosenzweig's *Star of
Redemption*, which might perhaps be described as variations on
these themes, eloquently attests to how a contemporary revival of
the age-old dicta might prevail. That this was possible only
within a framework of a recognition of the Jewish tradition
regarding the observance of the commandments of the Torah is
shown by the failure of related endeavors by Martin Buber, who
did without this framework and thus—in contradistinction to
Rosenzweig—became unacceptable to Orthodox Jews. That their
affirmation of God, in the forms appropriate to them, contained a
strong appeal for our age is certain—notwithstanding its fre-

quently doubtful exegetical character. It seems evident to me that faith (whatever nuance one may attribute to that word) in God has a particularly close connection with the conception of the world as Creation.

The famous question of why anything existed rather than there being nothing, posed by existential philosophers from Schelling to Heidegger, was not answerable outside and independent of the question about God, and this, of course, was the meaning it had originally, namely in Schelling. God as Creator was a more fundamental thesis than God in His capacity as Revealer or Redeemer. It is possible to imagine a theology in which the only Revelation is the Creation itself, and in fact many believers in Revelation conceived of it as such. An additional thesis—independent in the sense of not being deducible from the prior one—which was established by the monotheistic religions, though in most different forms, is that yet another Revelation of God to His creature took place beyond the single or repeated act of Creation which made the world process possible. Here the creature was the human being who, endowed with reason, no matter how limited his reason was thought to be, nevertheless possessed in it an instrument capable of accomplishing the highest things. In the religious sense, to be sure, this highest accomplishment was not what modern man, our contemporary, understands by it: the scientific penetration into the edifice of Creation itself. Rather it was the ability to perceive the Revelation, to assimilate it and to penetrate it. This ability could admittedly comprise the other one as well, and it is not by chance that the evaluation of reason has always been one of the central problems of religions based on Revelation.

An overestimation of reason, which provided a frequent common meeting ground for "rationalists" and "mystics" stood in contrast to a skeptical depreciation which emphasized and often enough exaggerated the limitations of reason. The latter sought to define Revelation and reason as two opposite poles, yet it could not evade the central fact that Revelation demanded that it should be accessible to the reason of man. Here, too, in Judaism the kabbalists were the ones in particular for whom there existed a specific affinity between Creation and Revelation, since both were conceived of as the language in which the divine Being communicated. And it was the kabbalists who regarded rational thinking as a linguistic process. I have developed these connections in greater detail elsewhere.[13] That the creative impetus is of a linguistic nature, that, therefore, an infinite multitude of languages suffuses the world, that all the structures we discover in it have a tendency toward language—this may be regarded as an extravagant formulation of the common basis of Creation and Revelation, yet it is a thesis which even in this provocative form has not lost its meaning even for us.

The same applies to another, no less essential point of Jewish theology, the prohibition against making images, whose fundamental significance can hardly be overestimated. The oneness of God, once it was confronted with the multiplicity of the mythical gods, was the condition for the fact that He was impossible to visualize. This was one of the most revolutionary steps in the history of mankind. The veneration of an imageless God simultaneously cast doubt on the visualizable character that seemed to pertain to everything created. Nothing created was worthy of representing what was beyond visualization. Therein was also virtually incorporated a possible conclusion which by far transcended the comprehension of the Biblical and medieval world. Is not the visualizable aspect of the world mere pretense; is what is visualizable not merely an approximation incapable of expressing the Creation? Is not Creation itself in its own way just as much beyond visualization as the Creator? Does not the thesis of a world in principle beyond visualization, which in the twentieth century revolutionized physics no less than the ideas of Copernicus and Newton did previously, correspond to the notion of Creation resulting from the idea of the unvisualizable oneness of God? The name of God, which the mystics rediscovered in all Creation and in all Revelation, was the unvisualizable factor transmitted by God to His creation or communicated therein. It deprived the visualizable aspect of the world of its power of evidence; such things could only be ascribed to the world metaphorically.

The oneness to which the name of God bore witness was

---

13. Cf. my essay *Der Name Gottes und die Sprachtheorie der Kabbala* in *Judaica* 3, *Studien zur Jüdischen Mystik* (Frankfurt-am-Main: Bibliothek Suhrkamp, 1973), pp. 7–70.

beyond such concepts as "static" or "dynamic." Its being was simultaneously movement. In the different stages of the traditional theology of Judaism it could therefore be conceived in one category as well as the other. Both are no more than one-sided aspects of the matter itself.

Corresponding to this is the basically sterile and endless discussion about the so-called attributes of God, into which I am not going to enter here. That applies above all to two theses which are connected to the traditional notions of the doctrine of the attributes and which could only come about through an utterly impractical transference to God of purely secular categories. Thus, of course, they immediately came into hopeless conflict with each other, a conflict impossible to resolve by any kind of verbal acrobatics.

What I have in mind are the attributes of omnipotence and providence, which are allegedly evident in God's acts and which are in sharpest contradiction with the human freedom of moral decision. This freedom of decision, however, is the basis of the moral world of Judaism, which stands and falls with it, today as it did 3,000 years ago. Nowadays, the least plausible of all "dogmatic" assertions of Jewish theology is the thesis of the providence of God, who in His infinite, all-embracing wisdom is supposed to have foreseen not only the meaning of Creation but also its development in every detail and at every stage. Even those convinced of God's existence will find it hard to come to terms with this doctrine. The living God of the Jewish religion, the Creator, who, having revealed Himself, can also be addressed, not only initiated the Creation but participates and is present in it every moment in a manner unfathomable to us. As the daily prayer puts it, "In His goodness He renews the work of Creation each day." But can the "goodness" mentioned here really produce any good that was not already accumulated in the first act of Creation? Does this process not contain moments in which something new, ever-fresh starts, can come into being? Is God's freedom in these ever-fresh starts not fully as unpredictable as that of man in his moral decisions?

The paradox necessarily engendered by investing God with human attributes is sterile; I doubt that it contributes anything to the religious attitude manifesting itself in the view of the world as

God's Creation. Nothing is gained by its dialectic dissection into "attributes." Remaining untouched by this discussion is the question as to the meaning of Creation, whether it has any meaning, and whether such meaning (which is not the same question at all) would also be intelligible to created beings—and that is still the question at the very core of religion. And even those who affirm the idea of Creation are undecided as to whether there really exists a framework within which all created things develop uniformly and in a definite sense (i.e., what Judaism refers to as a plan of Creation), or whether Creation consists of ever-new impulses which unfold only in development itself, and in which this Creation, moved by the ever-new, eventually reverts to itself.

With regard to the former assumption I would tend to share the opinion—despite its metaphorical character—of Erich Neumann, who said, "Why Creation? The answer 'so that, what unreflected would shine in itself only, should shine in endless diversity' is age-old, but it satisfies me." [14] In unmetaphorical language, of course, this means nothing other than that we cannot formulate this meaning, even though we affirm it. With regard to the second assumption, however, the idea of Creation is indeed unthinkable without being connected with that of Redemption. For that which definitively and perfectly unfolds in Creation would be nothing other than the state of Redemption. The ever-new in it would imply a promise in which it presents itself not as a hidden impulse but as open fulfillment. This development, which has its beginnings in the world as Creation, does not, to be sure, take a straight course. It is a dialectically constituted process, composed of contradictions and retarding factors, be their nature ontological or, on the human level, moral.

Before going into this aspect of Redemption as a concept which has a particular topical interest for us, I would like to say something more about the concept of Creation. The notion of continuous Creation is connected with an important concept through which the kabbalists have tried to grasp it intellectually by a bold maneuver. Since Creation was at the same time a

14. In a letter from Neumann to C. G. Jung, who was very displeased with this sentence, cf. C. G. Jung, *Briefe*, Vol. III (Olten: Walter Verlag, 1973), pp. 40–41.

miracle, they sought to render this miracle intelligible through the concept of *tzimtzum* (contraction)—though at a price, that of giving up the concept of the absolute immutability of God. This immutability, to be sure, much as it was dogmatically emphasized and formulated, was always only an expression of impotence in the face of the infinite variety of God, which (as I have already mentioned) could just as well be described in human metaphors as God's absolute mobility. The universe of space and time, this living process we call Creation, appeared to the kabbalists to be intelligible only if it constituted an act of God's renunciation in which He set Himself a limit. Creation out of nothing, from the void, could be nothing other than creation of the void, that is, of the possibility of thinking of anything that was not God. Without such an act of self-limitation, after all, there would be only God—and obviously nothing else. A being that is not God could only become possible and originate by virtue of such a contraction, such a paradoxical retreat of God into Himself. By positing a negative factor in Himself, God liberates Creation.

This act, however, is not a one-time event; it must constantly repeat itself; again and again a stream streams into the void, a "something" from God. This, to be sure, is the point at which the horrifying experience of God's absence in our world collides irreconcilably and catastrophically with the doctrine of a Creation that renews itself. The radiation of which the mystics speak and which is to attest to the Revelation of God in Creation—that radiation is no longer perceivable by despair. The emptying of the world to a meaningless void not illuminated by any ray of meaning or direction is the experience of him whom I would call the pious atheist. The void is the abyss, the chasm or the crack which opens up in all that exists. This is the experience of modern man, surpassingly well depicted in all its desolation by Kafka, for whom nothing has remained of God but the void—in Kafka's sense, to be sure, the void of God.

Redemption was at first a historical concept kept in a precarious balance between politically national and universal elements, but it subsequently became much more. The hope for the wholly new, permeating, and openly presenting itself, in Creation as such and Creation as the arena of history, here competed with the hope for the restitution of a lost whole that had broken to pieces. Such a state of paradise or national blissfulness was dreamed of as a past reality even though it never existed.

It seems to me particularly notable that the messianic idea, the third element in that trilogy of Creation, Revelation, and Redemption, exercises unbroken and vital power even today. Creation, so closely linked to the conviction of the existence of God, has to an extraordinary extent receded or vanished from contemporary consciousness. Outside the fundamentalist minority, Revelation persists only in enlightened or mystical reinterpretations which, no matter how legitimate they may be, no longer possess the original vehemence which promoted its enormous influence in the history of religion. Yet the messianic idea has maintained precisely this vehemence. Despite all attenuations it has proved itself an idea of highest effectiveness and relevance— even in its secularized forms. It was better able to stand a reinterpretation into the secular realm than the other ideas. Whereas more than 100 years ago such reinterpretation was still regarded as an utter falsification of the Jewish idea of Redemption and messianism—and just by the defenders of the historical school in Judaism—it has become the center of great visions in the present age. To be sure, the tensions among the possible conceptions of the content of the messianic idea were particularly strong in the course of the past two millennia. In their profusion, the sources of our tradition permitted the extrapolation of very different, even contradictory, elements at any time and the placing of them in the center. Elsewhere, I have dealt with several of these aspects in detail.[15]

The Jewish tradition preserves a constant conflict—never ending and never settled—among opposing elements in messianism. Even today it is the case that the exposition of such tendencies is likely to generate lively controversies. The principal ones among these are the conflict between apocalyptic tendencies and those aiming at their abolition, as well as between restorative and Utopian ones. Messianism could be represented soberly, almost in the manner of *Realpolitik*, with a slightly Utopian tinge, as it was by Maimonides, who regarded its

15. In the first four chapters of *The Messianic Idea in Judaism*, pp. 1–141.

apocalyptic and radically Utopian traits with great suspicion and who sought to eliminate them completely or at least reduce them to a minimum. Nevertheless, it was also possible to bring the apocalyptic elements to the fore, as in the impressive codifications of the works of Isaac Abarbanel and of the Maharal of Prague. Redemption could be understood as a historical process —as the culmination or breakdown of history—whose apocalyptic revolutions were necessary before the total newness of a renewed world could constitute itself or be formed by God. But Redemption could also be interpreted in a much broader sense: as Redemption of nature, of the multiformity of Creation striving for uniformity.

The vision of the Lurianic Kabbala went even further: it embraced all creation. In it the sum total of the world process, starting with *tzimtzum* (contraction), was represented as a gnostic drama, a drama of failure and reconstruction, but one needed to achieve what had been seminal in it and had never existed before. Here Redemption was not only the goal of history, which thus gave it meaning, but the goal of the whole universe as such. In this case, the Kingdom of God was no longer just the realization of the good on our earth, of a state in which the good would be done by a natural impulse. It was the actualization of this reign in all the infinite spheres of creation which are affected by the *shevirat hakelim* (the breaking of the vessels). As extravagant as this enthusiasm for the cosmic redemption of all that exists and is not in the right place but in exile strikes us, as vehement is the appeal inherent in this notion.

It is precisely the extravagant aspects of the messianic vision which played so great a role in its transformation into the profane and secular, as can be gathered even today from the writings of a thinker like Ernst Bloch. The optimism, even though only eschatological, which was preserved in the various forms of these secular reinterpretations overran the warning signals put up against it by reason and history. Messianism in our age proves its immense force precisely in this form of the revolutionary apocalypse, and no longer in that of the rational utopia (if one may call it that) of eternal progress as the Enlightenment's surrogate for Redemption. This version has only very little left in common with the concepts of the realization of ethical values in the ideal concept of a messianic future, such as was regarded central, for example, by Cohen, to the messianic idea.[16] Morality continues to appear in it only as a most distant frontier. It escapes the relativism of empirical moral concepts in an imperfect world by jettisoning them and by their nihilistic disavowal. This was already the case in the heretical messianism of the followers of Sabbetai Tzvi, which provided our history with an example of a messianism no longer theoretical but applied. Nor is it unrelated to this that the Utopia of the world-transforming revolution, which is to constitute the first real beginning of authentic human experience, develops its own moral code.

On one important point the secularized apocalyptic—or theory of catastrophe—of the revolution, which plays so great a role in contemporary discussions, remains related to the Jewish-theological impulse in which it originated (even though it refuses to admit as much). That is the rejection of the radical internalization of Redemption. Not that the history of Judaism was lacking in attempts—particularly in mysticism, as was only to be expected—to discover such a dimension in Jewish messianism as well. But in all its historical forms, Judaism has utterly rejected the thesis of an inwardness of Redemption that is as it were chemically pure. An inwardness which did not also manifest itself in the most external things which, indeed, was not thoroughly connected with them, counted for nothing here. The thrust toward the core was at the same time a thrust outward. After all, that restitution of all things to their proper place which is Redemption reconstructs a whole which knows nothing of such a separation between inwardness and outwardness. The Utopian element of messianism which reigns so supreme in Jewish tradition concerned itself with the whole and nothing but this whole.[17]

The difference between the modern "theology of Revolution," as it comes to us from so many directions and the messianic

16. Cohen (p. 291) went as far as the radical formulation: "The messianic future is the first conscious expression of the contrast to the empirical sensuality of ethical values." By this, I presume, is meant the temporary character demonstrated in the relativism of the application of such values in the imperfect world of history. As against this, then, the messianic future denotes a sphere which is removed from the restrictions of the experienced world and in which the values find their perfect, "absolute" realization.

17. Cf. my book *The Messianic Idea in Judaism*, p. 17.

idea of Judaism consists to an appreciable extent in a transposal of terminology. In its new form, history becomes prehistory; the human experience of which we have spoken turns out not to have been the authentic one, the latter being accessible only to a redeemed humanity. That simplified the discussions about the value, or lack of value, of previous history (which lacked the essential element of man's freedom and autonomy), and thus placed all discussions about real, authentic human values on the plane of eschatology. That opened door after door to an uninhibitedly optimistic Utopia, one not even to be described by the concepts derived from an unredeemed state of the world. That is the attitude behind the writings of the most important ideologists of revolutionary messianism, such as Ernst Bloch, Walter Benjamin, Theodor Adorno, and Herbert Marcuse, whose acknowledged or unacknowledged ties to their Jewish heritage are evident.

However, in the Jewish version of messianism, which, ever since the age of the Prophets, has not lost the vision of a renewed, liberated, and pacified humanity, such a vision remains closely connected with the Kingdom of God. The covenant which binds God and man not only in Revelation but anew in Redemption confirms both Revelation and Redemption as being two aspects of the same phenomenon. The true Kingdom of God is the actualization of true humanism. Unfortunately, the modern usage of the term "humanism" implies an unbearable and highly misleading double meaning. When in the eighteenth and nineteenth centuries humanism and humanity were mentioned, no contrast to a theistic orientation was intended. At that time the truly human was still the image of God in man which had to be brought forth and realized. Only much later did an opposing usage emerge, in which humanism presupposed an agnostic view of the world, an image of man in which there was no longer any room for God. Instead one gets an extravagant concept of the dignity of man, who accomplishes his own Redemption.

But there is another point on which the secularized and the religious conceptions of messianism—in their recent development—concur: the liquidation of the person of the Messiah as the bearer of the message of Redemption, which finds in him its expression and its realization. This personal element is undoubtedly connected with the historical origins of the messianic hope. It has now become immaterial for wide circles of Jews, even for some who harbor strong religious feelings, and its only remaining usefulness is symbolical, as a summation of everything implied by the messianic idea. For the religious consciousness, the "son of David," who would renew the Davidic reign and thereby at the same time establish the Kingdom of God on earth, did not constitute a necessary component of the messianic expectation. To be sure, certain features of messianism which had assured it great popularity were thereby eradicated. These are the features which in the prophecies of the servant of God as a messianic figure, had appealed to the religious sentiments of so many generations precisely by virtue of their disquieting and stimulating paradoxes.

Even though this figure was depicted here as most personal, even tragic, there had always been a tendency to see in it not the embodiment of a messianic personality, but one of the people of Israel as the bearer of this prophecy. In its historic destiny it would have to pay the high price for having kept faith throughout its history with the prophecy of a state transcending history, perhaps even disparaging history. Such reinterpretation opened the way to a further generalization. In a secularized world, suffering humanity itself, or the proletariat—proclaimed by the founders of socialism, in a fantastic *tour de force*, to be humanity's true representative—could take the place of the suffering servant of God. Yet, even without such "humanist" extension and reformulation, messianism has developed a destructive dialectic of its own within Judaism as well.

For a whole century it was the favorite pastime of the liberal theology of Judaism to use the messianic idea in order to forbid the Jews to live their lives on the historical level. In this they could, of course, base themselves upon a much more ancient tendency within Orthodox Judaism, which made a virtue of historical necessity and forbade the Jewish people any historic initiative, even though the alleged commandment of historical passivity was hardly compatible with the deepest impulses of messianism and, in fact, spelled its perversion. None of the many representatives has done better in expressing this in all its contradictoriness than Cohen, who could write: "The loss of the national state is already conditioned by messianism. But this is the basis of *the tragedy of Jewish peoplehood* [italics in the original—G.S.] in all historic depth. How can a people exist and fulfill its messianic task if it is deprived of the common human protection afforded by a state to its people? And yet, just this is the situation of the Jewish people, and thus it must needs be the meaning of the history of the Jews, if indeed this meaning lies in messianism." [18] A historical experience of incomparable intensity has unveiled the eerie character of these sentences (as of so many liberal theological axioms). This tragedy was too hollow and too cheap in its adaptations to an age of bourgeois illusions. Yet it remains undeniable that the discrepancy recognized, though perverted, by Cohen between the real history of the Jews, even in its reentry into contemporary history, and the messianic drive accompanying this history at the same time as it weakens it, represents a genuine problem which any Jewish theology in our time will find inescapable.

IV

I have been speaking of basic religious concepts which, even within a Judaism that does not repudiate its tradition, contain problems which appear to me unavoidable outside of fundamentalism. A number of their reinterpretations made concessions to the age of secularism. A number—above all those in the sphere of the conception of the world as Creation—cannot do without a fundamental and inescapable contradiction and confrontation of secularism. From the viewpoint of secularized humanism this is their weakness; from the viewpoint of a philosophy of history, which remains aware of the questionable nature of a totally secularized world, this is their strength.

These concepts, however, were not on the same level as the moral concepts underlying the commandments of the Torah insofar as the latter could be understood as meaningful and insofar as they also divulged such meaning in the sources themselves. Man's actions, even when they are directed toward

18. Cohen, pp. 311–12.

his fellow man and the community, are determined by concepts, by a scale of values, originating from man's relation to God.

The demands of religious ethics are in conflict with a secularized world. Such determinant values are the demands for the fear of God, the love of God, humility, and above all for sanctification, which cannot be imagined as unrelated to the religious sphere. Concepts such as reconciliation, justice, and faithfulness (*emunah*) have a meaning, though a very restricted one, on the purely social level; they can be imagined without any reference back to God. As regards holiness and sanctification, and perhaps more than anything else the fear of God, the highest values in Jewish ethics, they cannot be put into practice within the framework of a purely this-worldly ethics. The most prominent characteristics or aspects of the conception of God's actions in the world, namely severity and compassion, have, in the world in which we live, been transferred from the hands of God into those of the materialists and psychoanalysts.

Malcolm Muggeridge, a contemporary of ours with a gift of biting wit, has expressed this state of affairs as follows: instead of the old theological quibbles, he finds ours to be a time of "Freudians looking for their Marx and Marxists looking for their Freud." [19] Judaism certainly recognized the existence of a secular sphere to be infused with sanctity. Fear and love were powers which, under the dictate of the demand for the sanctification of human activity, attained a religious content reaching far beyond the experience given to man in his natural life. The profane sphere, which survived alone in an ever-spreading secularization of the human condition, had no use for a call such as the one for sanctification. For such a call presupposes a sphere which transcends the immanent values forming themselves in the course of development and necessarily remaining relative to the latter. This was the moral demand and call of Judaism.

The secularizing talk of the "sanctity of life" is a squaring of the circle. It smuggles an absolute value into a world which could never have formed it out of its own resources, a value pointing surreptitiously to a teleology of Creation which is, after all, disavowed by a purely naturalistic rationalistic view of the world.

19. Malcolm Muggeridge, *Chronicles of Wasted Time* (London: Colliers, 1972), p. 15.

But on the other hand, as far as one can see, this process of the secularization of all aspects of the human carries its own momentum and cannot be arrested; neither, therefore, can the dwindling of visible religious authority. Sociology, technology, and psychology seem to gain the upper hand. The uninhibited optimism inherent in the expectation that the application of scientific, progressive discoveries directed to the mastery of nature (the so-called technological revolution) would also solve problems of values is completely unfounded. Nevertheless, it seems as if it will have to spend itself until it will clearly recognize its limitations, which, of course, are necessarily the same as those of scientific knowledge in general. Such knowledge may still be able to lay bare deeply hidden facts or give these facts a theoretical coherence, but it cannot establish values. That, however, raises the question as to whether the progress in these areas, starting from the expectation of making them autarchic, could lead to the knowledge that they are either closed in themselves or open. In the present state of things this cannot be determined, although it could be of decisive importance.

If this "technological world" is closed in itself and leaves no room for other perspectives, then the conflict between such a world and the world of Judaism will persist with undiminished vehemence. In such a world man would be a helpless instrument of overpowering forces, and at the same time atomized and isolated, standing unprotected in the face of the loneliness and senselessness which oppress and suffocate him. If, to be sure, those areas which I have designated as technology, sociology, and psychology were open or porous, so that something else could become transparent in them, that would be a situation in which the religious attitude could develop in a fruitful dialogue with them.

The urgency of the question as to the significance of secularization for contemporary Judaism is evident. Can we adopt the view that Judaism has a positive stand toward such a process, that as it were it adds to it by complementing it and all this without coming into conflict with it? Could we perhaps say with Jacob Neusner: "The heavens tell the glory of God. The world reveals His holiness. Through mitzvot [good deeds] we respond to what the heavens say; through Torah we apprehend the revelations of the world. *Judaism rejoices, therefore, at the invitation of the secular city.* It has never truly known another world; and it therefore knows what its imperatives require" [italics mine, G.S.].[20] Against this, should it not be maintained that the demand, starting from the purely religious concept of sanctity, for the sanctification of the secular by way of a fulfillment of the Torah based on a divine legitimation, represents precisely the opposite of real secularization and is incompatible with the world-immanent values of the new scale of values which naturalism seeks to establish? In contemporary Jewish society this question, which obtrudes itself in the most varied facets, can in no way be circumvented.

If we live in a world in which Revelation as a positive possession has been lost, the first question is: Does this not mean the liquidation of Judaism insofar as Revelation is understood as a specific characteristic of the Jewish people, as the shape in which it has presented itself in world history? Is not then the slogan "like all the nations" not the solution, as many quarters pass it off as the meaning of Zionism? And, furthermore, how can the fear of God be not only a value *realizing* itself *in* the world as such—the same as most values on a religious level—but also a value *immanent* in, *originating* from the world? This was possible in the sphere called *theologia naturalis* by Christian theology, because here there was a rational theology of the knowledge of God that derived its arguments from meditation in the world itself. Jewish theology, although it avoided the expression "natural theology," followed the same line to a great extent.

Where, however, such a dimension of theology ceases to exist, as it does in the purely secular view of the world, it seems very difficult to anticipate a positive answer to this question. But can the purely naturalistic agnostic view, which admits secularism as the only possibility, be reconciled with the assertion made by so many thinkers that there is meaning even in the secular sphere? Much depends on the answer to this question, the discussion of which produces so many disputes.

The establishment of values depends on the acceptance of a

20. Jacob Neusner, *Judaism in the Secular Age* (London: Valentine, Mitchell and Company, 1971), p. 64.

meaning attributable to them. Philosophers of pure secularism, such as Guyau a hundred years ago and Walter Kaufmann today, have been trying to understand the phenomenon of meaning by way of naturalistic considerations. The argument that this was ultimately an attempt to pull oneself out of the mire by one's own bootstraps was rebutted by the neo-Hegelians and the neo-Marxists with an appeal to the dialectic, which allegedly puts an end to the dogmatism of such controversies. I consider it difficult to follow these arguments, but at any rate one ought to admit that on the basis of these presuppositions a fruitful meeting and discussion is possible between religion, whose message begins and ends with the meaningfulness of the world, and secularism. Indeed, if it were possible to follow the line of argument of the Jewish Reconstructionists, there might perhaps even be an understanding between the two. The developments of recent decades, however, did not justify the optimism which inspired expectations of this kind. The position of the man of the secularistic age vis-à-vis his society is more helpless than ever in his confrontation with naked nihilism.

It has often been said that in the course of millennia Judaism has proved itself infinitely adaptable without losing its original impetus. It has adjusted itself to very different forms of societies without essentially changing its values. It has proved its vitality in an agrarian society in antiquity, in a medieval society where the Jewish masses were urbanized and their living conditions were determined by entirely different occupations, in an absolutist society, and finally in an industrialist society. Why, then, should it not prevail in a technological age as well?

If technology is the domination and exploitation of the functional connection between things, it could be said of it that it does not so much negate the religious sphere as exclude it *per definitionem*. Even the most highly developed technology cannot make a statement about anything that does not enter into such functional connection. Its strength, although manifesting itself so overwhelmingly in everyday life, still remains subject to the conditions governing science in general and thus also its eventual limits. The priorities of such domination and exploitation, in other words the "morality" of technology and thus also the morality of a completely mechanized age—all this is still determined by interests which, no matter how one looks at it, stand beyond such technology. Bourgeois morality, the anarchistic morality of revolt, the combat morality of revolution—all of them derive their legitimation from sources *other* than scientistic or technical developments themselves.

Should, then, the values governing today's American "permissive society," for example, be accepted as a logical consequence of radical secularization? Or is there some chance for those forces which are resolved to oppose such a society with their own demands? Actually, even to pose this question would already mean to answer it affirmatively—if not for the skepticism, expounded above in greater detail, which is the result of the disintegration of the dogma of Revelation. Can that which we are able to learn from the sources of those three stages of Judaism discussed above persist unchanged, especially in its moral formulations and demands, when the sanction of Revelation has become dubious or when it can only be maintained in mystical forms? I consider it particularly urgent to pose this question for discussion.

I would like to say something about the above-mentioned slogan "like all nations," which became of the greatest contemporary interest through Zionism, through the construction by the Jews of a new society in their own land, a society bearing full responsibility for its success or failure, for our relations to the world around us as well as for the values which are to determine this construction. I have never been among those who accepted this as a legitimate formulation of the goal of Zionism. I am quite convinced that the realization of this slogan could only mean the transition to the decline or even disappearance of the Jewish people. The normalization, of which all of us who supported the Zionist cause had been dreaming, referred to the establishment of social conditions, in which the appeal of those imperatives which for millennia were the foundation, the justification, and in times of fatal catastrophes even the confirmation of our existence, would not be distorted, falsified, and rendered largely hopeless through the force of circumstances. Many of us believed that the forms in which those imperatives might appear could change; we never seriously believed that they would or even could disappear from the center of our existence. I admit that this unshakable belief in a specific moral center, which bestows meaning in world history on the Jewish people, transcends the sphere of pure secularization. I would not even deny that in it a remnant of theocratic hope also accompanies that reentry into world history of the Jewish people that at the same time signifies the truly Utopian return to its own history.

This hope would remain unaffected even by a process of complete secularization. For in an attempted liquidation of the values originating in the religious sphere, it would still become evident which of these values could resist liquidation. Such an attempt at liquidation, to be sure, is perilous like everything creative. It would lead to a point of the dissolution of everything that was specific to the Jews as a whole, or else to a point where this turned into something positive, more steadfast than all tradition, because it would be less expected and quite unforeseeable from the perspectives of the sphere of secularization.

I regard it as one of the great chances for living Judaism—indeed, the decisive chance—that it does not attempt to evade this choice with easy compromises, but rather that it faces it openly and in the unprotected arena of historical engagement. In other words, I am convinced that behind its profane and secular facade, Zionism involves potential religious contents, and that this potentiality is much stronger than the actual content finding its expression in the "religious Zionism" of political parties. Why? Because the central question about the dialectics of living Tradition—and in the context of Judaism this means above all the halakhic tradition—will be more fruitfully posed in Israel with an element of doubt than in the manner it is posed there from a position of strength, fortified today by cowardly laws. The secular character of the Zionist movement always contradicted its inescapable involvement with religious problematics. Subjected to violent attacks from both quarters, from the Orthodox on the one hand and from the liberals and assimilationists on the other, and condemned as allegedly un-Jewish by both sides according to their respective doctrines of salvation, it had to develop a vivid sense for what would occur in its confrontation with history, independent of its detractors.

As long as Zionism was in its rhetorical stage, it could provide a relatively peaceful home for the most varied slogans. At the moment when the Zionist vision was about to be realized, it soon became clear that its most active support came from the sector which inclined most strongly toward secularism. The state of Israel would never have become a reality without it. But the stronger that sector's position became, the stronger also became the tendencies toward the reconsideration of views. The attitude toward tradition, in construction or destruction, grew inescapably into a central question—truly burning and as yet unresolved—which still leaves everything open.

It goes without saying that on the religious level, too, the situation in Israel differs from that of the Diaspora. The shock suffered because of the Holocaust by every Jew who was conscious of his identity, and by many Jews who were not, has affected all centers of Jewish life. How deeply they were affected is not yet fathomable today, though we may assume that the after effects, repercussions, and reverberations of this event provide the background for, and are operative in, everything that is happening now. In the Diaspora these effects are rather diffuse. They did not visibly crystalize around a focus, though I would not say that they are therefore any less powerful. In Israel, however, where the activity of reconstruction provided a clear focus which was apt to crystalize the emotional shock—caused by the German murder of the Jews and the apathy of the world—around a new Jewish commonwealth, both the negative and positive aspects were fused into one whole, an entelechy. No event in Jewish history has so greatly transcended the dimensions discoverable in the previous experiences of that history as this event in which the slaughter of millions under the most horrible circumstances was linked with the most intensive effort for a new historical beginning.

Yet at the same time the discrepancy among the possible tendencies of the national rebirth was exacerbated by the situation outlined here. And that has prevented the formation of a pure crystalization or Gestalt in this rebirth. This applies above all to the religious level, on which a living Judaism could prove itself as much in the renewal of the halakhah as in the change of its historic Gestalt in which the values of Tradition must be reformulated in new contexts. Both these possibilities are in unresolvable contradiction to the secularization discussed here, in which a living Jewish people would resolve to renounce living Judaism as a binding order of values. These alternatives are, as far as I can judge, much less operative in the Diaspora.

The special circumstances prevailing in the Diaspora permit the almost peaceful coexistence of these alternatives. But in Israel that is impossible in the long run. Precisely the vitality of the Israeli enterprise—the high temperature, if I may say so, of all processes there—makes it impossible. Here, too, lies the cause for the increasing tension between Israel and the Diaspora in so many matters concerning the future of "Jewish life."

It would be a grave error if we were to deceive ourselves into ignoring this state of affairs. This tension does not, as is claimed often enough, have its principal source in the organization of the State of Israel and in its presumptive demand that its mundane interests should be identified with moral precepts. Such identification is manifestly impossible, not to mention that there can exist great differences of opinion about the true interests of the state in any given situation. It is not the state but the problems of Israeli society as a living reality which are relevant here. Whether, when, and in what form religion will be an effective force in society—that is indeed a decisive question whose consequences with regard to the Diaspora as well are unforeseeable even if we regard it as an indisputable fact that (as it certainly seems to me) such questions will also assume considerable importance in the conditions that will be prevailing in the Diaspora itself.

I consider a complete secularization of Israel to be out of the question so long as the faith in God is still a fundamental phenomenon of anything human and cannot be liquidated "ideologically." I consider a dialogue with such secularization about its validity, legitimacy, and limitations as fruitful and decisive. I could not designate the two parties to this dialogue any better than by two Talmudic words which probably constitute the most sublime synopsis of religious Judaism in the past, and possibly in the future as well. I mean the words living throughout 2,000 years of Jewish tradition: "the freedom of the tablets" of the Law and the "broken tablets," which still lie together with the holy tablets in the Ark of the Covenant—that is to say, within the religious dimension of Judaism.

On Eichmann

*Eichmann**

Eichmann has been executed. In its public and historical aspects the Eichmann case is at an end. All the lessons that might possibly be learned from the great trial which terminated in Eichmann's death sentence can already be studied in full. Now the time has come to embark on the soul-searching the affair demands, and there is no end to thoughts and questions, most of which are without answer.

Those who approved of Eichmann's being put before the bar of justice, those who upheld the trial itself as well as the form chosen for it by the authorities, those who saw in the trial a tremendous moral achievement in educating the nation toward a major historical reckoning—a task as necessary to undertake as it must necessarily fail—in short, all those who are primarily concerned with the public, moral, and historical aspects of the trial rather than with its legal side—they are the ones who are bound to ask themselves whether the execution of Eichmann was indeed the appropriate finish to this enormous issue. I am certain that many thousands and hundreds of thousands of the people of this land are still preoccupied with this question, and I propose to answer it as best I can.

There is no question but that Eichmann deserved the death penalty. I have no doubt he did. I have not come forth to find any merit in him, or, indeed, to discuss any aspect of his deeds and responsibility that pertains to the legal aspects of the trial. I assume that from the legal point of view nothing remains to be

* *Ammot* (August-September, 1962). Translated from the Hebrew by Miriam Bern-stein-Benschlomo.

said and that he deserved to die a thousand deaths each day. I come to plead on our own behalf, that is to say on behalf of Eichmann's potential (if not actual) victims.

The laws of human society are at a loss as to adequate punishment for Eichmann's crimes. On this point there is general agreement. There can be no possible proportion between this crime and its punishment. Neither could his execution serve to teach a lesson to other murderers of our people. The application of the death penalty for the murder of millions is not a "deterrent" and will not deter any potential murderer likely to arise against us in the days to come. It is not the deterrent power of the hanging of one inhuman wretch that will prevent catastrophes of this kind in the future. A different education of men and nations, a new human awareness—these will prevent it. To achieve such a human awareness was the purpose of the Eichmann trial.

Eichmann was an excellent example of the systematic destruction of the image of God in man, the "dehumanization" the Nazi movement preached by all possible means and practiced as far as possible. The significance of this trial consisted of revealing to the whole world the meaning of such dehumanization; its effects and the price paid by a whole nation which falls victim to this process. For one can very well say that in the strict sense two nations, not one, were the victims: the Jewish people, whose millions were murdered, and the German people, who became a nation of murderers when it allowed the Nazi doctrine to gain power over it. If we are "to do justice," to deter or avenge the bloodshed of our people, then it must be done to tens and hundreds of thousands whose hands are soiled with blood.

Which brings me to the main point: the application of the death penalty to Eichmann constituted *an inappropriate ending*. It falsified the historical significance of the trial by creating the illusion that it is possible to conclude something of this affair by the hanging of one human or inhuman creature. Such an illusion is most dangerous because it may engender the feeling that something has been done to atone for the unatonable. One man, who is only the corrupt product of the corrupt system which made his existence and activity possible, is to be hanged, and many millions, especially in Germany, will see it as an end to the whole business of the murder of our people. It will be said that the Israelis have captured the chief organizer of the murder; let them hang him and be done with it.

As Jews and as human beings we have no interest in such a phony "finis." It was an easy, slight ending in two senses: it was slight both as to significance and judgment. This hanging was an anticlimax, the satyr play after a tragedy such as had not been seen before. One fears that instead of opening up a reckoning and leaving it open for the next generation, we have foreclosed it. What superficially seems severity of judgment is in reality its mitigation, a mitigation in no way to our interest. It is to our interest that the great historical and moral question, the question probing the depths which this trial has forced all to face—How could this happen?—that this question should retain all its weight, all its stark nakedness, all its horror. The hangman who had to execute Eichmann's sentence added nothing to the situation, but he took away a great deal. As I have said before, he introduced the misplaced suggestion that this marked "the end of the story." It would have been better if we did not have the hangman stand between us and our great question, between us and the soul-searching account we have to settle with the world. Having gone through this trial we should ask ourselves: where do we stand now with this accounting? What do we really want to prove to the world? If we wanted to prove that justice is being done and that a great historical reckoning is being effected, then a living Eichmann—whether imprisoned by us or put into the hands of the Germans (who had good reasons for not wanting him)—was not likely to stand in the way of such a reckoning. But it is to be feared that an Eichmann who has been hanged will indeed stand in the way—very much in the way.

Letter to Hannah Arendt[*]

Jerusalem, June 23, 1963

Dear Hannah,

Six weeks have passed since I received your book on the Eichmann trial; and, if I write belatedly, it is because only now

* From *Encounter* (January 1964). Professor Scholem's letter is translated into English by John Mander.

do I have the leisure to devote myself to a proper study of it. I have not, let me say, gone into the question of the factual and historical authenticity of the various statements you make. To judge by your treatment of those aspects of the problem with which I happen to be familiar, however, I fear that your book is not free of error and distortion. Still, I have no doubt that the question of the book's factual authenticity will be taken up by other critics—of whom there will be many—and it is not in any case central to the critique I wish to offer here.

Your book moves between two poles: the Jews and their bearing in the days of catastrophe, and the responsibility of Adolf Eichmann. I have devoted, as you know, a good part of my time to a consideration of the case of the Jews, and I have studied a not insignificant volume of material on the subject. I am well aware, in common with every other spectator of the events, how complex and serious, how little reducible or transparent, the whole problem is. I am aware that there are aspects of Jewish history (and for more than forty years I have concerned myself with little else) which are beyond our comprehension; on the one hand, a devotion to the things of this world that is near-demonic; on the other, a fundamental uncertainty of orientation in this world—an uncertainty which must be contrasted with that certainty of the believer concerning which, alas, your book has so little to report. There has been weakness, too, though weakness so entwined with heroism that it is not easily unraveled; wretchedness and power-lust are also to be found there. But these things have always existed, and it would be remarkable indeed if, in the days of catastrophe, they were not to make their appearance once again. Thus it was in the year 1391, at the beginning of that generation of catastrophe; and so it has been in our own time. The discussion of these matters is, I believe, both legitimate and unavoidable—although I do not believe that our generation is in a position to pass any kind of historical judgment. We lack the necessary perspective, which alone makes some sort of objectivity possible—and we cannot but lack it.

Nevertheless, we cannot put these questions aside. There is the question thrown at us by the new youth of Israel: why did they allow themselves to be slaughtered? As a question, it seems to me to have a profound justification; and I see no readily formulated answer to it. At each decisive juncture, however, your book speaks only of the *weakness* of the Jewish stance in the world. I am ready enough to admit that weakness; but you put such emphasis upon it that, in my view, your account ceases to be objective and acquires overtones of malice. The problem, I have admitted, is real enough. Why, then, should your book leave one with so strong a sensation of bitterness and shame—not for the compilation, but for the compiler? How is it that your version of the events so often seems to come between us and the events—events which you rightly urge upon our attention? Insofar as I have an answer, it is one which, precisely out of my deep respect for you, I dare not suppress; and it is an answer that goes to the root of our disagreement. It is that heartless, frequently almost sneering and malicious tone with which these matters, touching the very quick of our life, are treated in your book to which I take exception.

In the Jewish tradition there is a concept, hard to define and yet concrete enough, which we know as *Ahavat Yisrael*: "Love of the Jewish people. . . ." In you, dear Hannah, as in so many intellectuals who came from the German Left, I find little trace of this. A discussion such as is attempted in your book would seem to me to require—you will forgive my mode of expression—the most old-fashioned, the most circumspect, the most exacting treatment possible—precisely because of the feelings aroused by this matter, this matter of the destruction of one-third of our people—and I regard you wholly as a daughter of our people, and as nothing else. Thus I have little sympathy with that tone—well expressed by the English word *flippancy*—which you employ so often in the course of your book. To the matter of which you speak it is unimaginably inappropriate. In circumstances such as these, would there not have been a place for what I can only describe with that modest German word—*Herzenstakt*? You may laugh at the word; although I hope you do not, for I mean it seriously. Of the many examples I came upon in your book—and came upon not without pain—none expresses better what I mean than your quotation (taken over without comment from a Nazi source!) about the traffic with the armbands with the Star of David in the Warsaw ghetto, or the sentence about Leo Baeck "who in the eyes of both Jews and Gentiles was the

'Jewish *Führer.*' . . ." The use of the Nazi term in this context is sufficiently revealing. You do not speak, say, of the "Jewish leader," which would have been both apt and free of the German word's horrific connotation—you say precisely the thing that is most false and most insulting. For nobody of whom I have heard or read was Leo Baeck—whom we both knew—ever a *"Führer"* in the sense which you here insinuate to the reader. I too have read Adler's book about Theresienstadt. It is a book about which a great many things could be said. But it was not my impression that the author—who speaks of some people, of whom I have heard quite different accounts, with considerable harshness—it was not my impression that Adler ever spoke of Baeck in this fashion, either directly or indirectly. Certainly, the record of our people's suffering is burdened with a number of questionable figures who deserve, or have received, their just punishment: how could it have been otherwise in a tragedy on so terrible a scale? To speak of all this, however, in so wholly inappropriate a tone—to the benefit of those Germans in condemning whom your book rises to greater eloquence than in mourning the fate of your own people—this is not the way to approach the scene of that tragedy.

In your treatment of the problem of how the Jews reacted to these extreme circumstances—to which neither of us was exposed—I detect, often enough, in place of balanced judgment, a kind of demagogic will-to-overstatement. Which of us can say today what decisions the elders of the Jews—or whatever we choose to call them—ought to have arrived at in the circumstances? I have not read less than you have about these matters, and I am still not certain; but your analysis does not give me confidence that your certainty is better founded than my uncertainty. There were the *Judenräte*, for example; some among them were swine, others were saints. I have read a great deal about both varieties. There were among them also many people in no way different from ourselves, who were compelled to make terrible decisions in circumstances that we cannot even begin to reproduce or reconstruct. I do not know whether they were right or wrong. Nor do I presume to judge. I was not there.

Certainly, there were people in Theresienstadt—as every

former inmate can confirm—whose conduct is deserving of the severest judgment. But in case after case we find that the individual verdict varies. Why was Paul Eppstein, one of these "questionable figures," shot by the Nazis, for example? You give no reason. Yet the reason is clear enough: he had done precisely that which according to you he could afford to do without serious danger—he told people in Theresienstadt what awaited them at Auschwitz. Yet he was shot twenty-four hours later.

Nevertheless, your thesis that these machinations of the Nazis served in some way to blur the distinction between torturer and victim—a thesis which you employ to belabor the prosecution in the Eichmann trial—seems to me wholly false and tendentious. In the camps, human beings were systematically degraded; they were, as you say, compelled to participate in their own extermination, and to assist in the execution of fellow prisoners. Is the distinction between torturer and victim thereby blurred? What perversity! We are asked, it appears, to confess that the Jews too had their "share" in these acts of genocide. That is a typical *quaternio terminorum*.

Recently, I have been reading about a book, written during the days of catastrophe in full consciousness of what lay ahead, by Rabbi Moses Chaim Lau of Piotrkov. This Rabbi attempted to define as precisely as possible what was the duty of the Jew in such extremities. Much that I read on this moving and terrible book—and it does not stand alone—is congruent with your general thesis (though not with your tone). But nowhere in your book do you make plain how many Jews there were who acted as they did in full consciousness of what awaited them. The Rabbi in question went with his flock to Treblinka—although he had previously called on them to run away, and his flock had called on him to do likewise. The heroism of the Jews was not always the heroism of the warrior; nor have we always been ashamed of that fact. I cannot refute those who say that the Jews deserved their fate because they did not earlier take steps to defend themselves, because they were cowardly, etc. I came across this argument only recently in a book by that honest Jewish anti-Semite, Kurt Tucholsky. I cannot express myself, of course, with Kurt Tucholsky's eloquence, but I cannot deny that he was right: if all the Jews had run away—in particular, to Palestine—

more Jews would have remained alive. Whether, in view of the
special circumstances of Jewish history and Jewish life, that
would have been possible, and whether it implies a historical
share of guilt in Hitler's crime, is another question.

I shall say nothing concerning that other central question of your
book: the guilt, or the degree of guilt, of Adolf Eichmann. I have
read both the text of the judgment delivered by the Court, and
the version you substituted for it in your book. I find that of the
Court rather more convincing. Your judgment appears to me to
be based on a prodigious *non sequitur*. Your argument would
apply equally to those hundreds of thousands, perhaps millions,
of human beings, to whom your final sentence is relevant. It is the
final sentence that contains the reason why Eichmann ought to
be hanged, for in the remainder of the text you argue in detail
your view—which I do not share—that the prosecution did not
succeed in proving what it had set out to prove. As far as that
goes, I may mention that, in addition to putting my name to a
letter to the President of Israel pleading for the execution not to
be carried out, I set out in a Hebrew essay why I held the
execution of the sentence—which Eichmann had in every sense,
including that of the prosecution, deserved—to be historically
wrong, precisely because of our historical relationship with the
German people. I shall not argue the case again here. I wish to
say only that your description of Eichmann as a "convert to
Zionism" could come only from somebody who had a profound
dislike of everything to do with Zionism. These passages in your
book I find quite impossible to take seriously. They amount to a
mockery of Zionism; and I am forced to the conclusion that this
was, indeed, your intention. Let us not pursue the point.

After reading your book, I remain unconvinced by your thesis
concerning the "banality of evil"—a thesis which, if your subtitle
is to be believed, underlies your entire argument. This new thesis
strikes me as a catchword: it does not impress me, certainly, as
the product of profound analysis—an analysis such as you gave us
so convincingly, in the service of a quite different, indeed
contradictory thesis, in your book on totalitarianism. At that time
you had not yet made your discovery, apparently, that evil is
banal. Of that "radical evil," to which your then analysis bore

such eloquent and erudite witness, nothing remains but this slogan—to be more than that it would have to be investigated, at a serious level, as a relevant concept in moral philosophy or political ethics. I am sorry—and I say this, I think, in candor and in no spirit of enmity—that I am unable to take the thesis of your book more seriously. With your earlier book in mind, I had expected something different.

GERSHOM SCHOLEM